Women and Rural Household Food Security

WOMEN AND RURAL HOUSEHOLD FOOD SECURITY

V. RADHA

Annamalai University, Tamil Nadu, INDIA

SERIALS PUBLICATIONS
NEW DELHI (INDIA)

First Published - 2009

ISBN: 978-81-8387-238-6

Published by

SERIALS PUBLICATIONS
4830/24, Prahlad Street, Ansari Road
Darya Ganj, New Delhi-110002 (India)
Phone : 23245225 Fax : 91-11-23272135
E-mail: serials@satyam.net.in

Contents

Foreword

The emphasis in contemporary population and infrastructural economics is on human resources. Investment in human capital increases the quality of human resource enhancement in human capital formation. In such a context, food and nutrition security are the vital necessities for human resource development and are integral to livelihood security in terms of capabilities, assets and activities required for living. In our country with rural population spread and reliance on women for food security, analytical studies on household food security from women's perspective inter-linked with socio-economic environment are considered essential to enhance the nutritional status of the rural population.

This book by Dr. V. Radha is a commendable endeavour in this direction and presents oodles of information, especially for the policy-makers, on household food security and nutrition security in Tamil Nadu. It is through such pioneering and grass-root studies, we can hope to get guidelines for proper decisions to triumph over food insecurity situations at the household level and nutritional deficiency at the individual level.

This study is an attempt to identify the general and the specific food security issues involved in the Indian context. Dr. Radha's focus of analysis in this book is on the inequality and variability in the food consumption pattern of the target population in the chosen regions of Tamil Nadu and listing of strategies adopted by these households to successfully manage food supply at vulnerable and crisis situations. The author's assessment of the potential tasks that women can perform at the household level and the nutrition security strategies that the government can chalk out at the national level is worthy to be recognized as guidelines for further course of action. This subject occupies an essential place in international research programmes like World Bank, IFAD and FAO.

I appreciate and congratulate the author for her contributions in this book to the fast developing science of gender studies in Economics.

N. Malathi

(Dr. N. Malathi)
Professor and Head
Department of Economics
Annamalai University
Annamalainagar-608 002

Preface

Food security is an important component of human welfare and considered the most important basic requirement for human resource development. Food security as a goal sets before itself the norms in regard to the availability of food, firstly, this should ensure basic existence of people and at the next level, it should serve the minimum nutritional standards for their active and healthy life. The present stage of development of India warrants the analysis to be made from the perspective of the latter norm.

The poverty level (as learnt from various studies) has come down in terms of Head Count Ratio (HCR), for both urban and rural areas. The results originate from the studies, keeping the yardstick so low that corresponded to just the minimum energy-intake. The variants of the measure, providing for differences in gender, occupation, age, etc., did not improve the standards set, beyond denoting minimum existence. Despite the fact, that even this lower standard is not yet reached by people fully, the stage of development (the rise in the extent of agricultural production, being a compelling reason) obtaining now, necessitate a higher nutritional standard being made available to people. It is because, the success of planning has to be construed from the angle of enhancing "capabilities" of people. The food security in the above sense, will correspond to insulating the people against, not only under-nutrition, but as well as against malnutrition.

It is startling to know that India has 204 million under-nourished people. The rate is alarming because China with a much larger population has only 164 million undernourished people. Particularly, child malnutrition rates in India continue to cause alarm. Around 60 per cent of children under five in India are found to be underweight due to poor economic conditions and inadequate proportion of nutritious food in the diet. A majority of them are afflicted with Protein Calorie Malnutrition. This implies that although availability of food is a necessary condition, it is not the sole yardstick to measure food security, because those who cannot afford to buy food are left hungry and undernourished. A direct indication of the extent of food deprivation (as observed by the expert committee) is that nearly fourteen percent of rural households are not getting two square meals a day for either part or whole of the year. So, ensuring nutritional security is a step ahead to food security.

In the present economic conditions, household food security depends more on the household's access to food than simply on availability. In relating the results to the causes of food insecurity, this study is indebted Sen's entitlement approach. A majority of studies dealing with the issue of food insecurity have viewed it only as a transitory problem. But transitory food insecurity is serious, if left unattended for long it may lead to chronic insecurity.

In the rural areas, poor households often face scarcity of both time and material resources. Women's daily chores in rural areas often are centred around food chain and food security activities. A broad understanding of women's role in food and nutrition activities will help to realise the potential of women for improving food security and nutritional security of rural households.

The invaluable contributions made by women need to be recognised and considered in development processes. This mindset would place the present study "Women and Rural Household Food Security" as essential and socially relevant. This study was conducted in the rural pockets of Sivaganga and Cuddalore Districts in Tamil Nadu. Its objective was to understand, recognize, establish and evaluate the contribution of women to achieve food security of rural household. Another added objective was to outline prospective approaches for improving women's opportunities and empowering them to ensure poverty reduction and promote food and nutritional security of individuals.

It can be strongly affirmed that the missing link in transforming national food self-sufficiency into adequate household food and nutrition security is the lack of information based decision-making in designing food and nutrition policy interventions. This study is based on first hand information. All sample households from the four study villages have been surveyed comprehensively. The findings of the study would provide the logistics and the vital empirical support required for any future rainbow study on women and household food security.

I wish to express my grateful gratitude to my Research Supervisor, Dr.N.Malathi, Professor of Economics, Annamalai University. Her creative and critical insights were of great help throughout, I am greatly thankful to Dr. R. Elango, Professor and Head (Retd), Department of Economics, Annamalai University for the initial idea and for the interest shown in the progress of this work.

I thank the Annamalai University which facilitated all my achievements.

I thankfully acknowledge the help rendered to me by Dr. M. S. Swaminathan, Research Scientist, M. S. Swaminathan Research Foundation, Chennai, for his valuable ideas, and my thanks are also due to Mr. Parasuraman, and the Librarian at M.S.Swaminathan Research Foundation.

I wish to express my sincere thanks to Dr. Mallika Arjuna Rao of the National Institute of Nutrition, Hyderabad and Dr. Shoba Rao for enlightening me on the methods of measurements of nutrition. I also thank the authorities of National Institute of Nutrition (NIN), and National Institute of Rural Development (NIRD), Hyderabad, for providing access to research materials in their libraries.

I thank with gratitude the sample population in the four study-villages who uninhibitively responded to my queries and shared with me their "short and simple annals". Without them this study would not have happened.

I acknowledge my thankfulness to my husband, Dr. V. Lakshmanan for his suggestions in show-casing the findings in a presentable format. I am thankful to my daughter, Dr. Sugirdha Prakash, and my son, Sai Charan, who sat for extended time on the computer and helped in data collection and tabulation. I also thank them for patiently enduring, during these days, my fluctuating disposition, and at times, neglect.

I want especially to record my gratitude to Serials Publication, New Delhi for undertaking the publication of this book.

The entire responsibility for the views expressed as also for any error of analysis of fact is solely that of mine.

I most humbly dedicate this work to my affectionate and loving parents wishing them long life and lasting happiness.

V. Radha

1

Introduction

Healthy human capital is the real asset to a nation. Sustainable human development is possible only with educated, healthy and well-nourished people. Food and nutrition security are the basic requirements for human resource development. By food and nutrition security, physical and economic access of food and nutrition to all sections of the society is meant. Food and nutrition security is integral to livelihood security in terms of capabilities, assets and activities required for living.[1] In practical and ramifactory terms, sustainable economic growth is possible only with sustainable human development, which, in turn is dependent on food and nutrition security. Thus food security is a priority concept in developmental economy.

While sufficiency of food is of prime concern to prevent social tension, nutrition security is equally important to foster a healthy population. Investing in nutrition makes good economic sense because it: reduces health care costs[2]; reduces the burden of non-communicable diseases[3]; and improves productivity and economic growth[4]; and promotes education, intellectual capacity and social development.[5] No other economic analysis, except food security analysis, can fully encompass the benefits of sustained mental and physical development from childhood into adult life.

More than 2,000 years ago, Hippocrates wrote: "Let food be thy medicine." And, indeed, that is exactly what is being endorsed by welfare economists to-day. A shift from a production orientation to a consumption or nutrition orientation is the analytical trend to-day.

Global financial institutions like the World Bank[6] contextualise the importance of investment in nutrition thus: "resources put into nutrition are an investment with significant returns, to-day and in the future."

The roots of concern with food security can be traced back to the Universal Declaration of Human Rights in 1948, which recognised the right to food as a core element for an adequate standard of living.[7] Such a rights-based approach is derived from the ethical position that all people are entitled to a certain standard of material well-being. About twenty-five years later, dismayed by the global food crisis of 1972-74, the World Food Conference was instantaneously convened in Rome in 1974. It was resolved that by 1984 no child, woman or man should go to bed hungry and no human being's physical or mental potential stunted by malnutrition. To-day, twenty-nine years after the resolution was made and nineteen years past the deadline "Over 700 million people go to bed hungry globally, 800 million suffer from chronic under-nutrition in less developed countries, and 200 million children under the age of five suffer from malnutrition in Asia."[8]

Every year, around 13.5 million children die in different parts of the world due to disease related to malnutrition.[9] The emerging need for global food security was felt by the Food and Agriculture Organisation (FAO). In 1990, one of its functional objectives was to ensure "the availability of sufficient quantity of food and sufficient means to purchase it." It is in this backdrop the FAO had convened the World Food Summit in 1996 to devise an internationally acceptable strategy for sustainable food security. In a review-study of this Summit's recommendations, Dr. M.S.Swaminathan, extends the emphasis to "focus on the ability to assure on a long term basis, that the food system provides the total population access to timely, reliable and nutritionally adequate supply of food."[10]

India has rightly placed achievement of food security high on the national agenda. India has moved from the famine situation of the 1940s to self-sufficiency in food production today due to timely exigent–initiatives like the Green Revolution during the late seventies and early eighties. As a result, food production has kept pace with the population increase during the past twenty-five years. The country is now holding a buffer stock of about 36 million tonnes of grains. On an average, in our country, the per head per day food availability has significantly increased from 359 gms in 1951 to 531 gms in 2000. In spite of the tremendous food self-sufficiency at the national level, the country has not attained food security at the household level, Chasmic variations across different strata and different sections of society continued to exist. A study by Prabha Gupta in 1999 shows that about seven per cent of rural households and about three per cent of urban households do not get even two squares meals a day for a whole year.[11] It is estimated that over 200 million children, women and men in India are still undernourished. Particularly, child malnutrition rates in India continue to cause alarm. A majority of them are afflicted with Protein Calorie Malnutrition. (PCM) According to a study made by the United Nations Development Programme (UNDP) in 1994, based on a database of 1990, sixty-three per cent of children under five in India were found to be underweight, the highest rate of any of the 127 developing countries listed.[12] This study further found that the percentage of children with severe malnutrition though decreases from about 14.2 per cent to 7.5 per cent, there is an increase in the proportion of mildly undernourished children; fifty per cent of adult population is reported to have Body Mass Index calibrated below normal.

From the foregone discussion, it can be comprehended that in India, even though food is available in abundance, the problem of food security continues to exist, indicating the problem is not one of food availability alone. Increased food resources do not automatically ensure access to food by the downtrodden sections of the society. A balanced distribution mode becomes obligatory. Studies on food distribution and food sharing mechanism in the different types of Indian households are very scarce. Hence widespread and in-depth studies have essentially to be carried out to determine relative risks from hunger and to reconstruct consumer-friendly distribution modes and to create socio-power structures with increased purchasability.

STATEMENT OF THE PROBLEM

Thanks to various programmes of poverty alleviation, the level of poverty in India has gone down significantly from 54 per cent in early seventies to 26.10 per cent in 1999-2000. This is a remarkable achievement when the country's population increased rapidly and crossed one billion mark.[13] However, most poverty reduction strategies fail to target food insecurity specifically. Consequently, a reduction of poverty in quantitative terms had little impact on the economy as the decline in quality had washed the percentage improvement.[14]

Rural Households

A report on nutritional trends in India has found that during the 10-15 years prior to 1993 there had been no significant change in consumption of food by the rural households. This report recognised the necessity that future food and nutrition policies should address the issues of poor access to food and low purchasing power of the household and aim at household food security to ensure adequate dietary intake by all members of the family.[15] To emerge victorious in the fight against food and nutrition insecurity, government policies will need to focus more attention on rural areas where 742 million out of total population of 1027 million live. These rural areas encompass a high proportion of food-deficit households and nutritionally high-risk groups. A case-study of Tami Nadu will help to illustrate the magnitude of the problem. In Tamil Nadu poverty ratio declined from 32.4 per cent in 1993–94 to 21.10 per cent in 1999–2000 which is much lower than the rural Indian average of 27.09 per cent[16] but the food intake level of this rural populations is precariously low. The food consumption per consumer unit is only 394 gms as against the Recommended

Level of 460 gms.[17] This implies that although availability of food is a necessary condition, it is not the sole yardstick to measure food security, because those who cannot afford to buy food are left hungry and undernourished.

Depending on the nature and extent of food insecurity and nutritional problems, policy and planning efforts in India range from emergency to short, medium and long-term food and nutrition intervention. Three broad categories of food and nutrition interventions that have been implemented in India are, labour-intensive public work programs in the form of food for work, market-oriented programmes such as subsidized food through public distribution systems[18] and special feeding programmes such as school feeding and supplementary feeding programmes.[19] But due to high implementation costs, leakages and poor administration the benefits of these intervention programmes did not reach the needy population.[20]

To-day, the need for target oriented measures is recognised. But lack of information on the characteristics of households that are badly in need of assistance and the impact of the benefits derived from such interventions have been a bottle-necks in designing targeted food and nutrition interventions. It can be strongly affirmed that the missing link in transforming national food self-sufficiency into adequate household food and nutrition security is the lack of information based decision-making in designing food and nutrition policy interventions.[21] Thoughtfully this study places its focus on the rural poor households, where except for the medium and large farmers, all others including the marginal and small farmers, agricultural and non-agricultural workers and artisans are vulnerable to seasonal fluctuations in employment, commodity, price and availability of food.

Role of Women

In India, in the present rural household configuration, women, play a pivotal role in family level food and nutrition security. All food related activities fall within their domain. They are not only responsible for feeding their families but have the added responsibilities of promoting, protecting and preserving the health of their family members also. IFPRI Food Policy Report clearly documents women's responsibilities in ensuring food and nutrition security at the household level.[22] It is imperative that any household food security and nutrition analysis should have a female perspective. This aspect receives particular attention in this study. It fully recognises women's important mediatory function between those economic processes which raise household resources and tasks and other processes which translate these resources into family meals, health care and concern for the vulnerable, especially children.

The FAO firmly acknowledges the contribution made by women to household food security and the multiple roles rural women play throughout the entire food chain. The FAO had evolved the theme "Women Feed the World" to mark the occasion of World Food Day on October 16, 1998. This is a timely reminder to governments and policy makers to reassess the capabilities and capacities of women to feed their families and to recommend corrective measures to eradicate obstacles in their way. Researchers like Bina Agarwal[23] and Ruth Dixon[24] amply cautioned us that rural development policies will not have the intended effect; in contrast, may have unintended negative impact if the position of women in rural households is not correctly analysed and taken into account.

International agencies like International Food Policy Research Institute (IFPRI), International Fund for Agricultural Development (IFAD) and Food and Agriculture Organisation (FAO) are funding research projects undertaken to comprehend women's role in agriculture and food security on a priority basis. The battle for household food security can be won only when, to quote the title of a novel by Kingston, the "Women Warriors" are in action. The invaluable contributions made by women need to be recognised and considered in development processes. This mindset would place the present study "Women and Rural Household Food Security" as essential, justified and socially relevant. This study was conducted in the rural pockets of Sivaganga and Cuddalore Districts in Tamil Nadu. Its objective was to understand, recognize, establish and evaluate the contribution of women to achieve food security of rural household. Another added objective was to outline prospective approaches for improving women's opportunities and empowering them to ensure poverty reduction and promote food and nutrition security of individuals.

ISSUES IN FOOD SECURITY

The concept of food security can be applied to analyse wide ranging issues pertaining to continental, inter-continental, national, household and individual level food and nutrition situations. But whatever the range, its ultimate focus will be on food security at the household and individual level.

Theoretical Issues

Food security, basically, is a consideration of the availability of food. It should assure basic existence for the people. In the next level, food security should assure them minimum nutritional standards for an active and healthy life.

Food security strategies include both supply and demand issues. Originally, there was a tendency to understand the concept of food security only from a supply point of view, but in 1979, the World Food Programme Report equated food security with an assurance of supplies and a balanced supply-demand situation of stable foods in the international market.[25] Food security at the national level was conceptualized as the outcome measure of agricultural policies. In a study by Reutlinger and Knapp[26] and another study by World Bank,[27] the focus was on the main staples, national storage of grains, and agricultural policies that ensured stability in supply all year round. However, increased aggregate food supply will not be a useful substitute for food consumption at the household level. Empirical studies tend to confirm the opinion that food self-sufficiency has no intrinsic value for eliminating food insecurity at the household level.[28] Adequate national or local food availability remains a necessary condition for household food security[29] for it cannot be taken for granted in the exigencies like continuous population growth, increased land scarcity and environmental degradation, Contrarily, a household perspective will give a different picture of the food situation of the same population. At such an ironical situation, the national level macro-approach of food-availability should be linked with micro-level household consumption to arrive at trustworthy conclusions.

The World Bank[30] has identified two forms of households food insecurity, transitory and chronic, based on time dimension of demand issue. Transitory food insecurity is temporary or transient, arising from temporary short-falls in food supply relative to requirements; or because of a temporary loss of adequate effective purchasing power for food. Even seasonal and annual fluctuations in production, natural catastrophes, the temporary loss of employment and similar factors can lead to transitory food insecurity at the household level. Chronic food insecurity is, on the other hand persistent, continuous, and almost intractable. Chronic food insecurity is a function of poverty.

A majority of studies dealing with the issue of food insecurity have viewed it only as a transitory problem.[31] But transitory food insecurity is serious, if left unattended for long it may lead to chronic insecurity. Like an omniscient study, the present analysis will be broad-based with its focus on the variability in food consumption pattern and enumeration of strategies adopted by households to successfully weather transitory shocks to food supply.

Conceptual Issues

The concept of food security at the household level is appropriately defined by IFAD[32] as "the capacity of a household to procure a stable and sustainable basket of adequate nutritious food." Though a slightly deviatory working definition is employed at times, as when the discussion shifts from the national to household level, there are no serious underlying contradictions to this definition in this study.

Food Security and the Household

The three key dimensions of household food security are availability of food, access to food and utilization of food.

A food secured household, as understood in this study, is one which not only satiates the hunger of its members but also satisfies their barest nutritional requirements. This dimensions of the study highlights the need to focus on various factors determining the level of food and nutrient consumption of households to decide whether a household is food secured or not.

Even at the household level, the food security strategy encompasses both supply and demand issues. It involves the production of food and therefore issues such as secured ownership of access to resources and services including land, labour, credit, extension; it involves the consumption of food and therefore issues such as nutrition, health, food storage and preparation, and access to income with which to purchase food. The link between poverty and food insecurity reflects a household's access to food, what A.K. Sen calls "Exchange Entitlements".[33] The entitlement approach concentrates on each household's entitlement to commodity bundles which includes food, and views food insecurity as resulting from a failure of the household to be entitled to a bundle of commodities with enough food.

Sen's theory of exchange entitlement explains why poverty and hunger act selectively. It could be because of lack of factor endowment (land labour, capital or entrepreneurial ability) or due to loss of entitlement or exchange based acquirement (loss or lack of employment, fall in wages, increase in food prices, reduction in social security provisions). In brief, lack of an adequate set of exchange entitlement has much to do with household food insecurity. Chronic food insecurity at the household level is caused by lack of resources; transitory food insecurity occurs with a temporary decline in the exchange entitlement set of a household particularly related to structural factors such as persistent lack of access to land or productive assets or highly skewed distribution of employment opportunities and income.

Access and security are the important core concepts in household food security. While access is defined by the entitlement to produce, purchase, exchange or receive food, the security concept refers to the balance between vulnerability, risk and insurance. As such, household vulnerability must be assessed in terms not only of immediate access but also of the stability and sustainability of those channels through which the household mediates its food access. In this context, the household food security needs to be concerned in relation to the various sources of their entitlements.

Another dimension of the problem of food security facing the household is consumption and utilization of food. Along with entitlement problem, family size and high dependency ratio may be considered as limiting factors in feeding the members. A household level food security concerns are associated with the capacities of individual's and household's day-to-day activities and decisions to produce, purchase and use food of right quantity and quality at various phases of the life cycle and seasons.

The amazing fact that the rural poor despite their food insecurity and malnutrition continue to survive, encouraged this researcher to investigate into the coping strategies adopted by women against the threat of transitory food insecurity.

Individual Food Security and Nutrition

Food security studies would become wholesome only when household production theory is employed. Intra-household vulnerability depends on women's roles and bargaining power. The household production economic theory would examine carefully what happens within the household and how resources are acquired, controlled, allocated and used. Hence, a discussion of intra-household food security dynamics has become indispensable.

The end objective of food security is to empower the individual to get adequate, balanced food throughout for an active and healthy life. While the logical level from which to analyse the problem of food access is the household, intra-household inequities and dynamics–particularly with regard to gender–too play a major role in determining individual food security. In other words, because a household is food secure, does not mean that all individuals in it are food secure; the most vulnerable in particular may not always get enough food. This observation has necessitated this study to focus on sex and age disparities in the distribution of food within the household and also their relation to disparities in nutritional status.

The nutritional efficiency of resources in the household depends on a number of inter-related factors including income control and allocation of resources within the household.[34] Because of women's dominant role in gaining access to food for the family, their decision-making role, their access to and control over resources, their education and nutritional knowledge matter much in measuring the nutritional status of the family members. Since ability to utilize food to their maximum benefit is influenced by factors like child care, access to health and favourable sanitary environment these receive due importance in the study. Inadequate food intake by household adults could be seen in low body mass indices and in children by levels of anthropometric characteristics. This concept has also been given due consideration in the statistical and econometric analysis of this study.

Armed with the theoretical framework discussed so far the following key research questions are attempted to be answered, through data and dialectics in this study:

1. Are the rural households secure enough in 'food' and 'nutritional' terms?
2. How does household food intake and dietary diversity influence household food security?
3. Are the households buying sufficient nutritory diets?
4. To what extent households/individuals provide for their food security in rural areas? How do they fight against food insecurity?
5. Can an appropriate and a reliable measure of food security be operationalized at the household level and nutritional security at the individual level?
6. How are intra-household dynamics critical to a household's food security and an individual's nutritional security?

The conceptualization of food security in this study makes divergent departures from the general perspective in composition, access, social and spatial dimensions. In composition, food is specified as a basket of commodities consisting of not just calories but a nutritionally balanced diet. By access, it recognizes not only physical access or availability but emphasizes equally economic access or entitlements to food. Socially, the study actualises an empowering environment for women with access to and control over resources, participation in decision making, inculcating and improving the ability of the household to achieve entitlement rights. It is spatially divergent because while reinforcing the economic access dimension it makes a remarkable shift in emphasis from a national to the household and to the individual level, thereby equating food security with livelihood security.

CHAPTER PLAN

Chapter-I: Introduction and relevance of the study, and discussion of statement of the problem with focus on rural households and role of women and main theoretical and conceptual issues.

Chapter-II: Presentation of a brief review of theoretical studies on demand side, supply side and gender perspective and empirical studies relevant to household food security and nutritional security with regard to socio-economic perspective and women perspective.

Chapter–III: Discussion of Research Design–Objectives, Hypotheses, Concepts, Survey Design and Limitations of the Study. Profile of Sivaganga and Cuddalore districts, focussing on Agro-economic and Demographic features.

Chapter–IV: Profile of sample households–analysis of background information in terms of household factors and maternal factors.

Chapter–V: Analysis of household entitlements and food security is in three sections (i) Household entitlements and food system and (ii) Operationalizing household food security and examination of the relationship between the entitlements and food security dimensions, and (iii) Entitlements and Dimensions of Food Security.

Chapter–VI: Analysis of women's role in the food chain through task and time allocation, their access to resources and participation in decision-making–Examination of the relationship between women empowerment and food security and women's food strategies.

Chapter–VII: Analysis of Individual Food Security (IFS)-Examination of: (i) Adequacy perspective of IFS (ii) Equity perspective of IFS and (iii) Efficiency perspective of IFS. Assessment of the relationship of the individuals' nutritional status with household and maternal factors.

Chapter–VIII: Integrated discussion and presentation of policy suggestions providing household food path model and scope for further research.

Chapter–IX: Conclusions.

NOTES AND REFERENCES

1. Chambers, R. and G. Conway (1992), "Sustainable Rural Livelihood: Practical Concepts for the 21st Century", IDS Discussion Papers No. 296, Brighton: 4.
2. Pelletier, D.L., E. A. Frongillo and J.P. Habicht (1993), "Epidemiologic Evidence for a Potentiating Effect of Malnutrition on Child Mortality", *American Journal of Public Health*, Vol. 83. No. 3, 1130-1133.
3. Scrimshaw, N. S. (1997), "Nutrition and Health from Womb to Tomb", *Food and Nutrition Bulletin*, Vol. 181: 1-19.
4. Soman, C. R. (1992), "Nutrition and Health Development–Lessons from Kerala", *Proceedings of the Nutrition Society*, Vol. 51: 81-92.
5. Pollitt, E. (1990), *Malnutrition and Infection in the Classroom*. UNESCO, Paris.
6. World Bank (1992), *Investing in Nutrition*, World Bank Assistance, World Bank, Washington, D.C., 6-7.
7. United Nations (1948), "Universal Declaration of Human Rights", Adopted and Proclaimed by General Assembly Resolution, 217/A (III) of 10, December.
8. Paroda, R. S., "Agricultural Research and Development Strategy in the Wake of Globalization", Paper Presented at the Planning Commission, Government of India, New Delhi.

9. Sundaram, S. I. (1996), "Feeding a Hungry World", *Social Welfare,* Vol. 43, No. 9: 17.

10. Swaminathan, M. S. (1998), "Sustainable Food and Nutrition Security for 1990's", *Agricultural Situation in India,* Vol. 32. No. 5: 363.

11. Prabha Gupta, S. (1999), "Nutrition–An Indian Perspective", *Indian Journal of Public Health,* Vol. 43. No. 1, January-March: 33-37.

12. United Nations Development Programme (1994), *Human Development Report 1994.* Oxford University Press, New York.

13. Economic Survey (2000-2001), Planning Commission, Government of India, Ministry of Finance, Economic Division: 194.

14. Khusro, A. M. (1993), "Poverty Declines in Production, So Does the Quality of Life", *Financial Times,* 5th July, 4.

15. Reddy, V., P. Rao, G. Sastry and K. Kashinath (1993), *Nutrition Trends in India.* National Institute of Nutrition, Hyderabad.

16. National Nutritional Monitoring Bureau (2000), *Twenty-Five years of National Nutritional Monitoring Bureau 1972-1997,* National Institute of Nutrition. ICMR, Hyderabad.

17. Economic Survey 2000-2001. *op.cit*

18. Alagh , Yoginder K. (1995), "Poverty and Food Security: Toward a Policy System for Food Security", *Economic and Political Weekly,* Vol. 30, No. 52: A 142-50.

19. Babu, S.C. and J.A. Hallam (1989), "Socio-economic Impacts of School Feeding Programs–Empirical Evidence from a South Indian Village", *Food Policy,* Vol. 1: 58-66.

20. Islam, Nurul (1992), "Poverty in South Asia: Approaches to its Alleviation", *Food Policy,* Vol. 17, No. 2, 109-128.

21. Rao, M.V. (1997), "Indian Agriculture, Future Challenges", *University News,* Vol. 35, No. 10: 12.

22. International Food Policy Research Institute, (1995), "Women's Roles in Food Security", *IFPRI Report,* Vol. 17, No. 3, October.

23. Agarwal, Bina (1985), "Women Agricultural Development Strategies and Ecological Imbalances: The Indian Context." Paper Presented at Asian Regional Conference on Women and the Household. Indian Statistical Institute, New Delhi, January 27-31.

24. Dixon, Ruth B. (1982), "Women in Agriculture: Counting the Labour Force in Developing Countries", *Population and Development Review*, Vol. 8, No. 3: 21.
25. *Ayalew@www.stanford.ac.uk*
26. Reutlinger, S. and K. Knapp (1980), "Food Security in Food Deficit Countries", *World Bank Staff Working Paper No. 393*, World Bank, Washington, D.C.
27. World Bank (1986), "Poverty and Hunger: Issues and Options for Food Security in Developing Countries", *World Bank Policy Study*, Vol. 11, No. 69, World Bank, Washington, D.C.
28. Schiff, M. and A. Valdes (1990), "The Link between Poverty and Malnutrition–a Household Theoretic Approach", *Working Paper* No. 536, World Bank, Washington, D.C.
29. Maxwell, S. and T. R. Frankenberger (1992), *Household Food Security: Concepts, Indicators and Measurements: A Technical Review*, UNICEF and FAO, New York and Rome.
30. World Bank (1986), op.cit.
31. FAO (1987), *Agriculture Towards 2000*. Rome.
32. International Fund for Agricultural Development (1992), *Rural Poverty Alleviation and Nutrition: IFAD's Evolving Experiences*, A Technical Paper. Technical Advisory Division: IFAD, Rome.
33. Sen, A.K. (1981), *Hunger and Poverty, Essays on Entitlement and Deprivation,* The Clarendon Press, Oxford.
34. Mc Guire, J. and B. Popkin (1988), "Increasing Women's Resources for Nutrition in Developing Countries", Paper Prepared for the U.N. Co-ordinating Committee's Sub-committee on Nutrition Symposium on Women and Nutrition.

2

Review of Literature

This chapter attempts to present a brief review of literature to decode views, trends and empirical results encoded in the works of various authors with reference to food security. This review is arranged in three modules. The first module would attempt to annotate literatures concerned with theories of food security from the supply, demand and gender perspectives in that order. The second module would survey literatures on Household Food Security and the third module, Nutritional Security. These two modules would individually and collectively highlight literatures concerned with socio-economic perspectives and women-related perspectives.

THEORIES ON FOOD SECURITY

This module would focus on macro-level studies in relation to supply and demand, and on micro-level studies in relation to gender.

Supply-side Perspective

Food security has been a theme of discussion even during the classical era when it was done at the macro-level from the supply parameter in terms of Food Availability Deficiency (FAD). Adam Smith (1776)[1] attributed the outburst of famine conditions to FAD. In his often quoted article "Digression Concerning the Corn Trade and Corn Laws," in Book IV of the *Wealth of Nations*, he theorised that famines could be caused only by a real scarcity situation, and a plenty of scarcity situations were caused by natural calamities like drought, flood and seasonal failures. But David Ricardo (1815) [2] contradicted Smith's views and proclaimed that famines could occur in situations of "super-abundance."

For many years thenceforth, rational discussion of the food problem was distracted by undue concentration on the comparative trend between population growth and expansion of output. In claiming a correlation between mass starvation and an excessive population growth that outstrips available food supply, Malthusian (1798)[3] theory explained famine through a direct and easily understood causal relationship. Malthus argued that as long as food output grew faster than the population, famine couldn't occur. He was concerned with formulating a kind of aggregate warning system through putting much emphasis on quantitative problem of population *vis-à-vis* food supply, which could enable a timely counteraction. A notable example is the approach of the Food and Agriculture Organisation, which operates on a balance sheet system relying on food and crop production statistics to forewarn food deficits.

Post-Smithian studies on supply-side approach present a uni-causal explanation for food insecurity and delve deep into the analysis of various causes, which lead to deficiency in food supply. Taking the lead from Adam Smith, authors like Brown *et al.* (1957)[4], Harrer (1963)[5] and Brown (1965)[6] analysed the world food situation and prospects of increasing food availability by improving technologies of food production. Moseman (1964)[7], Millikan and Hapgood (1967)[8], and a University of California study (1974)[9] examined the food availability problems of the less developed countries and concluded that technical progress could promote high yields. FAO (1970)[10] analysed the priority problems in agriculture with a view to improve food grain situation.

Masefield (1963)[11] and John (1975)[12] observed that acute food shortages led to starvation causing widespread diseases and deaths in restricted geographical areas of the world.

The World Food Conference (UN 1975)[13] identified the risk of the acute food shortages in the event of widespread crop failure, natural or other disasters, as well as the risk of fluctuations in production and prices. And many subsequent analyses quoted below in parenthesis similarly concentrated on risks to national food supply and the balance of payment (Minhas, 1976[14]; Reutlinger and Knapp, 1980[15]; and Valdes and Konandreas, 1981[16]).

Acharya (1983)[17] studied the food security situation in India and categorized various components of food security and accentuated the importance of each in the Indian context. George (1994)[18] explored the prospects of South Asian countries' food security situation. The study suggested increased food production by employing better technology, trading adequate buffer stock and enforcing target oriented programmes for the poor. Maurice (1991)[19] stated that theories of demographic trap were received with admiration even in the 1990s. Davies *et al.* (1991)[20] predicted alarming food insecurity situations and emphasised the necessity of data at the national and international levels for food security interventions.

Demand-side Perspective

Complementary to the supply perspective, which considered food availability as a matter of factual investigation, the demand side focus assumed importance in the food security equations.

Straffa (1971)[21] suggested that economists while concerned with food acquirement problem should also recognize the significance of command in the market (demand side focus). Smith's work, which focused on protecting the food insecure through marketing system by the laissez-faire approach, is debatable. Malthus, though made an early presentation of the theory of demand even before Keynes, his emphasis was on the quantitative problems of population against food supply.

Food Availability Deficiency (FAD) is based on population growth and physical access (agriculture stagnation) where as, 'economic access' is the phenomenon of the 1980s, largely resulting from the pioneering work of Amartya Sen (1981)[22] on food entitlements. Using the entitlement framework Sen demonstrated that food insecurity (famine in Sen's terminology) could occur in the absence of any change in production. Sen, while investigating the causes of various famines (Bengal in 1943, China in 1948 and Bangladesh in 1974) found that these famines took place when food was available in adequate quantities and in some part of the areas per capita availability of food was the highest during those years when compared to the earlier or subsequent years. Sen's Entitlement theory went beyond the narrow study of food availability.

According to FAD theory an individual is food insecure because there is not enough to eat, but according to Entitlement and Deprivation theory (E&D), food insecurity can also be seen as the characteristic of a person not having enough to eat. The latter could be the cause of the former, but it is not the only cause. The Exchange Entitlement concept implies that food insecurity at the household level is a result of inadequate demand for food. Based on the entitlement theory, by the mid-1980s the analysis of risk of inadequate access had become an important concern (World Bank, 1989).[23]

According to E & D thesis, if enough food were available and if people could access the food so available, there would be no food insecurity. But Mukherjee (1997)[24] discovered some splotches in the E&D thesis, and contested that even when these two conditions are satisfied, individuals can be food insecure. Quoting various analogical situations, he had explained that food insecurity could be caused in the absence of institutional sanction to access the food through exchange entitlement or transfer entitlement, and when people do not choose to access the available food. Mukherjee further established that the dimension of secondary food system was not taken cognizance of in both Sen's theory of E & D and in the theory of FAD.

However, identifying themselves with Sen's approach, many studies focused attention on the importance of the macro economic policies in ensuring food security of the poor due to deprivation of entitlements. Kumar (1987),[25] Krueger et al.

(1988)[26] and Pinstrup-Andersen (1990)[27] reviewed macro economic policies and suggested that policies for improving food security should not be limited to direct food-and agriculture-related policies. Also, non agricultural and economy wide policies, such as industrial protection and fiscal policies, are highly relevant for prices, income and employment of the poor and thus for food security in the short and long runs. In addition, Hussain (1990)[28] suggested that policies ranging from economy wide macro policies to community actions should be adopted. Policies based on the more targeted actions such as food subsidies and transfers, labour intensive public work and improved supplementary feeding programmes for food security should also be considered. Furthermore, nutritional improvement must not be formulated in isolation, but as components of a national food and nutrition strategy or of an appropriate development strategy.

Looking at food security only from the supply and demand perspectives would provide incomplete input to policy-makers. Another important input, namely that of the reaction of the household to the problem of food security must also be studied to seek solutions at micro level. This has made a discussion on gender perspective obligatory.

Gender Perspective

The Household is a fundamental production unit in every type of economy. The innumerable productive activities carried out by women within the household sector are of critical importance for its survival, growth and development. Women's effective labour was kept out of analytical framework for long. The foremost classical economist Adam Smith (1776)[29] considered labour as the true source of wealth but did not recognize the significance of women's labour. Adam Smith rationalised gender roles. To him women's reproductive and nurturing roles were important. John Stuart Mill (1879)[30] though did not see the productive contribution of women's work at home saw it as production of utilities. Later Feminists like Cadbury *et al.* (1907)[31] emphasised the disparity of incomes between sexes. Alfred Marshall (1930)[32] and Pigou (1952)[33] too addressed the issue of unequal wages. None of these earlier works recognised women's household labour, which is essential for the maintenance of family.

Household economics owes its origin to the seminal work of Becker (1965).[34] His revolutionary theory of the allocation of time defined household work and child rearing as productive activities, and households as units of both production and consumption. The New Household Economics sprang up in the 1960s. Economic modelling of the household followed two schools of thought. One based on a joint household utility function, which assumed that households maximized the joint welfare of their members by allocating income and other resources to the individuals. And the other Bargaining Theory Model while drew heavily on the work of co-operative games by Nash (1953).[35] Under this collective household model the welfare of the individual household members was not synonymous with over all household welfare. Resources were not necessarily pooled and the households acted as a collective, with members having their own preferences. This model helped to prove that the economic status of women outside the home influenced their part of the bargain in household decision making positively. This model helped to explain why gender inequalities persisted even though households' resources increased. These two theoretical approaches to Household Economics were framed in the context of the neo-classical theory of value. Both the approaches precluded the problem of gender bias. Nerlove (1974)[36] pointed out that household decisions about the allocation of resources had a profound effect in the food and nutrition, health care and education received by children.

Manser and Brown (1980),[37] McElroy and Horney (1981)[38] confirmed that decisions on allocating resources reflected the relative bargaining power of household members. They considered women's bargaining position as a prime factor in determining the well being of household members particularly children.

Sen (1984)[39] has shown that neither a family was a homogeneous mass, nor there existed altruism. Institutional approach to household decision-making hover around co-operative conflict. Sen (1990)[40] has been the moving spirit in accommodating power asymmetries among household members. This approach posed two simultaneous problems to households and its members. One involved co-operation (adding to total availabilities), and the other conflict (dividing the total availabilities) among the members of the households. In terms of resource distribution, there are many instances like wealth, food, nutrition and education distributed according to gender and age of the members. Distribution of resource itself got skewed according to who was in-charge of resource distribution (i.e., conflict will depend on the relative bargaining power of the different members of the household).

Women's role and bargaining power in any household framework are influenced by many factors. In very recent literatures, candidate proxies for bargaining power have included share of income earned by women (Haddad and Hoddinott 1994);[41] access to and control over resources (Doss 1996);[42] inherited assets (Quisumbing 1994);[43] and unearned income of women (Schultz 1990).[44] The participation in household decision-making has gained bargaining power and status for women. At household level, resource allocation decisions are made taking into account the households' resource endowment as well as their needs. But these are not gender equitable. Most often a situation of asymmetry can exist. Quisumbing and de la Briere (2000)[45] have ascertained that the bargaining power of men and women critically shaped the resource allocation decisions of households.

Studies were carried out on differential allocation between men and women within households with respect to income, work burdens, nutrition, health, mortality, morbidity, fertility decisions and education (Krishnaji 1987;[46] Sen 1995).[47] Bina Agarwal (1994)[48] and (1997)[49] used this model successfully to include the specific contours of social and cultural configurations in South Asia and had thus enriched and enabled this model to argue for land rights to women.

Women are not any more satellites orbiting around men. Some households are supported exclusively by women alone.

A supernova category, female-headed households, has emerged as a new field of inquiry. The present study parades over this aspect of household headship, and has identified it as an important variable in the distribution and improvement of food and nutrition security among the household members.

HOUSEHOLD FOOD SECURITY

The socio-economic environment of the household and the participative role of the women in the household largely govern household food security. Enormous literatures available on these two components have to be reviewed separately for effective comprehension.

Socio-Economic Perspective

Some studies have empirically proved that socio-economic factors tend to influence food security at the household level. Omawale and Rodrigues (1980)[50] in a study conducted in the Northwestern region of Guyana have confirmed the correlation between poverty and food consumption. In this study, land holding was found to be positively associated with both household expenditure on food and the quantity of self-produced food consumption.

Majumder *et al.* (1985)[51] identified that occupational status had a very clear impact on the dietary adequacy status of households. Acheson *et al.* (1980)[52] found that intake of edibles such as rice, milk roots and tubers, condiments and spices were almost the same during reference periods in families irrespective of their economic status. But Chadha *et al.* (1995)[53] noted significant difference in food consumption patterns, depending on income levels and occupational status. Another study by Davis (1982)[54] postulated a positive relationship between food expenditure and dietary status.

Hoddinott and Yisehac (2002)[55] examined from the data set for ten countries including India and found a significant association between dietary diversity and household per capita calorie availability in the rural areas.

Lipton (1983)[56] defined the ultra-poor households as those households, which consumed less than 80 per cent of recommended calories while spent more than 80 per cent of its income on food. Schiff and Valdes (1990)[57] found that increased per capita income had a positive impact on the number of meals and dietary status.

Kaur and Sood (1988)[58] in their study on dietary intake of non farm workers found that due to low income they subsisted on low cost vegetarian foods but their intake of various food items increased as their socio-economic status improved. Gray's (1982)[59] study identified income as the most important factor in the nutrient intake even though the income elasticity of food consumption was quite low. Alderman (1986)[60] found that increase in income resulted in increase in the intake of staple food especially for the rural poor households. It is also found to be true for non-staple food consumption especially meat. Bouis (1991)[61] was concerned with the effect of low-income on micronutrient food.

Von Braun and Pandya-Lorch (1991)[62] enumerated the various factors, which led to food insecurity in rural poor households. They found that food insecurity, measured in terms of low energy consumption, was higher among landless or quasi-landless households, who depended on riskier sources of income than farm income. Food insecurity was also found to be higher in households with more number of dependents and a young age composition.

Krishna (1992)[63] and Vyas (1993)[64] suggested that poor households inflicted with chronic food insecurity because of low economic status should be protected through social security networks like Public Distribution System. Basu (1993)[65] considered Employment Guarantee Scheme as the right social security component as it targeted the poor directly, ensured them a regular income, and increased their purchasing power, and enabled them to be food secured.

These empirical literatures provide conclusive evidence that resources are cardinal determinants of household food security.

Women Perspective

The literatures reviewed under this caption center around two relationships: the relationship between women's participation in food production and household food availability and the relationship between women's opportunities to control household food consumption and achieve food security.

FAO (1983)[66], ECA (1984)[67] and Okeyo (1985)[68] visualised emphatically the large contribution of women to the total household food availability in regions like Sub-Saharan Africa and also some places in Asia. They affirmed that women were mainly responsible for feeding their families.

Garibaldi Accati (1983)[69] found that women participation in farm and non-farm activities not only increased the total food supply to the household but also ensured dietary variations. In most rural households women were found to be responsible for growing different kinds of vegetables, roots and fruits. Wandel and Holmboe-Ottesen (1984)[70] found women in rural households to add relish to the diet in the form of wild foods, such as green leaves. Chaney (1985)[71] listed out a number of women's activities such as water and fuel collection and other food supporting activities that could contribute to increased food availability. Cairncross and Cliff (1987)[72] Magnani *et al.* (1984)[73] reported that women's time saved from bringing water supplies closer to their homes resulted in more time spent on food processing and food preparation.

Basiotis *et al.* (1983)[74] correlated household headship to dietary status. He adduced that joint headed households and female-headed household had significantly greater availability of food energy and other nutrients than households headed by males. He further suggested that headship variable should receive more research attention for effective policy-making.

Kumar (1985)[75] assessed that women in female-headed households work harder than in male-headed households but their output was lower. Some studies discovered male migration beneficial to women to meet their needs including the family food needs. Staudt (1979)[76] claimed that male absence enhanced control over products. In Jordan, male migration caused to have increased women's participation in the productive sector.

Evidences to support the greater impact of women's income on household food security are increasing. Detailed studies of rural women's and men's income and spending patterns were conducted in Zambia (Skjonsberg, 1981);[77] the Ivory coast and Nepal (Bério, 1984b);[78] Tamil Nadu and Kerala (Mencher, 1985).[79] The pattern that emerged from these studies was that even though women's cash income were generally lower than men's, a higher percentage of their earnings was allocated to household food. When home production was also taken into consideration, women's contribution was quite large in all these societies.

Safilios-Rotschild (1980),[80] deliberated on women's decision-making power as an important determinant of nutrition. Since women had the main responsibility for feeding their families on a day-to-day basis, they were more likely to make self-sacrifices for the sake of the health of their families, especially their children. In contrast, men tended to be more interested in spending on expensive non-food items. Piwoz and Viteri (1985),[81] identified women's income generating capacity as an ace variable in determining women's decision-making power and also in matters other than control over their own income. However, empirical studies on this aspect are lacking.

FAO (1993)[82] declared that intra-household inequalities in income and decision-making had increased recently and evidently it is because of the lack of women controlled resources. Agarwal (1994)[83] found that in poor households, having rights to land could alleviate both women's own poverty and the household risk of remaining poor. This study confirmed the views of various other earlier studies that women's access to economic resources had a positive effect on household welfare.

Garcia (1991)[84] examined the effect of women's income on household expenditure patterns and found that women spent higher proportion of their income on food consumption and health care of children than men. A recent study by Thomas and Chen (1994)[85] conducted in Taiwan found that with per capita household income at constant, women's income share had significant positive effect on household budget shares of staples and education but had significant negative effect on budget share allocated to alcohol and cigarettes.

The summary of these studies indicates that women's participation in food production and income-generating activities will enhance household food security tc a greater extent.

NUTRITIONAL SECURITY

Like household food security, achievement of individual nutritional security is also envisaged to be interrelated to socio-economic and women participation factors.

Socio-economic Perspective

Chopdar and Nabarro (1981)[86] found that poor socio-economic status is the reason for low weight of a new born baby. They indicated that mother's busy agricultural labour work and trading activities significantly reduced breast-feeding. A field study combining women's work and child-feeding patterns in Tanzania by Mascarenhas (1983)[87] confirmed this view of Chopdar and Nabarro. Mascarenhas found that in about half of the households studied, the preschool children got only one or two meals a day. Lack of mother's time was then considered to be the main reason for such a low frequency of child feeding. In a follow-up study Mascarenhas (1984)[88] found that nutrition sufficiency seemed to be worse in the household where women worked as casual labourers. Lack of food in their households during critical pre-harvest seasons compelled women to do casual work. This study ratified the poor socio economic condition to be both the cause of mother's working as well as of their children's nutritional condition. Rajagopalan et al. (1981)[89] recorded similar findings.

Visweswara Rao *et al.* (1994)[90] found access to health service and availability of safe drinking water to have high correlation with child nutritional status.

Gupta *et al.* (1988)[91] recorded income to be positively associated with energy intake and body weight of Indian women, and workload to be negatively associated with their energy intake and body weight.

Chavas and Keplinger (1983)[92] reported that no significant effect of money income was found in the nutritional status of very low-income households. Allen and Gadson (1982)[93] found household expenditure to have a positive impact on nutritional status of family members. Using the All India Large-scale Sample Survey, the NNMB (1989)[94] has demonstrated a clear correlation between income levels and decrease of malnutrition in rural children.

Women Perspective

Available women-related literatures confirm the view that women's earnings are spent preferentially on goods and services, which improve the health of children. This implies that both women's decision-making power and household health-related goods and services increase in tandem. Acharya and Bennet (1982)[95] claimed that women's direct access to cash had influenced their power in intra household dynamics and status. For example, a study on women participants in Maharashtra's Employment Guarantee Scheme reported that the nutritional status of children was better, when women received the cash or grain payments directly.

Bindinger *et al.* (1986)[96] in a detailed study of an Andhra village, exemplified that employment in the household in general, female members in particular, as the core factor which affected the energy intake of children under six years of age and the equitable allocation of food resources. This study found female employment to be a more significant determinant than income or land holding size.

Many studies in India have reaffirmed that women's employment had the potential to benefit household nutrition through an increase in household income. Gulati (1978)[97] found that daily nutritional adequacy in agricultural labourer households in Kerala was related more to women's employment than to men's employment. She calibrated that on days when both the male head of household and his wife were employed, their shortfalls in terms of calorie was 11 and 20 per cent respectively, while on days on which the women were unemployed, the shortfalls increased to 26 and 50 per cent respectively.

Thomas (1994)[98] and Doss (1997)[99] had found in their respective studies that female income had a greater impact than male income on pre-schooler's nutrient adequacy, their survival probabilities and their education.

Studies linking higher levels of maternal education with improved nutritional status are abundant. Sen and Sengupta's (1983)[100] study of two villages in West Bengal found a significant association between mother's education and children's nutritional status. Mothers with more education rarely had children with severe malnutrition. Devadas *et al.* (1991)[101] reiterated the axiom that educated mothers would provide a balanced diet and promote environmental hygiene.

Bairagi (1980)[102] studied the relationship between child nutrition and factors such as family income, maternal education and birth order. He found that income was not the only constraint on nutritional status, even in the lowest income group, maternal education had a significant influence on nutritional status. All the above-mentioned studies emphasise the pre-eminence of education over income.

A hypothesis that has advanced and often encountered in the literature is that gender and age based inequality in the intra household allocation of food. Evenson *et al.* (1979)[103] recorded from a series of household surveys in Philippines, the existence of sex-bias against females and age-bias against children. In both the cases, the female adults and female children were at a disadvantage. Levinson (1974)[104] identified food scarce situations ramifying to gender bias situations especially during conditions of seasonal scarcity or chronic poverty. Chen *et al.* (1981)[105] formulated that inequitable food distribution led to a higher incidence of severe malnutrition among women and girls and excess female infant mortality. He had also formulated that food scarcity alone would not explain sex disparities in mortality rate in the pre-school children. He identified even rich families with higher female child deaths. He advocated a more equitable allocation of food within the family in relation to its nutritional requirements.

Based on the nutritional surveys in India and Nigeria, Amartya Sen (1984)[106] quoted the incidence of sex-bias and age-bias in the intra household food allocation. Gopaldas *et al.* (1983)[107] postulated that the intra-household food distribution is related to cultural norm and socio-economic status.

Ware (1981)[108] was confounded that only a few traditional cultures recognised the increased nutritional needs of women during pregnancy and lactation. He reviewed weight-for-height data, taking it to be the measure of nutritional status, among male and female children and adults in different African villages, and found no coherent pattern of differences between the sexes. He had also identified "under investment in females" as a general feature in the Third World, pertaining not only to food but also to other basic needs such as education and health. She suggested that women might enjoy a better nutritional status on occasions when they play a major role in productive activities. Standing (1989)[109] also found that women who were non-earning dependents were worse off in terms of nutritional status then women who were earning members or heads of poor household.

Despite confirmed findings that household gender bias is a hazardous to nutritional well-being and health of women, prejudice continues to exist. Marcoux (2001)[110] in his recent study in developing countries identified the prevalence of gender bias.

A cross-country analysis by Ramalingaswami et al. (1996)[111], made on the database of 36 developing countries from South Asia (SA), Sub-Saharan Africa (SSA) and Latin America and Caribbean (LAC) established child malnutrition rate to be much higher is SA than SSA, though SA was performing better than SSA in accepted determinants of child nutritional status such as national income, food supplies, health services and education. The chasmic gap in the prevalence of malnutrition (termed "The Asian Enigma") is attributed to the extremely low status of women in SA compared with SSA. This analysis was carried out under the auspices of demographic and health surveys.

Much of the past research work were not concerned with relative allocation of food consumption among the members within the family but with direct comparison of gender by nutrition health status. In a study made by Jeyaraaj and Malathi (1996),[112] it was observed that in spite of efficient survival strategy hypothesis, there were wide differences in nutrition health status between school going children with reference to stunting and wasting malnutrition compared to pre-school children. This cannot really depict the magnitude of actual difference in the amount of food intake.

Interestingly enough, recent studies by Haughton and Haughton (1997)[113] and NNMB (1999)[114] report for Indians did not observe any sex-bias against females in the intra-familial allocation of food. This study also focuses on the relative allocation of food among individual members within the families.

The following issues emerge from the review of literature of household food security:

1. Entitlements of the households are more important than food availability for improving household food security.
2. Apart from entitlements, women's status is a priority factor in food security at the household level.
3. Women's education and nutritional knowledge are prime determinants of children and household nutritional well-being.

It is in the silhouette of these emerging issues, a micro level study of food security from women's perspective is attempted in this study. It is also assumed that socio-economic factors alone may not be able to achieve a food secured situation. Encouraging women participation in decision making and improving their status which have hitherto been little explored occupies an important stance in this study. Studies that deal with household headship and linking it with household food and nutrition security are rare and scarce. This study would attempts to provide the missing link.

NOTES AND REFERENCES

1. Smith, Adam (1776), *An Inquiry into the Nature and Causes of the Wealth of Nations*. Reprint 1976, Clarendon Press, Oxford.

2. Ricardo, David (1815), *An Essay on the Influence of a Low Price of Corn on the Profits of Stock.* John Murray, London.
3. Malthus, Thomas Robert (1798), *An Essay on Population* Ist ed.: 7.
4. Brown, Harrison, James Bonner and John Weir (1957), *The Next Hundred Years,* Viking Press, New York.
5. Harrer, J. George (1963), *Strategy for the Conquest of Hunger,* Rock Feller Foundation, New York.
6. Brown, Lester R. (1965), "Increasing World Food Output: Problems and Prospects." Foreign Agricultural Economics Report. No. 25. U.S. Department of Agriculture, Washington, D.C.
7. Moseman, Albert H. (1964), "Agricultural Sciences for the Developing Countries", American Association for the Advancement of Science, Washington, D.C.
8. Millikan, M and D. Hapgood (1967), *No Easy Harvest: The Dilemma of Agriculture in Underdeveloped Countries,* Little Brown, Boston.
9. University of California (1974), *A Hungry World: The Challenge to Agriculture,* Division of Agricultural Sciences, Berkeley.
10. Food and Agriculture Organisation (1970), *Provisional Indicative World Plan for Agricultural Development,* Vol. 2.
11. Masefield, G.B. (1963), *Famine: Its Prevention and Relief,* Oxford University Press, Delhi.
12. John D. Post (1975), *The Last Great Subsistence Crisis in the Western World.* The Johns Hopkins University Press, Baltimore.
13. United Nations (1975), *Report of the World Food Conference,* New York.
14. Minhas, B. S. (1976), "Presidential Address-Towards National Food Security", *Journal of Agricultural Economics,* Vol. 34, No. 4. October–December, 8-19.
15. Reutlinger, S. and K. Knapp (1980), "Food Security in Food Deficit Countries", *World Bank Staff Working Paper No.* 393, World Bank. Washington, D.C.
16. Valdes, A. and Panos Konandreas (1981), "Assessing Food Insecurity Based on National Aggregates in Developing Countries," in Alberto Valdes (ed.), *Food Security for Developing Countries,* Westview Press, Boulder.
17. Acharya, K.C.S. (1983), *Food Security of India,* Concept Publishing Company, New Delhi.

18. George, P. S. (1994), "Food Security in South Asia", *Economic and Political Weekly,* Vol. 29, April 18.
19. Maurice, King (1991), "Entrapment in India", *The National Medical Journal of India,* Vol. 4, No. 5, September, 101-103.
20. Davies, S. M., Buchanan-Smith and R. Lambert (1991), "Early Warning in the Sahel and Horn of Africa: The State of the Art. A Review of Literature." IDS Research a Report, Vol. 1, Brighton.
21. Straffa, P. (1971), *The Works and Correspondence of David Ricardo,* Vol. 5, Cambridge University Press, Cambridge.
22. Sen, A. K. (1981), *Poverty and Famines: An Essay on Entitlement and Deprivation,* Clarendon Press, Oxford, U.K.
23. World Bank (1989), *Gender and Poverty in India,* Washington, D.C.
24. Mukherjee, Amitava (1997), "Institutional Sanctions, Choice and Secondary Food System: Incompleteness of Sen's Entitlement and Deprivation Thesis as an Explanation for Hunger," in K.K. George, V. Sankaran Nair and Jose Jacob (eds.), *Economics, Development and the Quest for Alternatives,* Segment Books, New Delhi.
25. Kumar, S. K. (1987), "The Nutrition Situation and its Food Policy Links," in J.W. Mellor, C. I. Delgado and M.J. Blackie (eds.), *Accelerating Food Production in Sub-Saharan Africa.* Johns Hopkins University Press for the INFPRI, Baltimore: 39-52.
26. Krueger, Anne O., Maurice W. Schiff, and Alberto Valdes (1988), "Agricultural Incentives in Developing Countries: Measuring the Effect of Sectoral and Economy-wide Policies", *The World Bank Economic Review,* Vol. 2, September: 255-271.
27. Pinstrup-Andersen, P. (1990), "Macroeconomic Policy Reforms, Poverty, and Nutrition: Analytical Methodologies", Corenell Food and Nutrition Policy Program Monograph 3, Ithaca, New York, U.S.A.
28. Hussain, M.A. (1990), "Nutrition Policy and the Urban Poor in Developing Countries", *Food Policy,* Vol. 15, August: 186-192.
29. Smith, Adam (1776), *op.cit.*
30. Mill, John Stuart (1879), "The Subjection of Women", Reprinted in Alice Rossi (ed.), *Essays on Sex Equality,* Chicago University Press, Chicago.

31. Cadbury, Matheson E., M. Cecile and Shann George (1907), *Women's Work and Wages, A Phase of Life in an Industrial City,* Chicago University Press, Chicago.

32. Marshall, Alfred (1930), *Principles of Economics,* Macmillan, London.

33. Pigou, A. C. (1952), "Men's and Women's Wages." Reprinted in *Essays in Economics,* Macmillan, London.

34. Becker, Gary (1965), "A Theory of the Allocation of Time", In Alice Amalers, (ed.), *The Economics of Women and Work,* St. Martin Press, New York.

35. Nash, J. (1953), "Two-person Bargaining Games", *Econometrica,* Vol. 21, 128-140.

36. Nerlove, S. (1974), "Women's Workload and Infant Feeding Practices: A Relationship with Demographic Implications." *Ethnology,* Vol. 13: 207-214.

37. Manser, Marilyn and Murray Brown (1980), "Marriage and Household Decision-Making: A Bargaining Analysis", *International Economic Review,* Vol. 21: 31-44.

38. McElroy, Marjorie and Mary Jean Horney (1981), "Nash-bargained Household Decisions: Towards a Generalisation of the Theory of Demand", *International Economic Review,* Vol. 22, June: 333-49.

39. Sen, A.K. (1984), *Resources Values and Development: Family and Food Sex-bias in Poverty,* Oxford University Press, London.

40. Sen, Amartya (1990), "Gender and Cooperative Conflicts," in Irene Tinker (ed.), *Persistent Inequalities: Women and Development.* Oxford University Press, UK, 123-49.

41. Haddad, L. and J. Hoddinott (1994), "Women's Income and Boy-Girl Anthropometric Status in the Côte d'Ivoire." *World Development,* Vol. 22, No. 4, 543-553.

42. Doss, C. (1996), "Women's Bargaining Power in Household Economic Decisions: Evidence from Ghana", Staff Paper Series No. P. 96-11, Department of Applied Economics, college of Agricultural, Food, and Environmental Sciences, University of Minnesota.

43. Quisumbing, A.R. (1994), "Intergenerational Transfers in Philippine Rice Villages: Gender Differences in Traditional Inheritance Customs", *Journal of Development Economics,* Vol. 43. No. 2, 167-195.

44. Schultz, T.P. (1990), "Testing the Neo-classical Model of Family Labour Supply and Fertility", *Journal of Human Resources,* Vol. 25. No. 4: 599-634.

45. Quisumbing, A. R. and de la Briere (2000), "Women's Assets and Intra-household Allocation in Rural Bangladesh: Testing Measures of Bargaining Power", Food Consumption and Nutrition Division Discussion Paper 86, IFPRI, Washington, D.C.

46. Krishnaji, N. (1987), "Poverty and Sex Ratio: Some Data and Speculation", *Economic and Political Weekly,* Vol. 22, No. 23, June 6: 155-6.

47. Sen, Amartya (1995), "Gender Inequality and Theories of Justice," in Martha Nussbaum and Jonathan Glover (eds.), *Women, Culture and Development,* Clarendon Press, Oxford.

48. Agarwal, Bina (1994), "Gender and Command Over Property: A Critical Gap in Economic Analysis and Policy in South Asia", *World Development,* Vol. 22. No. 10: 1455-78.

49. Agarwal, Bina (1997), "Bargaining and Gender Relations: Within and Beyond the Household", *Feminist Economics,* Vol. 1, No. 5: 1-51.

50. Omawale and A.M. Rodrigues (1980), "Nutrition Consideration in a Cassava Production Programme for Guyana", *Ecology of Food and Nutrition,* Vol. 10: 87-95.

51. Majumder, P.P., P. Bharathi, D.C. Banerjee, and Basu (1985). "A Dietary Status of Mahishyas in Chakopta: Inter and Intra-Economic Group Variations", *Ecology of Food and Nutrition,* Vol. 17: 231-251.

52. Acheson, K.J., I.T. Campbell, O.G. Edholm, D.S. Miller, and M.J. Stock (1980), "The Measurement of Food and Energy Intake in Man-an Evaluation of Some Technique", *American Journal of Clinical Nutrition,* Vol. 33: 1147-1154.

53. Chadha, S. L., N. Gopinath, Indu Katyal, and S. Shekhawat (1995), "Dietary Profile of Adults in an Urban and a Rural Community", *Indian Journal of Medical Research,* Vol. 101:258-267.

54. Davis, C.G. (1982), "Linkages between Socio-economic Characteristics, Food Expenditure Patterns, and Nutritional Status of Low Income Households: A Critical Review", *American Journal of Agricultural Economics,* Vol. 64: 1017-25.

55. Hoddinott, John and Yisehac Yohannes (2002). "Dietary Diversity as a Household Food Security Indicator." Food and Nutrition

Technical Assistance Project, Academy for Educational Development, Washington, D.C.

56. Lipton, M. (1983), "Poverty, Undernutrition and Hunger", *World Bank Staff Working Paper* No. 597, World Bank, Washington, D.C.

57. Schiff, M. and A. Valdes (1990), "Poverty, Food and Malnutrition: Implications for Food Security in Developing Countries", *American Journal of Agricultural Economics,* Vol. 72: 1318-22.

58. Kaur, I.P. and B. Sood (1988), "Dietary Pattern and Nutritional Status of Spinning Mill Workers", *The Indian Journal of Nutrition and Dietetics,*Vol. 25: 315-319.

59. Gray, C.W. (1982), *Food Consumption Parameters for Brazil and Their Application to Food Policy,* Research Report 32, International Food Policy Research Institute, Washington, D.C.

60. Alderman, Harold (1986), *The Effect of Food Price and Income Changes on the Acquisition of Food by Low Income Households.* International Food Policy Research Institute, Washington, D.C.

61. Bouis, Howarth E. (1991), *The Determinants of Household-Level Demand for Micronutrients. An Analysis for Philippine Farm Households.* International Food Policy Research Institute, Mimeo, Washington, D.C.

62. Von Braun, Joachim and Rajul Pandya-Lorch (1991), "Income Sources of Malnourished People in Rural Areas: A Synthesis of Case Studies and Implications for Policy", *Working Papers on Commercialization of Agriculture and Nutrition,* No. 5. IFPRI, Washington, D.C. 1-46.

63. Krishna, T.N. (1992), "Population, Poverty and Employment in India", *Economic and Political Weekly,* Vol. 26: 46.

64. Vyas, V.S. (1993), "New Economic Policy and Vulnerable Sections: Rationale for Public Interventions", *Economic and Political Weekly,* Vol. 27, March: 26.

65. Basu, Kaushik (1993), "Structural Reform in India, 1991-93. Experience and Agenda", *Economic and Political Weekly,* November, 27: 2599-605.

66. Food and Agriculture Organisation (1983), "Women in Food Production", Report of the Expert Consultation held in Rome, FAO, Rome, December, 7-14 : 149.

67. United Nations Economic Commission for Africa (1984), "The Role of Women in the Solution of the Food Crisis in Africa." Paper

Prepared for the Third Regional Conference on the Integration of Women in Development, African Training and Research Centre for Women, UNECA, Addis Ababa.

68. Okeyo, Achola Pala (1985), "Women and Food Production", Special Report on the Crisis for African Children: The State of Africa's Child in 1985. Report Prepared for UNICEF.

69. Garibaldi, Accati Elena (1983), "Women's Role in Horticultural Production in Developing Countries", Prepared for the Expert Consultation on Women in Food Production, FAO, Rome.

70. Wandel, Margareta and Gerd Holmboe-Ottesen (1984), "Women's Perspective on Nutrition; Experience from a Village in Southern Sri Lanka", Report from a Work Conference, Norewegian Research Council, Secretariat for Research on Women, Munthesgt.

71. Chaney, Elsa M. (1985), "Women and Food Production: Variations on a Perennial Theme", in Rita S. Gallin and Anita (eds.), *Women Creating Wealth: Transforming Economic Development*, Spring Association for Women in Development, Washington, D.C., 61–64.

72. Cairncross, S. and J.L. Cliff (1987), "Water Use and Health in Mueda, Mazambique", *Transactions of the Royal Society of Tropical Medicine and Hygiene*, Vol. 81, No.1: 51-54.

73. Magnani, R.J., S.C. Tourkin and M.J. Hartz (1984), *Evaluation of the Provincial Water Project in the Philippines*. International Statistical Program Centre, U.S. Department of Commerce, Washington, D.C.

74. Basiotis, P., M. Brown, S.R. Johnson, and K.J. Morgan (1983), "Nutrient Availability, Food Costs and Food Stamps", *American Journal of Agricultural Economics*, Vol. 65: 685-93.

75. Kumar, Shubh K. (1985), *Women's Agricultural Work in a Subsistence-Oriented Economy: Its Role in Production, Food Consumption and Nutrition*, IFPRI, Washington, D.C.

76. Staudt, Katheleen (1979). "Women and Participation in Rural Development: A Framework for Project Design and Policy - Oriented Research." Rural Development Committee, Centre for International Studies. Cornell University, Ithaca, New York: 78.

77. Skjonsberg, Else (1981), "The Kefa Records: Every-day Life among Women and Men in a Zambian Village", Third World Seminar Publications No. 21, University of Oslo, Norway.

78. Bério, Ann-Jacqueline (1984), "The Use of Time Allocation Data in Developing Countries: from Influencing Development to Estimating Energy Requirements", Paper Delivered at the International Research Group on Time Budgets and Social Activities, Helsinki, FAO, Rome, August.

79. Mencher, Joan P. (1985), "The Forgotten Ones. Female Landless Labourers in Southern India," in R.S. Gallin and Anitha (eds.), *Women Creating Wealth: Transforming Economic Development*, Spring Association for Women in Development Conference, Washington, D.C.

80. Safilios-Rotschild, Constantina (1980), "The Role of the Family: A Neglected Aspect of Poverty", *Implementing Programmes of Human Development, World Bank Staff Working Paper,* No. 103, Washington, D.C.

81. Piwoz, Ellen Gail and Fernando Viteri (1985), "Studying Health and Nutrition Behaviour by Examing Household Decision-Making, Intra-household Resource Distribution, and the Role of Women in these Processes", *Food and Nutrition Bulletin,* Vol. 7, No. 4: 1-31.

82. Food and Agriculture Organisation (1993), "Rural Poverty Alleviation: Policies and Trends", *Economic and Social Development Paper,* No. 113, Rome.

83. Agarwal, Bina (1994), *A Field of One's Own: Gender and Land Rights in South Asia,* Cambridge University Press, UK.

84. Garcia, M. (1991), "Impact of Female Sources of Income on Food Demand among Rural Household in the Philippines", *Quarterly Journal of International Agriculture,* Vol. 30, No. 2, 109-124.

85. Thomas, D. and C.L. Chen (1994), "Income Shares and Shares of Income: Empirical Tests of Models of Household Resource Allocation", *Labour and Population Programme Working Paper,* The Rand Corporation, Santa Monica, California, USA: 94-108.

86. Chopdar, A. and D. Nabarro (1981), "Physical Parameters of the New Borns in Western Orissa", *Indian Pediatrics,* Vol. 18, 467-471.

87. Mascarenhas, Ophelia (1983), "Implications of Constraints in Women's Control and Utilization of Resources for the Food and Nutritional Status of their Families", Paper Presented at the TFNC/UNICEF Workshop on "Hunger and Society" Tanzania, December, 30.

88. Mascarenhas, Ophelia (1984), "Women's Allocation of Resources and Its Implications for the Nutritional Status of their Children", Report to the WHO/UNICEF Nutrition Support Programme for Iringa, Tanzania, 16.

89. Rajagopalan, S., P.K. Kyrnal and Pu-ai Pei (1981), "Births, Work and Nutrition in Tamil Nadu, India," in Chambers, Longhurst and Pacey (eds.), *Seasonal Dimensions to Rural Poverty*, Frances Pinter Ltd., London, 156-161.

90. Visweswara Rao K., N. Balkrishna, B.V.S Thimmayamma, and S. Veena (1994), *Interrelationship between Health and Nutritional Status of Children and their Mothers*. B.R. Publishing Corporation, Delhi, 29-38.

91. Gupta, S., B.L. Kawatra and S. Balaji (1988), "Comparison Energy Intake and Body Weight of Indian Adult Women from Different Socio-economic Groups", *Proceedings of Nutrition Society of India*, Vol. 34, 30-131.

92. Chavas, J.P. and K.O. Keplinger (1983), "Impact of Domestic Food Programs on Nutrient Intake of Low-Income Persons in the Untied States", *Southern Journal of Agricultural Economics*, Vol. 15 155-63.

93. Allen, J.E. and K.E. Gadson (1982), "The Influence of Selected Socio-economic Variables on at–Home Nutrient Intake", Paper Presented at the Annual Meetings of the SAEA, Orlando FL, February, 7-10.

94. National Nutrition Monitoring Bureau (1989), "Distribution of Pre-school Children According to Weight-for-Age Status (Gomes Grades), and Income Differentials", *Nutrition News*, Vol. 10, No. 2, 46-48.

95. Acharya, Meena and Lynn Bennet (1982), *Women and the Subsistence Sector Economic Participation and Household Decision-Making in Nepal*, The World Bank, Washington, D.C.

96. Bindinger, P., B. Nag and P. Babu (1986), "Factors Affecting Intra-family Food Distribution in a South Indian Village", A Report to the Ford Foundation, Mimeo.

97. Gulati, L. (1978), "Profile of a Female Agricultural Labourer", *Economic and Political Weekly*, Vol. 13: 12.

98. Thomas, D. (1994), "Like Father, Like Son, or Like Mother, Like Daughter: Parental Education and Child Health", *Journal of Human Resources*, Vol. 29, No. 4, 950-988.

99. Doss, C. (1997), *The Effects of Women's Bargaining Power in Household Health and Education Outcomes: Evidence from Ghana*, Williams College, Williamstown, Mass, USA.

100. Sen, A. and S. Sengupta (1983), "Malnutrition in Rural Children and the Sex-bias", *Economic and Political Weekly*, Vol. 18, 855-864.

101. Devadas, P., U. Chandrasekhar, S. Premkumari, and G. Geetha (1991), "Correlation between Female Literacy, Birth and Infant Mortality Rate", Paper Presented at the VI Asian Congress of Nutrition, Kuala Lumpur, Malaysia, September, 16-19.

102. Bairagi, R. (1980), "Is Income the only Constraint on Child Nutrition in Rural Bangladesh?", *Bulletin of the World Health Organisation*, Vol. 58, 767-772.

103. Evenson, R.E., B.M. Popkin and E. King-Quizon (1979), *Nutrition Work and Demographic Behaviour in Rural Philippines Households: A Synopsis of Several Laguna Household Studies*. Economic Growth Centre, New Haven, Connecticut, Yale University.

104. Levinson, J.F. (1974), *An Economic Analysis of Malnutrition Among Young Children in Rural India*, Cornell/MIT International Nutrition Policy Series.

105. Chen, L. C., E. Huq and S. D'Souza (1981), "Sex-bias in the Family Allocation of Food and Health Care in Rural Bangladesh", *Population and Development Review*, Vol. 7, No. 1, 55-70.

106. Sen, Amartya (1984), *op.cit.*

107. Gopaldas T., K. Saxena and A. Gupta (1983), "Intra-familial Distribution of Nutrients in a Deep Forest Dwelling Tribe of Gujarat, India", *Ecology of Food and Nutrition*, Vol. 43, 69-73.

108. Ware, Helen (1981), *Sex Differentials in Mortality and Morbidity, Women, Demography and Development*, Australian National University, Canberra: 35-75.

109. Standing, G. (1989), "Global Feminization Through Flexible Labour", *World Development*, Vol. 17, No. 7, 1077-95.

110. Marcoux, A. (2001), "The Feminization of Hunger: What do the Surveys tell us?" *Working Paper*, No. 2. Food and Agriculture Organisation of the United Nations, Social Development, Rome.

111. Ramalingaswami, V., U. Jonsson and J. Rohde (1996), *Commentary: The Asian Enigma*: In *The Progress of Nations* 1996, *Nutrition*. United Nations Children's Fund, New York.

112. Jeyaraaj, T. and N. Malathi (1996), "Child Health: Patterns and Perspective", *Journal of Annamalai University–Part A Humanities*, Vol. 42, 45-51.

113. Haughton, Dominique and Joanathan Haughton (1997), "Explaining Child Nutrition in Vietnam", *Economic Development and Cultural Change*, Vol. 45, 541-56.

114. NNMB (1999), *Report of Second Repeated Survey-Rural (1996-97)*, National Institute of Nutrition, ICMR, Hyderabad: 14.

3

Research Design and Area Profile

This chapter is divided into two sections. In the first section, the Research Design is presented and in the second section, a brief description of both the study areas, Sivaganga and Cuddalore districts, is done.

RESEARCH DESIGN

The present study is descriptive, diagnostic and exploratory.

Objectives

The specific objectives of the study are as follows:

1. To portray the exogenous factors of rural households.
2. To identify the determinants of household food system and to operationalize household food security.
3. To evaluate the participation of women in food chain activities.
4. To examine the adequacy, equity and efficiency perspectives of individual food security.
5. To assess the influence of household and maternal factors on nutritional security.
6. To suggest appropriate coping strategies to improve food security of rural households.

Hypotheses

Giving specific focus to the objectives, the following hypotheses are formulated:

1. Household entitlements and food security move together.
2. Women empowerment contributes positively to household food security.
3. Female headship reduces gender and age bias in individual food security.
4. Maternal factors have significant influence on individual nutritional security.

The significance of each of the hypothesis is further spelt out.

The first hypothesis has taken its lead from Sen's Entitlements approach,[1] which shifted the emphasis from supply perspective to command over food or food access. The focus of the hypothesis is on the main sources of entitlements which help to highlight the most influential variables in determining a food secure situation in the rural households. Its significance has also been recognised by authors like Adrian and Daniel[2] and Bina Agarwal[3] which are other sources of inspiration for this researcher.

The second hypothesis attempts to assess and provide evidence to the relationship between women empowerment and household food security. The synergy is based on studies made by Katona-Apte[4] and Tinker[5] which have tried to evolve a link between these two variables. The validation of this hypothesis would mean that improving women's status and potentiality in the household would have promotional effect on household food security.

The third hypothesis is to highlight the important proximate variable in reducing the gender and age-bias in the intra-familial food allocation, namely "female headship". This hypothesis is based on the findings of some researchers that there are differences in the food allocation (Abdulla[6] and Leslie[7]) among the individuals within the household. Results of some studies are seen to contradict the above views (NNMB report for Indians[8] and Haughton and Haughton[9]). To retest these results, this specific hypothesis is formed. The validation of this hypothesis might help to reemphasise the influential effect of female headship on individual food security.

The fourth hypothesis is to identify the dimensions of maternal factors and relate them to nutritional status. This is formulated on the basis of conclusions of Quisumbing and de la Briere[10] and Smith and Haddad[11] that the role and capabilities of women in poor households play a prominent part in promoting children's nutrition. The formulation of the hypothesis is also to ascertain the observed aphorism while interviewing the respondents that 'resources in the hands of women are resources for food security'. Testing this hypothesis would reveal women's important role in achieving nutritional security of household members.

CONCEPTS AND OPERATIONAL DEFINITIONS

Household: A single person or group of persons normally living together and sharing food from a common kitchen constitutes a household. The members of a household are related by blood, marriage or adoption.

Household Size: The size of the household is based on the number of consumption units. A person in particular sex-age group is converted into a number termed as 'consumer unit'. The total number of consumer units in a household is derived by adding consumer units obtained for each individual in the household after applying conversion factors as suggested by Indian National Sample Survey (NSS) (see p. 214 ref. no. 17). This is to account for per capita food consumption, income and expenditure on an adult equivalent basis.

Size of Landholdings: The sample marginal farmers owned both dry and wet lands. The productivity of the land varied among the two categories of land. Hence, the adjustment is used for standardising the wet and dry lands into a uniform single category of wet land such that landholding size groups are demarcated for further analysis. The ratio for adjustment was worked out as per the value of productivity of land as: 0.75 Acres of Dry Land = 0.45 Acres of Wet Land.

Task and Time Allocation: Total time spent or allocated for various activities was considered and the information was collected in a one day recall basis and the respondents were asked a number of probing questions to help them recall more accurately their participation in different activities and time spent on them. Activities included (i) Farm Related Activities (ii) Non-farm Activities (iii) Dairy Work (iv) Child-care Activities (v) Food Related Activities and (vi) Other Activities.

Women's Access to Resources: To assess the level of access to and control over various resources such as land, income, credit, water and fuel, health and sanitation and nutritional knowledge, score values were used (see Appendix-6, p. 331). Two point scale is considered by assigning 1 for 'yes' and zero for 'no'. All these were combined into a single index by summing up the actual scores for all these components. Taking the minimum (9) and maximum (29) score values out of 45, households were divided into three levels as low (9-15), low medium (16-22), and high medium (23-29). Since the obtained maximum score value was very low for women respondents in various households, high level access could not be assigned.

Household Headship: Headship of households is based on the level of participation of women in decision-making process of three areas namely: Food Related Activities (FORA), Family Administration (FAD), and Child Care Activities (CC). For each activity the extent of participation of women in these areas was analysed by taking the responses on a three-point scale i.e., 2 for full involvement, 1 for partial involvement and zero for no involvement. Score values were assigned accordingly (see Appendix-6, p.336). Answers were sought to various questions and they were scored and the total score values were taken for women's participation in decision-making.

Taking the minimum (6) and maximum (36) score values out of a total score of 36, obtained by the households, norms had been set to indicate low (6-15), medium (16-25) and high (26-36). The households securing maximum scores naturally come under the category of Female Headship as their level of participation in all activities is high and vice versa. On this basis, households were categorised into Male Headed Households

(6-15), Joint Headed Households (16-25) and Female Headed Households (26-36).

Women Empowerment: Women empowerment implies the ability to influence and make decisions covering the full range of personal and household affairs. Studies made by Jejeebhoy,[12] Bloom *et al.*[13] and Reddy[14] found that the participation of women in decision-making and access to control over resources as the crucial indicators of women empowerment. In the present study the researcher attempted to measure women empowerment through these two most important components. The total score values obtained for women's participation in decision-making and access to resources were combined and fixing the minimum (22) and maximum (57) score values out of 81, they were divided into three levels of empowerment group as Low Empowered Households (22-33), Moderately Empowered Households (34-45) and Highly Empowered Households (46-57).

Protein Calorie Malnutrition (PCM): A marked dietary deficiency of both energy and protein resulting in under-nutrition is defined as having a dietary energy and protein intake below the minimum requirement level (according to ICMR norms)[15] to maintain the balance between actual intake and acceptable levels of expenditure. Calorie is the unit used to indicate the energy value of foods expressed as Kcals and Protein is measured in grams.

Nutritional Status: It is the physiological state of an individual that results from the relationship between nutrient intake and requirements and from the body's ability to digest, absorb and use these nutrients.

(i) Stunting malnutrition refers to low height-for-age, reflecting a sustained past episode or episodes of under-nutrition.

(ii) Wasting malnutrition refers to low weight-for-height, generally the result of weight loss associated with a recent period of starvation or disease.

(iii) Body Mass Index (BMI) is the ratio of weight-for-height to estimate the body fat and is obtained by dividing the weight (in kilograms) by the square of the height (in metres).

THE SURVEY DESIGN

A four-tier sampling design is a unique feature of this study. The first stage of sampling involved selection of two Districts in Tamil Nadu, based on sex-ratio and agro-climatic conditions. Cuddalore District was randomly selected out of nine districts with developed agro-climatic conditions (rainfall >800mm) and low sex-ratio (<1000) and Sivaganga District (see Figure 2) was randomly selected out of nine districts with under-developed agro-climatic conditions (rainfall <800mm) and high sex-ratio (>1000) (see Table 1).

FIGURE 1

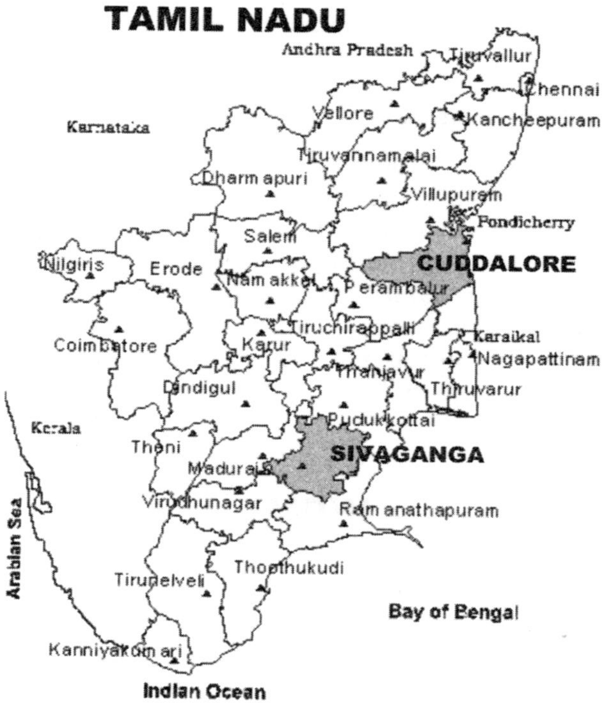

FIGURE 2

In the second stage, one block in each of the selected two districts, representatively possessing the characteristic regional qualities of the respective district, was selected by the area sampling method. The factors considered were rainfall, cropping pattern, percentage of area under irrigation, sex-ratio, female literacy, and female labour participation rate. For this purpose, the relative indices for the blocks were worked out with respect to District average for these factors to every block in the District. Using these indices the respective absolute deviations from the district level for all these six factors where computed from which the average absolute deviation was derived. The block with the minimum value shows its least variation. This is considered as the block representing the District according to area sampling method.

Table 1
District-wise Rainfall and Sex-ratio in Tamil Nadu

Districts	*Rainfall*in mm*	*Sex-ratio***
1. Nilgiris	1399.6	1015
2. Kanyakumari	1312.0	1013
3. Kancheepuram	1033.0	961
4. Chennai	1028.0	951
5. *Cuddalore*	*1015.0*	*984*
6. Thiruvallore	1004.7	970
7. Thanjavur	993.0	1020
8. Nagapattinam	988.8	1014
9. Perambalur	968.0	1007
10. Thiruvarur	881.4	1013
11. Dharmapuri	875.8	938
12. Theni	865.2	979
13. Salem	844.0	929
14. Erode	816.5	971
15. Villupuram	809.4	983
16. Ramnad	804.6	1033
17. Virudhunagar	802.1	1011
18. Karur	785.0	1010
19. Trichy	778.0	1000
20. Dindigul	762.4	986
21. Ariyalur	760.0	1007
22. Madurai	754.0	978
23. Thoothukudi	736.6	1049
24. Thiruvannamalai	726.7	996
25. Vellore	716.4	997
26. Tirunelveli	673.1	1042
27. Coimbatore	657.4	959
28. Pudukottai	638.4	1015
29. Namakkal	634.9	967
30. *Sivaganga*	*631.0*	*1043*
Tamil Nadu State	932.4	985

Note: *Actual average rainfall for five years period (1996-97 to 2000-2001).
Source: Indian Meteorological Department, Chennai. 2001
** Government of Tamil Nadu (2001), Human Development Report 2001.

Tables 2 and 3 show respectively the District and Block-wise characteristics of Sivaganga and Cuddalore districts. In Sivaganga district, Kallal block (see Figure 3) shows the least absolute deviation with the characteristics of the district at 2.63 and hence this block is chosen for the present study. In

Cuddalore district, Keerapalayam block (see Figure 4) which shows the minimum average absolute deviation at 9.11 is selected for the study.

Table 2
Block-wise Characteristics in Sivaganga District

Name of the Block	*Average Rainfall (in mm.)*	*% of Area under food crops*	*% of Area under irrigation*	*Sex-Ratio*	*Female Literacy (%)*	*Female Labour participation rate (%)*
Devakottai	657.5	62.7	63.2	1074	54.2	29.4
9.8	(104.2)	(86.5)	(111.2)	(103.0)	(108.9)	(118.0)
Ilaiyangudi	654.3	74.2	62.5	1063	50.1	20.2
6.33	(103.7)	(102.3)	(110.0)	(102.0)	(101.0)	(81.0)
Kalayarkoil	627.8	70.1	60.3	1047	47.2	24.1
3.16	(99.5)	(96.7)	(106.2)	(100.4)	(95.0)	(96.4)
Kallal	*636.0*	*72.1*	*54.5*	*1054*	*50.4*	*26.9*
2.63	*(100.8)*	*(99.4)*	*(96.0)*	*(101.1)*	*(101.3)*	*(108.0)*
Kannangudi	577.4	79.4	53.4	1005	49.1	23.4
5.75	(91.5)	(109.5)	(94.1)	(96.4)	(99.0)	(94.0)
Manamadurai	575.4	57.3	54.1	940	44.4	20.2
12.36	(91.2)	(79.0)	(95.2)	(90.1)	(89.3)	(81.0)
Sakkottai	662.0	65.0	59.1	1042	49.0	25.1
3.45	(104.9)	(89.6)	(104.0)	(100.0)	(99.0)	(100.4)
Singampunari	629.1	83.0	60.2	1045	54.1	19.7
8.46	(99.7)	(114.5)	(106.0)	(100.2)	(108.8)	(79.0)
Sivaganga	633.5	84.4	50.2	1053	45.1	25.1
6.5	(100.4)	(116.4)	(88.4)	(101.0)	(90.7)	(100.4)
S. Pudur	596.2	72.7	59.2	1038	48.2	21.0
4.9	(94.5)	(100.3)	(104.2)	(99.6)	(97.0)	(84.0)
Thiruppathur	656.2	81.6	67.8	1022	49.3	32.4
11.4	(104.0)	(112.6)	(119.3)	(98.0)	(99.1)	(129.6)
Thirubuvanam	667.6	64.8	50.1	986	52.2	32.1
9.73	(105.8)	(89.5)	(88.2)	(94.6)	(104.9)	(128.4)
Sivaganga	*631.0*	*72.5*	*56.8*	*1043*	*49.74*	*25.0*
District	*(100)*	*(100)*	*(100)*	*(100)*	*(100)*	*(100)*

Source: Directorate of Economics and Statistics, Chennai.

Note: Figures in parentheses denote relative indices of the block to the district value computed as (Block value / District) value x 100 Figures in Italics are Average absolute deviation from the District values.

Table 3
Block-wise Characteristics in Cuddalore District

Name of the Block	*Average Rainfall (in mm.)*	*% of Area under food crops*	*% of Area under irrigation*	*Sex-Ratio*	*Female Literacy*	*Female Labour participation rate*
Annagramam	845.4	40.7	60.5	977	43.3	33.3
13.81	(83.3)	(56.2)	(100.5)	(99.3)	(96.0)	(83.25)
Bhuvanagiri	1197.7	90.6	72.1	977	51.1	34.1
15.22	(118.0)	(125.1)	(119.76)	(99.3)	(113.0)	(85.2)
Cuddalore	996.7	59.7	84.3	936	44.6	37.1
12.15	(98.2)	(82.4)	(140.1)	(95.1)	(98.8)	(92.7)
Kammapuram	856.6	55.7	55.4	978	40.6	68.5
21.46	(84.4)	(76.9)	(92.0)	(99.4)	(89.8)	(171.3)
Kattumannarkoil	720.6	76.9	69.74	991	48.2	48.7
13.33	(71.0)	(106.2)	(115.8)	(100.8)	(106.4)	(121.8)
Keerapalayam	1049.5	83.2	61.4	996	48.2	50.7
9.05	(103.4)	(114.9)	(101.9)	(101.2)	(106.6)	(126.7)
Kumaratchi	1187.5	94.1	76.2	967	48.4	40.7
14.18	(117.0)	(130)	(126.5)	(98.3)	(107.1)	(101.7)
Kurinjipadi	906.4	62.3	67.0	975	47.3	33.5
9.65	(89.3)	(86.1)	(111.3,	(99.1)	(104.6)	(83.7)
Mangalur	712.5	31.8	59.1	1009	41.1	45.1
18.15	(70.2)	(43.9)	(98.1)	(102.6)	(91.0)	(112.7)
Nallur	731.8	65.2	67.3	1012	38.3	30.7
14.45	(72.1)	(90.0)	(111.7)	(102.9)	(84.8)	(76.8)
Panruti	844.4	36.7	24.6	982	41.6	30.5
26.2	(83.2)	(50.7)	(40.9)	(99.8)	(92.0)	(76.2)
Portonovo	1386.4	77.0	69.7	1045	50.6	24
19.4	(136.6)	(106.4)	(115.7)	(106.2)	(112.0)	(60.0)
Vridhachalam	898.2	58.4	51.9	1018	47.4	41.7
9.2	(88.5)	(80.7)	(86.2)	(103.5)	(105.0)	(104.2)
Cuddalore	1015.0	72.4	60.2	984	45.2	40.0
(100)	(100)	(100)	(100)	(100)	(100)	

Source: Directorate of Economics and Statistics, Chennai.

Note: Figures in parentheses denote relative indices of the block to the district value computed as (Block value/District value) x 100 Figures in Italics are Average absolute deviation from the District values.

The third stage of sampling involved the selection of two villages at random in each of the selected blocks of the two districts. In selecting the villages thus, the proximity of

SIVAGANGA DISTRICT

FIGURE 3

CUDDALORE DISTRICT

FIGURE 4

marketing outlets was given due consideration. One village, in the selected block of each of the district, situated close (within 5 km.) to the marketing centre and another village located relatively away (beyond 10 km.) from the marketing centre, was selected. In this respect Devapattu and Vetriyur were selected in Sivaganga district; Kannangudi and Orathur were selected in Cuddalore district. They are referred to as V_1 (Village 1) and V_2 (Village 2) respectively.

The fourth stage of sampling was the selection of households in each of the four villages on the basis of their prime occupation categorising them as Marginal Farmers (MF), Non-Farm workers (NFW) and Landless Agricultural Labourers (LAL). In order to obtain a symmetrically representative sample of rural households, a random selection of ten households in each of the above three occupational categories in each of the two villages of the two districts was made. As such 120 households were covered as the sampling group for the study at the rate of 60 households for each selected district. Among the cross-section of respondent households, each of the three occupational categories had 40 respondents.

The cross-sectional data for analysis of household food security for the period July 2000 to June 2001 were collected. A Pilot survey was conducted in 20 per cent of the households in the chosen villages to finalise the interview schedule and questionnaire.

Data Collection

Data were collected through the direct in-field enquiries from the 120 households by using pre-tested interview schedule and questionnaire method. Spot observation method was also adopted to gather specific information. Comprehensive details were collected with respect to:

- Household demographic data on age, sex, family size, family type, education, number of earners in the household, nature of employment and days worked.
- Economic status indicators at the household level like asset structure, sources of income, expenditure pattern and home production of food items.

- Data on household food stores, usage patterns, food habits and women's coping strategies.
- Women's access to and control over resources, level of participation in decision-making and task and time allocation pattern of women in food chain activities.
- The quantity of various edibles purchased and used during lean and busy seasons to measure the dietary adequacy status of the households.
- Food consumption data for twenty-four hour period using a food-weighing method for each member of the 120 households (a total of 574 individuals).
- Anthropometric data for height, weight and arm circumference for each member of the 120 households (a total of 574 individuals).

Diet Survey

Information regarding the quantities of different raw food items consumed by households was recorded to assess the households' food adequacy status by 24-hour recall method.

For measuring an individual's nutrient intake, it was suggested that any single day or two days' food weighment method would be equally efficient as that of week days' record method.[16] Accordingly, the researcher, in a pilot survey, had administered a questionnaire to obtain food intake information using a 24-hour recall method on two different occasions. The two-day intake assessment was restricted to 20 per cent of the sample households in each of the selected district and no considerable variation in daily nutrient intake levels across the two observation days was found in the pilot survey. The relative validity was also worked out using food weighing method. Based on the invariability, the one day food weighment method, recorded to be reliable, is chosen for the dietary survey of individuals. Local volumetric measures were used to record food intake and later converted to grams and nutrients (see Appendix-1). In this study, all care is taken to reduce non-sampling errors.

Tools of Data Analysis

Primary data collected from the respondent-households were cross-tabulated and simple averages and percentages were computed for scientific presentation of the data.

Households were categorised based on occupation, headship and empowerment, for further statistical analysis.

Dietary Adequacy Ratio (DAR), Protein Calorie Malnutrition (PCM) and Relative Nutrient Allocation (RNA) were calculated and compared with the ICMR (Indian Council of Medical Research) norms.

Weight-for-height index, Height-for-age index and Body mass index were computed to calibrate the nutritional status of children and adults.

To test the hypotheses, techniques like (i) Multiple Linear Regression Model, (ii) Fisher's Two-way Analysis of variance (ANOVA), (iii) Student's t-test for Difference between mean values and (iv) Chi-square Analysis of Association of Attributes were used.

Limitations of the Study: Consumption surveys involve wide ranging data collection exercise and a study often will not be able to capture all the detailed aspects to household food security. In this study, nutritional security is assessed both directly and indirectly, directly by nutrient intake levels and indirectly by anthropometric measurements.

Direct consumption assessment usually involves the conversion of the consumed food items to various nutrients like calorie, protein, vitamins, calcium, iron etc. But this study limits the assessment to two nutrient components, calorie and protein as calorie is prioritised as the measure of energy the body needs and protein as the qualitative measurement of food which abundantly helps the growth process. For indirect measurement, three anthropometric indices namely (i) weight-for-age (ii) height-for-age (iii) weight-for-height are commonly used. But, weight-for-age is generally recommended to assess changes in the magnitude of malnutrition over a time.[17] It cannot distinguish wasting and stunting. So, weight-for-age measurement is excluded from this study since this is restricted only to an examination of malnutrition at a given point of time.

In other words, since this is a synchronic study of malnutrition, diachronic aspects are excluded.

PROFILE OF TAMIL NADU

Tamil Nadu, the southernmost state of India, nestles in the peninsula between the Bay of Bengal in the east, Indian Ocean in the south and the Western Ghats and the Arabian Sea on the west. In the north and west the state adjoins Karnataka, Andhra Pradesh and Kerala. Tamil Nadu shows rich variety and diversity in its geography and climate with coastal plains co-existing with tropical rain forest, river valleys and hill stations.

According to the 2001 census, the State's population is approximately 62 million. The sex ratio works out to 986. The density of population in Tamil Nadu, a true indicator of population distribution, is 478 persons per sq. kilometer. In Tamil Nadu, 56.14 per cent of the population live in rural areas. The state per capita income, which was below national average in 1980's, crossed that mark in 1991-92 and has maintained the trend. At Rs. 19,889, it ranks fourth, after Maharashtra, Punjab, and Haryana.

Agriculture has been the mainstay of the economy since independence with more than 65 per cent of the population depending on this sector for a living. Agricultural growth holds the key for economic development and for reduction in the incidence of poverty. Major food crops grow.. are paddy, millets, pulses and cash crops such as groundnut, cotton and sugarcane. Yearly per capita foodgrains availability in Tamil Nadu works out to 168.21 kgs. This is lesser than the normal requirements of foodgrains as recommended by the National Institute of Nutrition, Hyderabad at 182.50 kgs. The per capita net availability of food grains per day works out to 431 grams which is lower than the National availability of 466 grams per day.[18] The estimates of poverty made by the Union Commission in 1999-2000 shows that 21.12 per cent of the State's population live below the poverty line which is less than the All-India average of 26.10 per cent.

Comparison of some major health indicators of Tamil Nadu with all-India figures shows that the State has made impressive strides. The annual population growth rate during 1981-1991 was 2.14 per cent for all-India, while it was 1.43 per cent for Tamil Nadu, second only to Kerala (1.34 per cent). Infant mortality rate has decreased from 63 per 1000 population from in 1990 to 49 in 2000. Even when mortality is controlled nutritional status did not improve. The National Nutrition Monitoring Bureau data show a high percentage of under weight children in India below three as under weight, stunted and wasted. Making Tamil Nadu malnutrition free state is one of the objectives of the Tenth plan. In spite of a number of schemes being implemented to tackle malnutrition problem in the State, the recent National Family Health Survey (2000-2001) assessment on the basis of weight-for-age, height-for-age and weight-for-height, observed that in Tamil Nadu, 37 per cent of the children under the age of three years are under weight, 29 per cent are stunted and 20 per cent are wasted. Undernutrition is higher in rural than urban areas and it is particularly high among children from disadvantaged socio-economic group.

PROFILE OF CUDDALORE AND SIVAGANGA DISTRICTS

The Tamil Nadu state has a total geographical area of 1,30,058 sq.kms. Of these, 2.83 per cent (3678 sq.kms.) is occupied by Cuddalore district whereas Sivaganga district covers 3.14 per cent (4086 sq.kms). Evidently, the present study covers nearly 6 per cent of the total area of Tamil Nadu state. The density of population in Sivaganga district is 275 persons per sq.km, whereas in Cuddalore district, it is 628 persons per sq.km. Data on total forest area show that Cuddalore district has nearly 0.4 per cent (percentage to the total geographical area of the district) whereas in Sivaganga district, the total forest area is 8.91 per cent. In each district there are three revenue divisions. Cuddalore district consists of six taluks and Sivaganga district comprises of nine taluks. Cuddalore district is divided into 13 Community Development Blocks, whereas Sivaganga district has 12 Community Development Blocks.

Geographical Features

Cuddalore district is, for the most part, a flat plain sloping from the west to the sea on the east and also from the north to the south except for a strip of high ground running across the district from Pondicherry to Vriddhachalam. The district has fairly rich mineral deposits. Limestone is found in Parur and in the north-west regions of Vriddhachalam. The region can be distinguished into the following natural divisions. The eastern region consists of red soil tracts and wide spread paddy fields and green groves of fruit bearing trees. The southern region of the district, particularly Chidambaram taluk and a few parts of Vriddhachalam taluk, is comparatively green and fertile and is made up of even expanse of irrigated land which resembles, to a great extent, the deltaic part of Thanjavur district.

The Sivaganga district is situated in the south-eastern part of the state. It is bounded on the north by a small portion of Tiruchirappali and the district of Pudukkottai, on the east by the district of Pudukkottai and Ramanathapuram, on the south by the district of Ramanathapuram and Virudhunagar and on the west by the district of Madurai and a small portion of Tiruchirappalli. Large portions of Tiruppattur and Sivaganga taluks in the district are covered by hard red laterite. This soil here is poor and the large tracts of thorny jungles are not suited for cultivation. The area comprising Tiruppattur taluk and the northern portions of the Sivaganga taluk can be classified under the red soil region and is known as Chettinad. Some portions of Sivaganga district are plains, and have black cotton soil or regar, locally known as *Karisal*. This soil is mostly used for growing cotton and cultivation of dry crops. The familiar landscape is of palms and acacias. Except Piranmalai in Tiruppattur taluk, no hill is found in this district. With regard to minerals, white clay is the basic mineral in Sivaganga district. Besides, graphite is also available in plenty in Sivaganga district.

Agro-Economic Features

Cuddalore district occupies an important place in the field of agriculture, since agriculture is the mainstay of the people of this district. The crops grown in the district can be conveniently grouped into two, viz., the cereals and pulses which come under food crops, and others which come under cash crops or commercial crops. 72.4 per cent of the total sown area in the district covers food crops. The principal cereal crops of this district are paddy, *varagu, cholam, cumbu* and *ragi*. Important varieties of pulses are red gram, green gram and black gram. Black gram is one of the important pulses grown in Tamil Nadu and is grown during both Kharif and Rabi seasons and it occupies nearly of 40 per cent of the total area under pulses. Blackgram is extensively grown in ten districts and Cuddalore district one among them. Other varieties of pulses raised in the district, viz., bengal gram, red gram and horse gram are predominantly cultivated as rainfed crops.

The chief commercial crops of the district are groundnut, sugarcane and gingelly. Paddy is cultivated in all the taluks of the district and more extensively in Chidambaram. Oil seeds are grown throughout the district as a summer crop. Among oil seeds, groundnut, gingelly and castor occupy important places.

Other crops grown in the district are cashew, tobacco, and cotton. Bananas, Mangoes and Jack fruits are the important fruits cultivated in the district.

The prominent role that Cuddalore is now playing in the Agricultural sector in the State is due mostly to its irrigation facilities. More than half of the net area sown in the district is under irrigation. The chief source of irrigation in the district is the rivers supplemented by a large number of rained tanks, wells and spring channels. The principal rivers that serve the region are the Coleroon, Vellar, Manimukthanadhi and Ponnaiyar. All these rivers run in valleys and have been harnessed for irrigation purposes by anicuts built across them at various stages of their course. Tanks are fed by river channels and rain water. Most important among major tanks of the district are the Veeranam tank, Wallajah tank and Ponneri tank.

Paddy is the important food crop of Sivaganga district. It is grown on wet lands irrigated by rivers, channels, tanks and wells. *Cumbu, Cholam, Ragi, Varagu, Samai* and *Kudiravali* are the millets produced in the district. Of the commercial crop, the most important is cotton, which is grown in the area having black cotton soil. Chief commercial crops of the district are chillis, gingelly, groundnut, and coconut. Banana, Mangoes and Jack fruits are also cultivated in the district.

There are no perennial rivers in Sivaganga district. The river Vaigai is the only major river which centers the districts near Thiruppuvanam and flows through Sivaganga Taluk. The other seasonal rivers flowing in the districts are Bambar, Thennar, Sarugani, Uppargundar and Kottagudi.

Land use pattern, shown in Table 4, makes a comparison of how effectively the two districts are utilising its available land.

Table 4
Land Use Pattern in Sivaganga and Cuddalore Districts

	Sivaganga district		*Cuddalore district*	
Land use	*Hectare*	*%*	*Hectare*	*%*
Total Geographical area	438827	–	367781	–
Forests	39349	8.96	1415	0.38
Barren and Uncultivable Land	17941	4.08	14647	3.98
Land put to Non-agricultural Use	52683	12.00	47372	12.88
Cultivable Waste	17470	3.98	7283	1.99
Permanent Pastures and other Grazing Lands	5120	1.16	720	0.19
Land under misc. tree crops & groves not included in the net area sown	6738	1.53	19190	5.21
Current Fallow	53447	12.17	34770	9.45
Other Fallow Lands	64343	14.68	11705	3.18
Net area sown	130071	29.64	230679	62.72
Area sown more than once	234	0.05	64519	17.54
Gross cropped area	130305	29.69	295198	80.26

Source: Statistical Hand Book 1999-2000, Sivaganga and Cuddalore.
Note: % values are to the total Geographical Area.

The livestock population of Cuddalore district includes bullocks, cows, buffaloes, sheep, pigs and poultry. Milk production is comparatively higher in Cuddalore district than Sivaganga district. The position of livestock in Sivaganga district is found to be an allied activity of agriculture in the district. Livestock and poultry population in Sivaganga district is considerably less when compared with that of Cuddalore district.

The Cuddalore district is one of the backward areas in industrial development. The Neyveli Lignite Corporation, a government of India enterprise, is the agency engaged in mining in the district. Lignite, which lies under an overburden of about 180 to 200 feet covers an area of about 100 sq. miles. Associated with lignite, there is a vast reserve of white refractory clay. Laterite is found over a wide belt of the country between Pondicherry and Vriddhachalam. Important mineral based industries in the district are Lignite and refractories. Brick manufacturing is another important industry in the district. It is found mainly in Panruti, Vallambadugai and Sethiathope. Black smithing, wood carving, oil pressing, hand pounding of rice, bee-keeping and honey extraction are some of the common cottage industries found in the district. Handloom industry has been a traditional occupation of this district.

Compared to Cuddalore district, Sivaganga district is industrially a backward district. Brick manufacturing, gold smithing, wood carving, weaving and food processing are some of the cottage industries found in the district.

Demographic Features

Some of the important demographic features of the study districts are given in Table 5 furnished below:

Table 5
Demographic Features in Sivaganga and Cuddalore Districts

Demographic Features	*Sivaganga District*	*Cuddalore District*
Population (in lakhs)	11.50	22.80
Sex Ratio (females per 1000 males)	1043	984
Density per sq.km	275	628
Percentage of Rural Population	71.82	67.00
Female Literacy Rate (%)	49.7	45.2
Birth Rate (per 1000 population)	18.52	20.0
Death Rate(per 1000 population)	6.1	6.8
Infant Mortality Rate(per 1000 live births)	27	34
Maternal Mortality Rate(per 1000 alive children)	0.8	1.0
Bed Population Ratio	1:1287	1:1882
Doctor Population Ratio	1:8461	1:12394

Source: 1. Statistical Hand Book 2000-2001, Sivaganga and Cuddalore.
2. Government of Tamil Nadu (2001). *Tamil Nadu Human Development Report*. Department of Evaluation and Applied Research, Kuralagam, Chennai.

It is seen from Table 5 that Cuddalore district has a higher density of population (628 per sq.km.) when compared to Sivaganga district (275 per sq.km.) which may be due to the higher gross cropped area in Cuddalore district which is 80.26 per cent whereas, it is low at 29.69 per cent in Sivaganga district. In terms of literacy and health statistic data Sivaganga district is found to be slightly better. Data on the nutritional status of children (below three years of age) show 9.5 per cent in Cuddalore district to be moderately malnourished as against 6.1 per cent for Sivaganga district. Whereas, the severely malnourished account for only 0.2 per cent in each of the study districts. The Government of Tamil Nadu, over the last two and a half decades, has created and continued a massive network of nutrition, health and child development centres at the grass root level in rural and urban areas.

Table 6
Occupational Pattern in Sivaganga and Cuddalore Districts

Occupation	*Sivaganga District*	*Cuddalore District*
Cultivators	185828	257142
	(43.82)	(20.8)
Agricultural Labourers	122894	333897
	(28.98)	(27.01)
Household Industry Labourers	85492	18681
	(20.16)	(1.51)
Other Workers	29834	626380
	(7.04)	(50.68)
Total Workers	424048	1236100
	(100)	(100)

Source: Statistical Hand Book 1999-2000, Sivaganga and Cuddalore.

The occupation-wise classification of workers between the study districts in Table 6 reveal that in Sivaganga district, 43.52 per cent of the workers are cultivators which is much higher than that of Cuddalore district which is 20.81 per cent. Next to cultivators, the agricultural labourers constitute 28.98 per cent in Sivaganga district whereas in Cuddalore district, it is 27.01 per cent. In Cuddalore district the other workers constitute the higher percentage of 50.68 which surpasses the level in Sivaganga district which is 7.04 per cent. The contribution of household industry labourers in Cuddalore district is only marginal at 1.51 per cent but in Sivaganga district it is considerably higher at 20.16 per cent.

The first Human Development Index (HDI) report for Tamil Nadu was prepared in 2001. It facilitates comparison of human development across districts. The quality of life of people in Tamil Nadu, as measured by the three indicators of the HDI, namely longevity of life, education and income, have improved in Tamil Nadu and its districts due to development activities. Similarly, Gender Development Index (GDI) is measured to assess gender equality. Sivaganga district is seen to be better placed than the Cuddalore district indices.

Indicators	*Sivaganga district*	*Cuddalore district*	*Tamil Nadu*
HDI	0.615 (16)	0.596 (24)	0.631
GDI	0.608 (17)	0.593 (23)	0.626

Source: State Planning Commission 2001 Chennai.
Note: Figures in parentheses denote respective HDI and GDI ranks of the districts.

This provincial description of the study districts is supplemented in the next chapter by a detailed description of the study-villages and the socio-economic characteristics of the respondent households.

NOTES AND REFERENCES

1. Sen, A. K. (1981), *Poverty and Famines: An Essay on Entitlement and Deprivation*. Clarendon Press, Oxford, U.K.
2. Adrian, J. and R. Daniel (1976), " Impact of Socio-economic Factors on Consumption of Selected Food Nutrients in the United States", *Journal of Agricultural Economics*, Vol. 58: 31-38.
3. Agarwal, Bina (1994), "Gender and Command Over Property: A Critical Gap in Economic Analysis and Policy in South Asia", *World Development*, Vol. 22, No.10, 1455-78.
4. Katona-Apte, Judith (1983), "A Socio-cultural Perspective on the Significance of Sex Roles in Agriculture", in *Nutritional Impact of Agricultural Projects*. Papers and Proceedings of a Workshop Held by the UN Administrative Committee on Co-ordination (ACC)/ Sub-committee on Nutrition, 28-43.

5. Tinker, Irene (1979), "New Technologies for Food Chain Activities: The Imperative of Equity for Women", Office of Women in Development, AID, Washington, D.C.

6. Abdulla, Mohammad and Erica F. Wherrel (1985), "Seasonal Variation and the Intra-household Distribution of Food in a Bangladesh Village", *American Journal of Clinical Nutrition,* Vol. 41, 305-313.

7. Leslie, J. (1991), "Women's Nutrition: The Key to Improve Family Health in Developing Countries?", *Health and Policy Planning,* Vol. 6, No. 1: 9.

8. National Nutrition Monitoring Bureau (1999), *Report of Second Repeated Survey-Rural 1996-1997,* National Institute of Nutrition, ICMR, Hyderabad.

9. Haughton, Dominique and Joanathan Haughton (1997), "Explaining Child Nutrition in Vietnam", *Economic Development and Cultural Change,* Vol. 45, 541-56.

10. Quisumbing, A.R. and de la Briere (2000), "Women's Assets and Intra-household Allocation in Rural Bangladesh: Testing Measures of Bargaining Power", Food Consumption and Nutrition Division Discussion Paper, No. 86, Indian Food Policy Research Institute, Washington, D.C.

11. Smith, L.C., U. Ramakrishnan, A. Ndiaye, L. Haddad, and R. Martorell (2003), "The Importance of Women's Status for Child Nutrition in Developing Countries", Research Report, No. 20, International Food Policy Research Institute, Washington, D.C.

12. Jejeebhoy, Shireen (1998), "Measuring Contraception: An Overview of New Approaches", Paper Presented at the United Nations Expert Group Meeting in Methodologies for Measuring Contraceptive Use Dynamics.

13. Bloom, S. Shelah, David Wy Pij, and Monica Das Gupta (2001), "Dimension of Women Autonomy and the Influence on Maternal Health Care Utilization in a North India City", *Demography,* Vol. 38, No 1, 67-68.

14. Reddy, G. N. (2002), *Building Capacities for Sustainable Development,* Krishna Publishers, New Delhi.

15. Indian Council of Medical Research (2002), *Nutrient Requirements and Recommended Dietary Allowance for Indians: A Report of the Indian Council of Medical Research.* National Institute of Nutrition, Hyderabad: 11.

16. Visweswara Rao, K. (1975), "Diet Surveys by Weighment Method -A Comparison of Reference Periods", *Indian Journal of Nutrition and Dietetics*, Vol. 12: 9-16.

17. Collins, S., A. Duffield and M. Myatt (2000), "Assessment of Nutritional Status in Emergency-affected Population: Adults", July, ACC/SCN, Geneva.

18. Government of Tamil Nadu (2002), Tamil Nadu–An Economic Appraisal 1999-2000. Department of Evaluation and Applied Research, Kuralagam, Chennai.

4

Profile of Sample Households

This chapter presents a demographic and socio-economic profile of the sample households and identifies exogenous factors for food security. Since the basic component of this study is food and nutrition security at the household and individual level, a complete grasp of the key household and maternal characteristics is very essential to comprehend the diagnostic aspects of food and nutrition security.

In this profile the village households have been classified into three main household categories on the basis of their principal source of income as Marginal Farmers (MF), Non-Farm Workers (NFW) and Landless Agricultural Labourers (LAL). Here the discussion is restricted to the differences in characteristics of the sample homeholds by the Household Category in all the four villages selected for the study in Sivaganga and Cuddalore districts. Apart from this, a general analysis of household characters by household headship is also made. As mentioned earlier this is a uniqueness of this study to reveal interesting findings in the latter part of analysis.

HOUSEHOLD CHARACTERISTICS

Household factors in the profile of sample villages further enable worthwhile comparisons between variables taken for analysis in the two districts.

Religion and Community

Several social scientists have analysed differentiation and inequalities among rural households in India by using the concept of caste and religion, which is considered to be deep-rooted and all pervasive in the Indian Society[1]. The distribution of households by religion (Table 1) reveals that majority of the respondents are Hindus and this percentage is much higher in Cuddalore district than Sivaganga district (95.0 per cent and 78.3 per cent respectively). Christians constitute 20.0 per cent in Sivaganga district and a mere 3.3 per cent in Cuddalore district while one Muslim household is found in each of the two districts. Both these Muslim households belong to NFW category.

From Table 2, it can be observed that in Sivaganga district, the major community is the backward community (BC), which constitutes 56.7 per cent. Of this 40.0 per cent belong to MF households. Most Backward Community (MBC) and Schedule Caste (SC) account for 25.0 per cent and 16.6 per cent respectively. Forward Community (FC) constitutes the lowest at 1.7 per cent. But in Cuddalore district, the sample shows equal representation of both MBC and SC at 31.7 per cent. Thirty per cent of the samples in Cuddalore district belong to BC category and FC is represented the lowest at 6.6 per cent. An interesting observation is that 60 per cent of the LAL households belong to MBC and SC category and none of the FC household found in this LAL category.

Food insecurity is generally considered as the function of poverty. Studies on poverty have shown that the incidence of poverty is related to caste hierarchy and the poverty level increased as the households become marginalised in the caste hierarchy. But researchers like

Kathleen Gough[2] have established that economic differentiation has affected almost every caste and that the community/ caste is no longer homogenous in occupation and wealth.

Family Type

Table 3 shows that majority of the households, comprising 76.7 per cent and 73.7 per cent belong to nuclear family in Sivaganga

Table 1
Religion wise Distribution of Sample Households

Category		*Sivaganga District*				*Cuddalore District*			
		Hindus	*Christians*	*Muslims*	*Total*	*Hindus*	*Christians*	*Muslims*	*Total*
V_1	MF	7	3	-	10	10	-	-	10
	NFW	9	1	-	10	10	-	-	10
	LAL	7	3	-	10	10	-	-	10
OVERALL		23	7	-	30	30	-	-	30
V_2	MF	7	3	-	10	9	1	-	10
	NFW	8	1	1	10	9	-	1	10
	LAL	9	1	-	10	9	1	-	10
OVERALL		24	5	1	30	27	2	-	30
Grand Total		47	12	1	60	57	2	1	60
		(78.3)	(20.0)	(1.7)	(100)	(95)	(3.3)	(1.7)	(100)

Source: Computed
(Figures in Parentheses are Percentage to Total)

Table 2
Caste wise Distribution of Sample Households

Category		*Sivaganga District*					*Cuddalore District*				
		FC	*BC*	*MBC*	*SC*	*Total*	*FC*	*BC*	*MBC*	*SC*	*Total*
V_1	MF	1	7	1	1	10	2	3	3	2	10
	NFW	0	5	4	1	10	1	4	3	2	10
	LAL	0	5	3	2	10	0	3	3	4	10
OVERALL		1	17	8	4	30	3	10	9	8	30
V_2	MF	0	6	2	2	10	0	2	3	5	10
	NFW	0	6	2	2	10	1	3	5	1	10
	LAL	0	5	3	2	10	0	3	2	5	10
OVERALL		0	17	7	6	30	1	8	10	11	30
Grand Total		1	34	15	10	60	4	18	19	19	60
		(1.7)	(56.7)	(25)	(16.6)	(100)	(6.6)	(30)	(31.7)	(31.7)	(100)

Source: Computed
(Figures in Parentheses are Percentage to Total)

and Cuddalore district respectively, and the remaining households (23.3 per cent and 26.7 per cent) live in extended family system.

Table 3
Family Type wise Distribution of Sample Households

		Sivaganga District			*Cuddalore District*		
Category		*Nuclear*	*Extended*	*Total*	*Nuclear*	*Extended*	*Total*
V_1	MF	6	4	10	5	5	10
	NFW	8	2	10	6	4	10
	LAL	8	2	10	8	2	10
OVERALL		22	8	30	19	11	30
V_2	MF	8	2	10	8	2	10
	NFW	8	2	10	8	2	10
	LAL	8	2	10	9	1	10
OVERALL		24	6	30	25	5	30
Grand Total		46	14	60	44	16	60
		(76.7)	(23.3)	(100)	(73.3)	(26.7)	(100)

Source: Computed.
(Figures in Parentheses are Percentage to Total).

Krishnaji[3] observes that the labour market, characterised by a high degree of unemployment, does not confer any special advantage to a joint family. On the other hand uncertainty of finding work, especially in the lean seasons, may make intra-family income sharing difficult for joint families. That is why families get divided more frequently among the poor than the non-poor. This is also the finding of the researcher while interviewing the women respondents of the LAL households, particularly in V_2 of Cuddalore district, where the tendency is more towards the nuclear family.

Household Debt

An examination of the data from Table 4 will show that the largest amount of borrowings are made by MF Category in all the study villages except MF households in V_2 of Sivaganga district. The purposes of borrowing as stated by the MF category in V_1 of Sivaganga district include cultivation, marriage expenses and purchase of milch animals. MF households in V1 of Cuddalore district stated almost the same reasons. It is interesting to note that among the LAL households 25 per cent in Sivaganga district and 27 per cent in Cuddalore district reported that they borrowed to repay the old debts. The rest of the LAL households mostly borrow to meet out family expenditure. Even in NFW category, 50 per cent of the households borrowed money to meet out their excess expenditure. Only one household reported that it obtained loan for husband's medical expenses.

Table 4
Average Debt for the Sample Households

		Sivaganga District		*Cuddalore District*	
Category		*Amount of Debt (Rs.)*	*% of Debt to total asset*	*Amount of Debt (Rs.)*	*% of Debt to total asset*
V_1	MF	3700	2.6	4500	2.8
	NFW	800	3.4	750	1.9
	LAL	1030	5.6	1470	11.6
OVERALL		1843.3	3.03	2240	3.2
V_2	MF	930	1.2	4300	3.1
	NFW	960	3.2	1310	2.5
	LAL	1090	6.5	900	8.7
OVERALL		993.3	2.1	2170	3.03

Source: Computed
(Figures in Parentheses are Percentage to Total)

An analysis of the sources of borrowing, among all the three categories, indicates that private moneylenders in the near-by town finance them to a large extent. Banks and Co-operatives account for the least share of borrowing patronised by only very few MF households. A few LAL households said that their membership in the Self-Help group helped them to borrow money easily and on easily payable instalments.

The analysis in terms of percentage share of debts over the asset reveals striking differences between LAL category and other categories. The burden of debt in terms of asset is maximum for LAL households in V_1 (11.6 per cent) and V_2 (8.7 per cent) of Cuddalore districts, while it is less than 3 per cent for other categories in that district. Similar are the figures for Sivaganga district. Over all, the analysis shows that amount borrowed for consumption purpose per household is higher in the case of poor households living far below the poverty line.

Sex-Ratio

The number of females to thousand males would showcase the biological characteristics of the population and structural composition of the society in a particular village. It has also served as an essential tool for regional analysis and as a calibrator to measure the socio-economic conditions of the target region. It could be observed from Table 5 that the sex-ratio (female/male) among adult and children population is higher for both the villages in Sivaganga district (1.11 and 1.40 for adult and children population respectively) and it is lower for both the groups in both the villages of Cuddalore district (0.8 for adult and 0.84 for children respectively). This population sex ratio

Table 5
Category-wise Sex Ratio of Sample Households

Sivaganga District													
		Adult				*Children*				*Over All*			
Category		*M*	*F*	*Total*	*SR*	*M*	*F*	*Total*	*SR*	*M*	*F*	*Total*	*SR*
V_1	MF	14	18	32	1.28	4	8	12	2.00	18	26	44	1.40
	NFW	19	20	39	1.05	6	6	12	1.00	25	26	51	1.04
	LAL	14	17	31	1.21	4	8	12	2.00	18	25	43	1.40
OVERALL		47	55	102	1.17	14	22	36	1.57	61	77	138	1.30
V_2	MF	18	18	36	1.00	3	4	7	1.30	21	22	43	1.04
	NFW	17	20	37	1.17	6	7	13	1.16	23	27	50	1.20
	LAL	16	16	32	1.00	7	9	16	1.28	23	25	48	1.10
OVERALL		51	54	105	1.05	16	20	36	1.25	67	74	141	1.10
Grand Total		98	109	207	1.11	30	42	72	1.40	128	151	279	1.20
Cuddalore District													
V_1	MF	24	20	44	0.83	5	5	10	1.00	29	25	54	0.86
	NFW	17	15	32	0.88	12	8	20	0.66	29	23	52	0.80
	LAL	18	13	31	0.72	9	6	15	0.60	27	19	46	0.70
OVERALL		59	48	107	0.8	26	19	45	0.73	85	67	152	0.78
V_2	MF	17	17	34	1.00	6	6	12	1.00	23	23	46	1.00
	NFW	21	14	35	0.63	9	8	17	0.88	30	22	52	0.70
	LAL	14	11	25	0.78	10	10	20	1.00	24	21	45	0.87
OVERALL		52	42	95	0.80	25	24	49	0.96	77	66	143	0.84
Grand Total		111	90	201	0.80	51	43	94	0.84	162	133	295	0.81

Source: Computed
M-Male F-Female SR-Sex Ratio=Female/Male

data correlated with the macro level data: according to 2001 census 1043 females per 1000 males are recorded in Sivaganga district, where as it is low in Cuddalore district at 984 females per 1000 males.

Demographers have attributed the low female-male sex ratio to factors such as dowry and marriage practices and high female mortality rate. High female mortality rate is the result of poor nourishment and neglected health of female children due to gender bias[4]. It is worth recalling here Sen's comparison of female–male mortality rates in China and India, where he mentions that more than 100 million women are missing.[5] Low status of women also account for the lower number of females against males, which is the cause and consequence of the gender bias towards females.

Family Size

Size of the household has impact on the economic bearing of the household. The distribution of household size in Table 6 shows that a larger proportion of respondent households have medium size families (55 per cent and 58.4 per cent in Sivaganga and Cuddalore districts respectively). Large size families are not found in the sample households of Sivaganga district and negligible in Cuddalore district with only two households (3.3 per cent). Family size in relation to food expenditures has received wide attention for its effect on the nutrient intake of individuals. But, it has its limitations too. Though, this variable is important in determining the level of living of a household, it should also be noted that large households need not necessarily be marked by destitution.[6]

Age Composition

The age composition of the members of the respondent families affects greatly the maintenance of the household. A "bulging age distribution" may exert an influence by its effect on the ratio of dependents to productive elements in the working population. The age composition of the sample households in Sivaganga and Cuddalore districts is given in the following paragraphs.

Table 6
Family Size wise Distribution of Sample Households

Category		Sivaganga District				Cuddalore District			
		Small 0 - 4	*Medium* 5 - 7	*Large* 8 +	*Total*	*Small* 0 - 4	*Medium* 5 - 7	*Large* 8 +	*Total*
V_1	MF	3	7	-	10	4	4	2	10
	NFW	3	7	-	10	3	7	-	10
	LAL	7	3	-	10	5	5	-	10
OVERALL		13	17	-	30	12	16	2	30
V_2	MF	7	3	-	10	5	5	-	10
	NFW	4	6	-	10	2	8	-	10
	LAL	3	7	-	10	4	6	-	10
OVERALL		14	16	-	30	11	19	-	30
Grand Total		27	33	-	60	23	35	2	60
		(45)	(55)		(100)	(38.3)	(58.4)	(3.3)	(100)

Source: Computed.
(Figures in Parentheses are Percentage to Total)

A comparison of the proportion of children population (0-14 years), working population (15-59 years), and 60 + population is detailed in Table 7. The proportion of children population in the age group 7-14 years is large for both districts than the proportion of children population between 0-6 years. In village V_1 of Sivaganga District it is 20.3 per cent as against 5.8 per cent and in V_2 it is 18.4 per cent as against 6.4 per cent. Though the proportion of children between 0-6 years age group is slightly higher in Cuddalore district, than in Sivaganga district, it is comparatively lower than the proportion of children population between 7-14 years. The skewed age-wise population distribution found in these villages reflects the contemporary national level scenario because the proportion of the population below 15 years to the overall population is gradually declining in the country.

The family composition is generally held to be the second best determinant of household consumption next to income. This variable influences not only the quantum of consumption, but also the composition of household demand and magnitude of the "Engel Elasticities".[7] Of the surveyed households around 65 per cent are found to be in the active age group. Around 11 per cent of the population belongs to the geriatric age group of sixty plus in both the districts.

The age structure of the Indian population is an issue of great concern to planners. It has been found that nutritional problems affect mainly children in the pre-school age (1–5 years) particularly among the poor socio-economic groups of the population.[8] Differentials in under-nutrition can be observed while comparing different age groups of the sample population. The findings from such type of analysis would help the planners to devise short-term strategies to improve the nutritional status of the vulnerable groups in the population.

Working Composition

This demographic variable in terms of number of earning members against dependents in a household is considered to be a strong determinant of income and as a scale measure the nutritional well being of the family members. It was observed

Table 7
Age Composition of Sample Household Members

Category		Sivaganga District 0-6	7-14	15-59	60+	Total	Cuddalore District 0-6	7-14	15-59	60+	Total
V_1	MF	6	6	28	4	44	5	3	42	4	54
	NFW	1	11	39	-	51	7	12	31	2	52
	LAL	1	11	25	6	43	6	9	28	3	46
OVERALL		8	28	92	10	138	18	24	101	9	152
		(5.8)	(20.3)	(66.7)	(7.2)	(100)	(11.8)	(15.8)	(66.4)	(6.0)	(100)
V_2	MF	1	6	30	6	43	5	7	30	4	46
	NFW	6	6	37	1	50	5	12	27	8	52
	LAL	2	14	27	5	48	5	16	22	2	45
OVERALL		9	26	94	12	141	15	35	79	14	143
		(6.4)	(18.4)	(66.7)	(8.5)	(100)	(10.5)	(24.4)	(55.3)	(9.8)	(100)

Source: Computed.
(Figures in Parentheses are Percentage to Total).

from the field survey that no child below the age of 15 years was found to be an earner. The dependent-to-earner ratio (which is the result of the combination of differences in age-structure in the household and in labour force status of working age members) worked out in Table 8 for V_1 and V_2 of Sivaganga district is shown to be lower at 0.91 and 0.93 respectively, where as in Cuddalore district, it is higher at 1.05 for V_1 and1.48 for V_2. Households which are dependent on a single wage earner experienced a higher risk of food insecurity.

Another observation made from this Table is that more female earners are found in Sivaganga district (53.1 per cent) than in Cuddalore district (41.6 per cent) with male earners constituting 46.9 per cent and 58.4 per cent in the respective districts.

The female labour participation rate (FLPR) was also worked out. This indicates a higher ratio for LAL category in both the districts. It is customary to associate high FLPR with low economic status.[9] The FLPR is higher in Sivaganga district at 0.71 and lower in Cuddalore district at 0.61.

MATERNAL CHARACTERISTICS

The nutritional well-being of the individuals is influenced not only by access to food at the household level but also by maternal factors such as women education, work participation, their control over the income earned, their decision-making level and their status as heads of households. Level of education as a signifier of social progress is important in identifying demographic and economic changes. It has been widely and frequently observed in the available empirical literature that there have been dramatic changes in fertility levels and related factors due to the singular impact of maternal education.[10]

Household Headship

Distribution of households according to household pattern presented in Table 9 shows that 36.7 per cent of households in Sivaganga district is headed by women; in all such Female Headed Households (FHH), the spouse was present and he was a constituent part of the household. Joint Headed Households

Table 8
Workers Composition of Sample Households

Category		Sivaganga District						Cuddalore District					
		FE	*ME*	*TE*	*DP*	*DPE*	*FLPR*	*FE*	*ME*	*TE*	*DP*	*DPE*	*FLPR*
V_1	MF	14	12	26	18	0.7	0.77	9	17	26	28	1.07	0.45
	NFW	12	13	25	26	1.04	0.60	9	14	23	29	1.26	0.60
	LAL	13	8	21	22	1.04	0.76	11	14	25	21	0.84	0.85
OVERALL		39	33	72	66	0.91	0.71	29	45	74	78	1.05	0.60
V_2	MF	12	13	25	18	0.7	0.66	8	10	18	28	1.55	0.47
	NFW	12	11	23	27	1.17	0.60	8	12	20	32	1.65	0.57
	LAL	14	11	25	23	0.9	0.88	10	10	20	25	1.25	0.91
OVERALL		38	35	73	68	0.93	0.70	26	32	58	85	1.48	0.62
Grand Total		77	68	145	134	0.92	0.71	55	77	132	163	1.24	0.61
		(53.1)	(46.9)	(100)				(41.6)	(58.4)	(100)			

Source: Computed
(Figures in Parentheses are Percentage to Total)

Note: FE–Female Earners , ME–Male Earners , TE–Total Earners, DP–Dependent , DPE–Dependent Per Earner, FLPR–Female Labour Participation Rate

Table 9
Headship wise Distribution of Sample Households

		Sivaganga District				*Cuddalore District*			
Category		*FHH*	*JHH*	*MHH*	*TOTAL*	*FHH*	*JHH*	*MHH*	*TOTAL*
V_1	MF	4	4	2	10	2	3	5	10
	NFW	4	3	3	10	1	4	5	10
	LAL	4	4	2	10	1	4	5	10
OVERALL		12	11	7	30	4	11	15	30
V_2	MF	3	4	3	10	2	4	4	10
	NFW	3	5	2	10	4	3	3	10
	LAL	4	5	1	10	3	3	4	10
OVERALL		10	14	6	30	9	10	11	30
Grand Total		22	25	13	60	13	21	26	60
		(36.7)	(41.7)	(21.7)	(100)	(21.7)	(35.0)	(43.3)	(100)

Source: Computed
(Figures in Parentheses are Percentage to Total)

Note: FHH–Female Headed Households, JHH–Joint Headed Households, MHH–Male Headed Households

(JHH) constitute 41.7 per cent and Male Headed Households (MHH) constitute the lower proportion of 21.7 per cent in this district. But Cuddalore district shows a different picture where MHH constitute 43.3 per cent and JHH 35 per cent and FHH constitute only 21.7 per cent. Female headship is a useful targeting indicator for anti-poverty programmes.[11] This headship variable in the two districts provided opportunities to compare the variations in the food intake and nutritional status of family members in the two districts.

Educational Status

Literacy and schooling are important indicators of the quality of life, which help to measure the poor's ability to take advantage of the income-earning opportunities, which in turn, may influence food intake and health-seeking behaviour.

Table 10 gives the educational background of the sample households. The overall literacy level among husbands is higher for Cuddalore district at 83.4 per cent and lower for Sivaganga district at 71.7 per cent. It can be observed that no one in the LAL category is found to have attained high school level literacy. It can also be observed that no one in Sivaganga district has attained higher secondary level but in Cuddalore district seven of the males constituting 12 per cent in MF and NFW category have attained higher secondary level.

But with regard to women's literacy it is greater at 70 per cent in Sivaganga district and lower at 65 per cent in Cuddalore district. Women education is considered important for they have greater role in household decision-making. In this aspect, Sivaganga district seems to be well poised for growth.

Among the sample literate population, the largest concentration is found in the distribution of primary education. The diffusion of general primary education has a long-run cumulative effect on economic development. According to UNESCO "functional literacy is normally reached at the end of four or more years of schooling".[12] This means that a person who has completed at least four years of schooling may not relapse into illiteracy.

Table 10
Education wise Distribution of Sample Households (Husband/Wife)

Category		*Husband's Education*											
		Sivaganga District						*Cuddalore District*					
		No schooling	*Primary*	*Middle*	*HS*	*HSS*	*Total*	*No schooling*	*Primary*	*Middle*	*HS*	*HSS*	*Total*
V_1	MF	2	4	1	3	-	10	3	1	1	4	1	10
	NFW	4	6	-	-	-	10	1	4	1	3	1	10
	LAL	2	6	2	-	-	10	-	8	2	-	-	10
Overall		8	16	3	3	-	30	4	13	4	7	2	30
V_2	MF	4	5	1	-	-	10	2	2	1	2	3	10
	NFW	2	2	4	2	-	10	1	5	-	2	2	10
	LAL	3	7	-	-	-	10	3	6	1	-	-	10
Overall		9	14	5	2	-	30	6	13	2	4	5	30
Grand Total		17	30	8	5	-	60	10	26	6	11	7	60
Wife's Education													
V_1	MF	3	4	2	1	-	10	3	2	2	3	-	10
	NFW	5	4	1	-	-	10	3	4	2	-	1	10
	LAL	1	7	2	-	-	10	3	6	1	-	-	10
Overall		9	15	5	1	-	30	9	12	5	3	1	30
V_2	MF	4	5	1	-	-	10	3	5	1	1	-	10
	NFW	2	4	1	3	-	10	3	4	3	-	-	10
	LAL	3	6	1	-	-	10	6	3	1	-	-	10
Overall		9	15	3	3	-	30	12	12	5	1	-	30
Grand Total		18	30	8	4	-	60	21	24	10	4	1	60

Source: Computed
Note: HS–High School, HSS–Higher Secondary School

Husband/Wife Age-wise Classification

Table 11 presents the age-wise classification of wives and husbands. It is categorized into four age groups- 20-30, 31-40, 41-60 and above 60 years. It could be seen that the age group 31-40 years is highly represented in both the villages of Sivaganga and Cuddalore districts. Women's age factor is taken as a variable in the later parts of this study to know whether it has an influencing effect in the level of participation of women in decision-making.

Socio-Economic Status

Table 12 presents some important socio-economic characteristics of households by household headship. The results show that in the case of per centage of nuclear households, majority families are living independently irrespective of the household headship. Households, which live as joint or combined families, are in minority. The FLPR (the ratio of total adult females participating in work to total adult working population) shows that it is higher for households in Sivaganga district than Cuddalore district. Participation in labour gives women an opportunity to earn additional income to ensure additional resources to maintain the household. A significant feature of women's work participation in these rural areas is, as reported by women respondents themselves, their substantial contribution to income.

The data in Table 12 further shows that the earner-dependent ratio is comparatively lower for Sivaganga district. In Cuddalore district, headship wise analysis shows that the number of dependents per earner is higher for FHH (1.6 inV_1 and 2.08 in V_2 respectively) and it is lower for JHH (1.3 in V_1 and 1.65 in V_2 respectively). In such resource poor households, the higher dependency ratio may have an unfavourable influence on nutrition intake. With regard to number of days employed, it is the highest for women in FHH in both the villages of Sivaganga district (210 days and 214 days respectively) and in Cuddalore district it is 141 days and 182 days respectively. Further, women in FHH have comparatively longer days of work followed by women in MHH in both the

Table 11
Age-wise Classification of Sample Households (Husband/Wife)

Wife's Age											
		Sivaganga District					*Cuddalore District*				
Category		*20-30*	*31-40*	*41-60*	*60+*	*Total*	*20-30*	*31-40*	*41-60*	*60+*	*Total*
V_1	MF	2	3	5	0	10	1	2	6	1	10
	NFW	0	4	6	0	10	4	4	2	0	10
	LAL	0	7	3	0	10	3	4	3	0	10
Overall		2	14	14	0	30	8	10	11	1	30
V_2	MF	0	2	5	3	10	2	6	2	0	10
	NFW	1	3	6	0	10	1	5	3	1	10
	LAL	1	5	4	0	10	1	6	3	0	10
Overall		2	10	15	3	30	4	17	8	1	30
Grand Total		4	24	29	3	60	12	27	19	2	60
Husband's Age											
V_1	MF	0	2	8	0	10	2	6	2	0	10
	NFW	0	1	9	0	10	1	5	4	0	10
	LAL	0	3	6	1	10	0	5	4	1	10
Overall	0	6	23	1	30	3	16	10	1	30	
V_2	MF	1	6	3	0	10	3	6	1	0	10
	NFW	0	3	7	0	10	0	2	7	1	10
	LAL	0	4	4	2	10	0	4	6	0	10
Overall		1	13	14	2	30	3	12	14	1	30
Grand Total		1	19	37	3	60	6	28	24	2	60

Source: Computed

districts. Mean income of women corresponds to the number of days employed.[13] It is interesting to observe that the share of female income in household income is greater than male income in FHH of Sivaganga district (53.2 per cent and 53.1 per cent in V_1 and V_2 respectively). More over, women in FHH of Cuddalore district bring in a good share of total income (44.7 percent and 47.3 per cent in V_1 and V_2 respectively). This may be valid data in influencing women's participation in household decision-making process and empowering them to attain a status in the family.

Table 12
Socio-economic Characteristics of Sample Households: Headship wise

	Sivaganga District								
Headship category		*%NH*	*FLPR*	*EDR*	*WDE*	*MI*	*SFWI*	*%FE*	*%BPL*
V_1	FHH (n=12)	75	0.70	1.05	210	5638	53.2	66.7	58.3
	JHH (n=11)	82	0.71	1.03	146	4329	45.2	67.4	54.5
	MHH (n=7)	57	0.72	0.98	166	4800	38.1	70.3	85.7
V_2	FHH (n=10)	80	0.59	0.9	214	5896	53.1	74.4	70.0
	JHH (n=14)	78	0.85	1.07	202	5073	44.7	71.8	85.7
	MHH (n=6)	83	0.66	0.9	211	5228	46.0	84.6	83.3
Cuddalore District									
V_1	FHH (n=4)	75	0.66	1.6	141	4275	44.7	64.5	25
	JHH (n=11)	55	0.68	1.3	129	4392	30.1	73.6	72.7
	MHH (n=15)	66	0.61	1.44	124	4109	33.1	79.1	80
V_2	FHH (n=9)	55	0.61	2.08	182	5676	47.3	74.6	66.6
	JHH (n=10)	100	0.76	1.65	111	3605	40.9	80.8	90
	MHH (n=11)	72	0.62	1.67	138	4790	33	85.1	63.6

Source: Computed

Note: %NH- %of Nuclear households, FLPR-Female labour participation ratio, EDR-Earner-dependent ratio, WDE-Women's days employed, MI-Mean income of Women (Rs. per year), SFWI-Share of female wage income, %FE-% of income on food expenditure, BPL-% of households below poverty line.

With regard to percentage income spent on food expenditure, it is comparatively lower for female-headed households in V_1 (66.7 per cent) and V_2 (74.4 per cent) of Sivaganga district. Almost the same result is obtained in the Cuddalore district also. This observation leads to the generalisation that when the percentage of households below poverty line increases, the percentage of income for food expenditure also increases.[14] This analysis also suggests that poverty and female headship are not strongly linked. Since the relationship between headship and food insecurity is a relatively unexplored area in India, the present analysis would provide useful findings, which in due course, could lead to make effective policy suggestions.

Key Findings

- Majority of the respondents are Hindus in both the districts. Major community concentration in Sivaganga district is Backward Caste (BC) and in Cuddalore district it is Most Backward Caste (MBC). Most of the households are nuclear families in both the districts.
- Main source of borrowing is form private moneylenders. Borrowing for consumption purposes is higher in poor households.
- Sex-ratio is higher for Sivaganga district and lower for Cuddalore district. Most of the households in both districts belong to medium size families.
- More female earners are found in Sivaganga district than Cuddalore district.
- Female-headed households are found comparatively more in Sivaganga district.
- Female literacy is greater in Sivaganga district there Cuddalore district
- Middle-aged population is greater in the sample households of both the districts.
- Dependent ratio is lower for Sivaganga district.
- The female labour participation rate shows that it is higher for households in Sivaganga district than Cuddalore district.

NOTES AND REFERENCES

1. Bailey, F.G. (1957), *Caste and the Economic Frontier*, Manchester University Press, Manchester.

2. Gough, Kathleen (1971), "Castes in a Tanjore Village," in E.R. Leach (ed.), *Aspects of Caste in South Asia India, Ceylon and North West Pakistan*. Cambridge University Press, Cambridge.
3. Krishnaji, N. (1980), "Agrarian Structure and Family Formation: A Tentative Hypothesis." *Economic and Political Weekly*, Vo1. 15, A. 38–A.43.
4. Bardhan, Pranab (1988), "Sex Disparity in Child Survival in Rural India," in T. Srinivasan and Pranab Bardhan [eds.], *Rural Poverty in South Asia*. Columbia University Press, New York.
5. Sen, Amartya (1990), "More Than One Hundred Million Wómen Are Missing: Women's Survival as a Development Problem", *New York Review of Books*, December 20: 61-66.
6. Haijiang, Ma and B.M. Popkin (1995), "Income and Food Consumption Behaviour in China: As Structural Shift Analysis", *Food Nutrition Bulletin*, Vol. 16. No. 2, 155-165.
7. Currie, J. M. (1972), *The Analysis of Family Budgets: The Demand for Food*, Manchester University Press, Manchester: 17-36.
8. Evenson, R. E., B.M. Popkin and E. King-Quizow (1979), "Nutrition, Work and Demographic Behaviour in Rural Philippine Households", A Synopsis of Several Laguna Household Studies. Economic Growth Center, Yale University, Connecticut, New Haven.
9. Bardhan, Kalpana (1986), "Stratification of Women's Work in Rural India: Determinants, Effect and Strategies," in *Social and Economic Development in India: A Reassessment*, Sage Publication, New Delhi.
10. Robert, T. Michael (1973), "Population Education and the Derived Demand for Children", *Journal of Political Economy*, Vol. 2: 28.
11. Buvinic, M. and G. Gupta (1997), "Female-Headed Households and Female-Maintained Families: Are they Worth Targeting to Reduce Poverty in Developing Countries?". *Economic Development and Cultural Change*, Vol. 45, No. 2: 259-80.
12. Hanumantha Rao, G. (1977), *Caste and Poverty: A Case Study of Scheduled Castes in a Delta Village*. Savitry Publications.
13. In concurrence with the previous studies eight hours work was calculated into one day work.

    See, Jain, Devaki and Malini Chand (1982), *Report on Time Allocation Study: Its Methodological Implications*. Institute of Social Studies Trust, New Delhi.

14. The Researcher has used the Planning Commission, Government of India's revised statistics of Rs. 11,000 per household during Ninth Plan as per 1992-93 prices as poverty line income. This figure is suitably inflated by using wholesale price index number worked out to Rs. 20,742 at 2000–2001 prices and rounded off to Rs. 20,700.

    See also, Karuppaiyan, E. (2002), *Rural Development Programmes and Externalities: A Study of Seven Villages in Tamil Nadu*. The Planning Commission, Government of India, New Delhi, 185.

5

Household Entitlements and Food Security

Any analysis of issues in individual food security needs to be conducted at the household level because it is where decisions about production and consumption converge. It is indispensable to analyse the family food system because this provides the framework within which the food requirements of individuals are met. This chapter attempts to analyse household entitlements and food security in two sections. The first section deals with identification of factors contributing to household food entitlements. It focusses on each component of household food system and aims to comprehend all household level information regarding the functional elements of the household food system. In the second section an attempt is made to operationalize the prime determinants of food security at the household level so that household vulnerability to entitlement behaviour is substantially reduced.

HOUSEHOLD ENTITLEMENTS AND FOOD SYSTEM

In rural areas the household food system functions inefficiently leaving very often many poor people inadequately fed. This insufficiency is because of the lack of well-equipped network to connect determinants like employment status, income, food-pricing and other services. Asset Structure, Primary and Secondary Food System, Sources of Income, Household Expenditure Pattern, Monthly Food Consumption Frequency,

Household Food Habits and such idiosyncrasies are the variables which would help identify the high risk households. These are important indicators of household food security and they have to be understood clearly for targeting proximate variables for policy suggestions. The data gathered for these indicators are analysed in this section.

Asset Structure

Lack of an adequate asset base has much to do with poverty and in turn food insecurity. Table 1 makes a detailed description of the different types of assets, held by different categories of the sample population. Assets are classified into five broad categories, namely, (a) Income Generating Assets (IGA) comprising of land (LV), livestock (LSV) and trees (b) Financial Assets (FA) (c) Liquid Assets (LA) comprising of small livestock and jewellery (d) Household Durables (HD) and (e) Household Structures (HS).

Table 1 shows large variations in the possession of household assets among the household categories. IGA constitutes the major form of asset, which is around 60 per cent in Sivaganga district and 70 per cent in Cuddalore district for MF households alone. The second larger share of assets is provided by household structures (HS), which constitute the major form of asset for NFW and LAL categories. Next in order comes household durables (HD), and financial assets is shown to be meagre for all categories. (Financial assets relate to savings through insurance and banking). LAL households are found to be with extremely low level of ownership of assets with cumulative asset value of less than twenty-thousand rupees for each of the four villages. Scarce assets may make these poor LAL households vulnerable to food insecurity.

Lack of land asset is the most commonly cited reason for food insecurity among rural households. Observations and interviews further reveal that for many households, including landless households, animal ownership is their real asset which they use to generate income. Large livestock in the form of milch animals and drought animals are possessed by 23 households in Sivaganga district and a majority of households

Table 1
Average Household Wealth of Sample Households

(Rs.)

Sivaganga District										
Category		*LV*	*LSV*	*TREES*	*IGA*	*FA*	*LA*	*HD*	*HS*	*HW*
V_1	MF	67550	5010	3400	75960	1573	17204	10541	35335	140613
		(48.0)	(3.6)	(2.4)	(54.1)	(1.1)	(12.2)	(7.5)	(25.1)	(100)
	NFW	-	-	555	555	965	5455	5152	10926	23053
				(2.4)	(2.4)	(4.2)	(23.7)	(22.3)	(47.4)	(100)
	LAL	-	1480	690	2170	551	2287	3775	9676	18459
			(8.0)	(3.8)	(11.8)	(3.0)	(12.4)	(20.4)	(52.4)	(100)
V_2	M	48950	1930	1130	52010	287	3167	3865	19650	78979
		(62.0)	(2.4)	(1.4)	(65.8)	(0.4)	(4.0)	(4.9)	(24.9)	(100)
	NFW	-	1500	765	2265	1325	6172	8390	12088	30240
			(5.0)	(2.5)	(7.5)	(4.4)	(20.4)	(27.7)	(40.0)	(100)
	LAL	-	800	373	1173	160	2181	5650	7565	16729
			(4.8)	(2.2)	(7.0)	(1.0)	(13.0)	(33.8)	(45.2)	(100)

Contd...

Cuddalore District										
Category		*LV*	*LSV*	*TREES*	*IGA*	*FA*	*LA*	*HD*	*HS*	*HW*
V_1	MF	106750	7050	2020	115820	799	5749	9220	29320	160908
		(66.3)	(4.5)	(1.2)	(72)	(0.5)	(3.6)	(5.7)	(18.2)	(100)
	NFW	-	2250	730	2980	2010	6279	9160	18260	38689
			(5.8)	(1.9)	(7.7)	(5.2)	(16.2)	(23.7)	(47.2)	(100)
	LAL	-	960	480	1440	690	1149	3820	5550	12649
			(7.6)	(3.8)	(11.4)	(5.4)	(9.1)	(30.2)	(43.9)	(100)
V_2	MF	86700	2250	3875	92825	1240	4604	5390	30936	134995
		(64.2)	(1.7)	(2.9)	(68.8)	(0.9)	(3.4)	(4.0)	(22.9)	(100)
	NFW	-	3300	945	4245	1735	14995	10660	20050	51685
		(6.4)	(1.8)	(8.2)	(3.3)	(29.1)	(20.6)	(38.8)	(100)	
	LAL	-	-	448	448	150	1884	2530	5352	10364
				(4.3)	(4.3)	(1.4)	(18.2)	(24.5)	(51.6)	(100)

Source: Computed
(Figures in Parentheses are Percentage to Total)

which possess this asset is in MF category. In Cuddalore district 19 households possess milch animals. Here again, the majority of such households are in MF category.

Liquid assets like small livestock are found in 22 households in Sivaganga district and 19 households in Cuddalore district. Liquid assets in the form of goats and chicken are more relevant to a household for they reflect a household's ability to cope with short term food shortage. Small livestock is the most common form of liquid asset for LAL category. In MF and NFW households, liquid asset in the form of jewellery is owned by respondents in both the districts. However, in Sivaganga district, some households reported reluctance to liquidate the jewellery asset as they have acquired it for their daughter's marriage. But in Cuddalore district, respondents said that this asset often help them to get released out of debt or help them to raise money to fund their food needs or other necessities.

Household durables (HD) in the form of gadgets like radio and television is found in a few households of both MF and NFW categories. Though the ownership of these gadgets may not always indicate a food secured household, the inability of the households to purchase any of these durables provide some useful data to locate the food insecure household. Scrutinizing the occupation wise asset structure of households, it is found that a majority of LAL households fall in the lowest asset group. This strengthens the view that land possession is a very reliable indicator of asset status.

Primary Food System

For rural households, the agricultural sector is an important source of livelihood activities which also provides direct access to food. Their primary sources of food supply are a combination of factors like home production, wage in kind, market dependence, and Public Distribution System. Of the surveyed households, MF category respondents derive their food entitlement (staple food) from their own production.

Table 2 reveals the large difference in the pattern of land ownership and area under cultivation among MF households in the study area. Average land holdings are small (< 0.75 acres) for seven households in Sivaganga district (35 per cent) and five households in Cuddalore district (25 per cent). On an average in V_1 of Sivaganga district only 89 per cent of the land area is under cultivation. For the other three villages the percentage area cultivated account for 100 per cent. Eight households in Sivaganga district (40 per cent) and six households in Cuddalore district (30 per cent) own land area in the range of acres 0.76 and < 1.5 acres. But the cultivable land in Sivaganga district accounts for nearly 91 per cent whereas in Cuddalore district it accounts for 100 per cent. Only five households in Sivaganga district (25 per cent), and nine households in Cuddalore district (45 per cent) own an area ranging from 1.6 to 2.5 acres. In this category, on an average, a maximum of 90 per cent (in V_2 of Sivaganga district) and minimum of 63 per cent (in V_2 of Cuddalore district) of the total area is found to be under cultivation.

Table 2
Average Area Under Cultivation (in %)

	Sivaganga District		*Cuddalore District*	
Area in Acres	V_1	V_2	V_1	V_2
< 0.75	89 (3)	100 (4)	100 (2)	100 (3)
0.76 - 1.5	95 (4)	88 (4)	100 (3)	100 (3)
1.6 - 2.5	83 (3)	90 (2)	88 (5)	63 (4)

Source : Computed.
Figure in Parentheses denote numbers.

Rice is by far the most important food crop for all the Marginal Farmers. Respondents reported that anticipating adverse conditions, they like to grow paddy for this would ensure them a certain moderate level of food adequacy and also they would be ensured against riskier portfolio choices. Very few households informed that they indulge in crop diversification to reduce the risk against food entitlement failures. Information collected from them on crop diversification, show that two households in each of the districts grow chillies and three households in Sivaganga district and two in Cuddalore district grow groundnut. They choose these crops since they yield better even in dry weather and poor soil conditions. It is further found that one household in Sivaganga district grows *ragi,* seven households in Cuddalore district grow black gram (as an inter-crop) and three households in Sivaganga and two in Cuddalore districts engage in vegetable production. For the vegetable growers lack of water during dry season is the major constraining factor.

The relationship between food production and food security (sustainability) depends on the food stocks available at the household level. Table 3 presents the marketed surpluses of food crops. For those households with land holding of <0.75 acres, the marketed surplus is nil. Of the respondents belonging to this land holding group, some state that the food stock they produce was just enough to feed the household members for 3-4 months. Often the retained food stocks are sold away to

Table 3
Average Marketed Surplus of Food and Cash Crops (in %)

	Sivaganga district		*Cuddalore district*	
Items	V_1	V_2	V_1	V_2
Marketed Surplus of Grains				
< 0.75 Acres	0	0	0	0
0.76 - 1.5 Acres	28	26	24	26
1.6 - 2.5 Acres	0	65	31	14
Marketed Surplus of Pulses				
< 0.75 Acres	-	-	60	-
0.76 - 1.5 Acres	58	-	51	57
1.6 - 2.5 Acres	-	-	62	64
Marketed Surplus of Vegetables				
< 0.75 Acres	-	-	-	-
0.76 - 1.5 Acres	90	93	-	-
1.6 - 2.5 Acres	84	95	-	90
Marketed Surplus of Chillies				
< 0.75 Acres	93	-	-	-
0.76 - 1.5 Acres	-	-	-	90
1.6 - 2.5 Acres	90	-	-	-
Marketed Surplus of Groundnut				
< 0.75 Acres	-	-	-	-
0.76 - 1.5 Acres	83	95	95	-
1.6 - 2.5 Acres	84	-	-	-

Source: Computed.

purchase other food and non-food items and to fund unexpected expenditure. Respondents belonging to MF households, holding 0.76 to 1.5 acres are found to have sold one fourth of the produce immediately after harvest. The marketed surplus for households owning land between 1.6 and 2.5 acres is found to be nil for households in V_1 and 65 per cent for households in V_2 in Sivaganga district. The corresponding figures for V_1 and V_2 of Cuddalore district are shown to be at 31 per cent and 14 per cent respectively. Many poor farmers reported that lack of storage facility compels them to sell their crops soon after harvest even though prices are lower and to buy food grains during the dry season at higher prices. More than half of the produce of pulses is sold in the market, and in the case of marketed surpluses of vegetables and cash crops it is 90 per cent. It is observed that for households which produce more and retain the ample stock for the entire year's consumption, food availability is not a problem. But MF households with poor resources along with NFW and LAL households are reported to depend on open market or Public Distribution System (PDS).

Table 4 furnishes data for source-wise share of food consumption, showing the minimum, maximum and mean value. To know the nature of deviation in the mean value among the households, the co-efficient of variation is computed. The findings show that the majority of rural households depend on PDS and this dependency is higher for LAL households at 40.3 per cent and 47.4 per cent in V_1 and V_2 of Sivaganga district and 35.2 per cent and 26.0 per cent in V_1 and V_2 of Cuddalore district respectively. However, the obtained CV value shows less variability around the mean value to the tune of 17.4 per cent in V_1 of Sivaganga district implying highly consistent percentage of PDS consumption among the households.

For MF households, the main source of primary food is home production (HP), which are around 70 per cent for both the villages of each selected district. The extent of variability value is shown to be comparatively lower at 19.5 per cent for V_1 of Cuddalore district. For LAL households, a known source

Table 4
Source-wise Share of Food Consumption of Sample Households (%)

Sivaganga District

Category		PDS			HP/WIK			MKT		
		MIN	MAX	MEAN	MIN	MAX	MEAN	MIN	MAX	MEAN
V_1	MF	0	52	30 (69.3)	48	100	70 (30.1)	0	12	1.2 (308.3)
	NFW	29	44	37.2 (17.4)	0	9	2.4 (133.3)	49	70	60.4 (13.1)
	LAL	33	44	40.3 (10.7)	17	29	23.4 (17.9)	27	50	36.3 (21.4)
V_2	MF	0	55	28.4 (73.2)	45	100	70.8 (30.1)	0	8	0.8 (312.5)
	NFW	22	45	32.1 (23.4)	0	20	2.8 (23.2)	35	78	65.1 (18.9)
	LAL	33	66	47.4 (26.6)	11	29	18.8 (29.2)	17	46	33.8 (28.4)

Contd...

Cuddalore District										
		PDS			HP/WIK			MKT		
Category		MIN	MAX	MEAN	MIN	MAX	MEAN	MIN	MAX	MEAN
V_1	MF	0	34	18.9 (71.4)	55	100	79 (19.5)	0	12	1.5 (253)
	NFW	24	48	31.7 (29.6)	0	0	0 (0)	52	76	68.3 (13.7)
	LAL	20	53	35.2 (28.9)	15	40	25.8 (29.1)	23	65	39 (39.7)
V_2	MF	14	33	22.8 (23.2)	15	78	61.3 (38.2)	0	71	15.9 (169.2)
	NFW	0	44	23.8 (60.9)	0	15	5.2 (113.4)	41	90	72.4 (24.7)
	LAL	20	33	26 (17.3)	8	17	10.5 (23.8)	50	72	63.5 (10.4)

Source: Computed.

(Figures in Parentheses denote co-efficient of variation = $\frac{\text{Standard Deviation}}{\text{Mean}} \times 100$)

of food is wage-in-kind (WIK) which satisfies around 23.4 per cent and 18.8 per cent of their total cereal needs in V_1 and V_2 of Sivaganga district. In Cuddalore district, dependency of LAL households on this source is at 25.8 per cent and 10.5 per cent for V_1 and V_2 respectively.

Market dependency (MKT) is greater for NFW households at 60.4 per cent and 65.1 per cent in V_1 and V_2 of Sivaganga district and 68.3 per cent and 72.4 per cent in V_1 and V_2 of Cuddalore district. The lower variability observed around the mean value shows consistency in the mean value of the market dependency of the households. The percentage of market dependency is less for MF households. LAL households depend on market very much. Studies have shown that for larger part of the purchase the poor people have to depend on open market than on PDS [1]. And this is the case with the households in the study area with a large family size. It is known from the findings that for LAL households the open market source is 36.3 per cent and 33.8 per cent for V_1 and V_2 of Sivaganga district and for Cuddalore district it is 39.0 per cent and 63.5 per cent for V_1 and V_2 respectively. A few MF households in both pockets of the study area reported that they do not require PDS rice for they retain their home grown stock.

PDS is considered an important component to solve the problem of food insecurity in rural India. The utilisation of PDS at the household level is determined by the respective household's purchasing power, production of grains, entitlement to the PDS, prices and quality of rice and other commodities available from the PDS in relation to that of open market. In both the study areas the basic food items such as rice, wheat, sugar and edible oil are marketed at subsidised price by the PDS. 20 per cent of the households in Sivaganga district and 24 per cent in Cuddalore district reported that the PDS gives a safety net at least in ensuring cereal security to them. Though wheat is supplied at the PDS it does not make any significant change in the pattern of food grain consumption of the households. Among the food items, people prefer to buy only rice and edible oils. Some households reported that they could not purchase their entire quota in one day because of fund constraints. Daily wage earners sometimes have to borrow money to buy from the PDS or have to depend on the open market to fulfil their requirements.

LAL households reported that their monthly purchases from PDS form the lowest share of their food consumption and PDS does not substantially support them. Studies have also shown that the poor get only marginal benefits from PDS in rural India.[2-3] Many respondents reported inefficiencies in the distribution operation since for most of the time the shops remain closed. However, many of the households want the coarse cereals like *ragi* and other millets to be distributed through PDS and they want to be allowed to make fractional purchases of grains and pulses. They want their rice quota to be increased. Above all, they want the PDS shop to operate customer-friendly like the shops in the open market, allowing them to make purchases in the smooth way. From this analysis, it is inferred that the state-arranged sources of entitlement to food hardly provided creditable food security to the poor.

Secondary Food System

In addition to primary sources of food availability, food was also available from the adjoining fields and forests in the study area. The existence of such food sources is not a new phenomenon in the Indian context.[4-5]

It is very interesting to find that people in Sivaganga district consume a variety of plant and animal products. They ate green-leaf edibles such as *Mayilikeerai, Kurinjakeerai, Ponnanganni, Pirandai* and roots and tubers like *Kottikizhangu* and *Kannikizhangu,* fruit varieties like *naval* and wood apples and vegetables like *Kovaikai and Mithukangkai.* They pickle or dry these edibles and consume with rice during the busy season or when women have less time for cooking. Many in Sivaganga district reported that these green leaves are collected while returning home from the fields and these help them to save their time which they normally spend to purchase food.

Another source of secondary food is access to 'bush meat' which is a complement to household food security and nutrition. Two NFW households in V_1 and V_2 of Sivaganga district belonging to hunter family, are seen to hunt birds like *'Ullan'*, *'Kadai'*, *'Kavuthari'* and small animals like rabbits. These poor hunter families manage to get their protein requirements mainly through this source. As this 'bush meat' is available in the villages at a price lower than the food items in the market, they are purchased and consumed by other poor households of the villages. The respondents informed that the fruit and nut varieties are available from March to May, whereas edible roots and tubers are available from January to March. MF households and LAL households make use of it to a greater extent. Thus secondary food items serve as an integral source of household food security to the very poor households in Sivaganga district.

But in Cuddalore district the access to forest food is low. The findings show that a very few green-leaf varieties are gathered from the fields. Some LAL households reported that they catch fish and crabs from ponds during summer when they dried up.

The variations in the access to this food source in the two districts can be attributed to the macro data on forest converge discussed in the chapter on Area Profile (see p. 69). It is confirmed that food derived from this secondary food source provides essential vitamins, proteins and calories and is essential for a family's food security strategy especially during the scarce situation of primary food.

Sources of Income

The shift in household food security paradigm from food supply to food access has led many policy makers and development practitioners concerned with food and nutrition issues, to emphasize the role of household income as a determinant of food security. It is worth recalling Sen[6] again, whose work focussed attention on the lack of access to food by households and individuals because of low incomes. Source-wise share of average annual income of the sample households is given in Table 5. The data show striking differences both in the amount of total income and in its composition, across villages and between different household categories.

Table 5

Source-wise Average Annual Income of Sample Households

(Rs.)

Sivaganga District										
Category		*CI*	*LSI*	*TI*	*RI*	*FWI*	*MWI*	*TWI*	*IS*	*HI*
V_1	MF	6777	1873	534	630	6463	8885	15348	1382	26544
		(25.5)	(7.1)	(2.0)	(2.2)	(24.4)	(33.5)	(57.9)	(5.3)	(100)
	NFW	-	72	194	180	7520	10135	17655	200	18301
			(0.4)	(1.0)	(0.98)	(41.1)	(55.4)	(96.5)	(1.12)	(100)
	LAL	-	1558	375	0	5602	5765	11367	502	13802
			(11.3)	(2.7)	(0)	(40.6)	(41.8)	(82.4)	(3.6)	(100)
V_2	MF	4595	1248	251	0	5590	5980	11570	1273	18938
		(24.2)	(6.6)	(1.3)	(0)	(29.5)	(31.6)	(61.1)	(6.8)	(100)
	NFW	-	1305	301	146	7924	7670	15594	400	17746
			(7.36)	(1.7)	(0.83)	(44.66)	(43.2)	(87.86)	(2.25)	(100)
	LAL	-	771	130	0	5663	6364	12027	80	13008
			(5.93)	(1.0)	(0)	(43.53)	(48.92)	(92.45)	(0.62)	(100)

Contd...

Cuddalore District										
Category		*CI*	*LSI*	*TI*	*RI*	*FWI*	*MWI*	*TWI*	*IS*	*HI*
V_1	MF	6174	4734	344	0	4485	6640	11125	0	22377
		(27.6)	(21.16)	(1.53)	(0)	(20.04)	(29.67)	(49.71)	(0)	(100)
	NFW	-	1338	124	106	3882	9190	13072	3300	17940
			(7.46)	(0.69)	(0.59)	(21.64)	(51.23)	(72.87)	(18.39)	(100)
	LAL	-	534	306	0	5815	8300	14115	540	15495
			(3.4)	(2.0)	(0)	(37.5)	(53.6)	(91.1)	(3.5)	(100)
V_2	MF	5880	1439	930	0	4880	7075	11955	150	20354
		(28.9)	(7.07)	(4.57)	(0)	(24.0)	(34.76)	(58.76)	(0.7)	(100)
	NFW	-	2701	304	290	4086	12670	16756	1780	21831
			(12.37)	(1.39)	(1.33)	(18.71)	(58.04)	(76.75)	(8.16)	(100)
	LAL	-	57	313	0	5034	5560	10594	622	11586
			(0.5)	(2.7)	(0)	(43.43)	(48)	(91.43)	(5.37)	(100)

Source: Computed.

(Figures in Parentheses denote co-efficient of variation = $\frac{\text{Standard Deviation}}{\text{Mean}} \times 100$)

In addition to producing food, majority of MF households gain access to income by generating sufficient revenue through sale of own produced crop and other income generating assets. For them, the shares of wage income from agriculture and crop income (CI) are in higher proportion. For NFW households, major share of income is from wage employment in the non-farm sector and also from petty trading and livestock rearing. Female wage income (FWI) and male wage income (MWI) from agriculture dominate the source-wise share of income for LAL households which is at nearly 90 per cent of their total income. This proves the proverbial myth that labour is the poor man's most valuable asset. Diversification of income sources is often indicated as an important part of households' strategy to reduce the risk of entitlement failure. [7] But in this analysis, the researcher found that only income from livestock provides a substantial amount that too for a few households, whereas Income from Trees (TI), Rental Income (RI) and Income from other Sources (IS) do not generate a substantial amount.

The tabulated data further identifies the LAL households as characterised by lesser income and asset which make food security of these households more risky.

Household Expenditure Pattern

Household food expenditure pattern is an excellent indicator of existing economic condition of a community and behaviour of variables like food consumption and calorie/protein intake in relation to the level of food expenditure is the important input of nutritional analysis.[8]

The household expenditure can be defined as the cumulative monetary values of consumption of various groups of food items such as Cereals (VC), Pulses (VP), Vegetables (VV), Green Leaves (VGL), Fruits (VF), Oils and Fats (VOF), Meat Products (VOMP), Milk and Milk Products (VMMP), Sugar (VC), Spices and Condiments (VSC) and Beverages (VB) and Consumption of various groups of non-food items such as Fuel and Lighting (VFL), Clothing and Cosmetics (VCC), Education (VE), Medical Expenses (VME), Recreation (VREC),

Transport (VTR), Household Maintenance (HM), Narcotics (NAR) and Social and Religions Expenditure (SRE).[9]

The percentage of monthly income spent on food by the respondent households is presented in Tables 6, 7 and 8 by household category. From these tables the highest and the lowest items of food consumption can be identified. Co-efficient of variation is also calculated and utilized for accounting the extent of inequality in the expenditure pattern among the three categories of sample households.

Table 6

Average Monthly Expenditure Pattern of Food Items in MF Households

(Rs.)

	Sivaganga District				*Cuddalore District*			
	V_1		V_2		V_1		V_2	
Items	*Mean*	%	*Mean*	%	*Mean*	%	*Mean*	%
VC	588	39.0	444	38.3	771	46.7	578	44.8
	(27.5)		(17.0)		(35.6)		(28.2)	
VP	120	8.0	109	9.4	136	8.1	102	7.9
	(18.4)		(28.8)		(31.2)		(15.8)	
VV	212	14.0	189	16.3	249	15.0	216	16.7
	(17.1)		(20.1)		(40.4)		(25.0)	
VGL	27	1.7	24	2.1	35	2.1	27	2.1
	(30.4)		(20.2)		(61.9)		(31.7)	
VF	38	2.5	33	2.8	32	1.9	24	1.9
	(30.7)		(51.1)		(41.8)		(59.5)	
VOF	109	7.1	76	6.5	114	6.8	82	6.3
	(12.5)		(16.6)		(40.7)		(13.8)	
VOMP	121	7.9	78	6.7	93	5.5	85	6.6
	(35.3)		(54.8)		(69.0)		(25.5)	
VMMP	140	9.2	69	6.0	138	8.3	81	6.3
	(93.2)		(71.1)		(92.7)		(104.5)	
VS	32	2.1	20	1.7	23	1.3	20	1.5
	(14.9)		(54.4)		(70.2)		(79)	
VSC	65	4.2	6	5.2	39	2.3	36	2.8
	(19.3)		(39.0)		(30.7)		(43.8)	
VB	66	4.3	58	5.0	34	2.0	40	3.1
	(63.6)		(53.4)		(61.5)		(58.7)	
Total	1518	100	1160	100	1664	100	1291	100

Source: Computed.

(Figures in Parentheses denote co-efficient of variation = $\frac{\text{Standard Deviation}}{\text{Mean}} \times 100$)

Table 7
Average Monthly Expenditure Pattern of Food Items in NFW Households

(Rs.)

	Sivaganga District				Cuddalore District			
	V_1		V_2		V_1		V_2	
Items	*Mean*	*%*	*Mean*	*%*	*Mean*	*%*	*Mean*	*%*
VC	409.0	37.8	409	36.4	374	32.5	432	33.7
	(14.5)		(18.0)		(24.2)		(23.5)	
VP	96.5	9.0	91	8.1	112	9.7	115	9.0
	(29.8)		(13.1)		(20.0)		(18.4)	
VV	148.0	13.7	160.5	14.3	165	14.3	163	12.7
	(22.4)		(14.0)		(24.7)		(16.0)	
VGL	24.5	2.3	21	1.9	20	1.7	25	2.0
	(31.0)		(29.0)		(28.5)		(37.6)	
VF	21.5	2.0	29.5	2.6	22.5	2.0	25	2.0
	(55.8)		(28.1)		(58.5)		(70.8)	
VOF	81.0	7.5	94	8.4	96	8.3	95	7.4
	(27.1)		(11.38)		(15.6)		(16.6)	
VOMP	76.0	7.0	73	6.5	77	6.7	91	7.1
	(25.7)		(40.8)		(38.1)		(53.8)	
VMMP	74.0	6.8	81.5	7.2	99	8.6	151	11.7
	(94.5)		(56.7)		(68.6)		(89.4)	
VS	17.5	1.6	20	1.8	29	2.5	18.5	1.4
	(70.5)		(52.5)		(44.8)		(91.3)	
VSC	68.0	6.3	67.5	6.0	62	5.4	73	5.6
	(23.5)		(21.1)		(16.1)		(19.1)	
VB	65	6.0	76	6.8	96	8.3	95	7.4
	(20.7)		(73.9)		(79.1)		(52.6)	
Total	1082	100	1123	100	1152	100	1283	100

Source: Computed.

(Figures in Parentheses denote co-efficient of variation = $\frac{\text{Standard Deviation}}{\text{Mean}} \times 100$)

The results show that the average monthly food expenditure is the highest in MF households of both districts at Rs. 1518 and Rs. 1160 for V_1 and V_2 of Sivaganga district and Rs. 1664 and Rs. 1291 for the villages in Cuddalore district. NFW households spend Rs. 1082 (V_1) and Rs. 1123 (V_2), Rs. 1152 (V_1) and Rs. 1283 (V_2) in Sivaganga and Cuddalore districts respectively. In LAL households the expenditure is the lowest at Rs. 756 and Rs. 807 in V_1 and V_2 of Sivaganga

Table 8
Average Monthly Expenditure Pattern of Food Items in Lal Households

(Rs.)

	Sivaganga District				*Cuddalore District*			
	V_1		V_2		V_1		V_2	
Items	*Mean*	%	*Mean*	%	*Mean*	%	*Mean*	%
VC	291 (22.5)	38.5	341 (24.6)	42.2	362 (28.7)	34.8	400 (21.3)	43.4
VP	79 (20.2)	10.4	75 (17.3)	9.3	94 (26.5)	9.0	71 (29.5)	7.7
VV	101 (17.8)	13.4	104 (12.5)	12.9	153 (24.8)	14.7	101 (18.3)	11.0
VGL	19 (20.5)	2.5	19 (20.6)	2.4	22.5 (45.0)	2.2	26 (23.0)	2.8
VF	22.5 (45.4)	3.0	21.5 (46.5)	2.7	20 (20.4)	1.9	19.5 (71.7)	2.1
VOF	59.5 (15.4)	7.9	61 (15.7)	7.6	80 (23.5)	7.7	61.5 (22.6)	6.7
VOMP	41 (21.9)	5.4	36 (26.6)	4.4	83 (51.0)	8.0	54.5 (53.7)	5.9
VMMP	40 (80.0)	5.3	35 (108.5)	4.3	90.5 (60.0)	8.7	62 (88.7)	6.7
VS	19 (52.6)	2.5	17.5 (70.5)	2.2	20 (50.0)	1.9	17.5 (68.5)	1.9
VSC	44 (19.0)	5.8	54 (18.5)	6.7	53 (15.0)	5.1	38 (26.3)	4.1
VB	40.0 (42.5)	5.3	43 (47.6)	5.3	63 (147.6)	6.0	71 (69.0)	7.7
Total	756	100	807	100	1041	100	922	100

Source: Computed.

(Figures in Parentheses denote co-efficient of variation = $\frac{\text{Standard Deviation}}{\text{Mean}} \times 100$)

district and Rs. 1041 and Rs. 922 for Cuddalore district. The striking variations in the level of expenditure among the three categories reflect the prevailing gross inequalities in income.

A glance at the food group shows that expenditure on cereals occupies the highest priority, with more than 36 per cent of the total food expenditure. Since rice is the staple food of the study area its consumption is naturally high. Next to cereals, vegetables are consumed largely. The proportion exceeds 14 per cent for MF households and more than 12 per cent for NFW and LAL categories in both the districts. The expenditure on milk and milk products occupies a third place in priority for MF households in V_1 of both Sivaganga and Cuddalore districts. Generally pulses and legumes occupy a relatively lesser position in the analysis of total food expenditure. But in V_2 of both the districts, expenditure on pulses occupy the third position with 9.3 per cent and 7.8 per cent respectively.

The share of expenditure on expensive food items like meat and milk products are higher for MF and NFW households and lesser for LAL households. Mean expenditure on oil and meat products occupy a relatively lesser proportion. Lowest share of expenditure is made on micro nutrient rich foods like green leaves and fruits which account for only around two per cent in all the sample households. Analysing the degree of dispersion of expenditure, greater inequality is found among the respondents in the consumption expenditure of milk and fruits. Many families in both the districts do not consume any fruit or drink any milk (see Table 12). A great variation of mean expenditure on foods like milk products, fruits and beverages is noticed among the households in each district. Level of expenditure on qualitative food is found to be low for LAL category, endorsing the view that these families consume food just enough for survival.

Expenditure on non-food items tabulated for all the three occupational categories in Tables 9, 10 and 11 shows that for MF households in both the districts, larger proportion of expenditure is on clothing and cosmetics (VCC), followed by expenditure on fuel and lighting (VFL). But for LAL and NFW households it is the reverse. The level of expenditure on education (VE) for all the categories does not exceed even 10 per cent. It is the highest for LAL category and this may be due to the reason that there are more school-going children in the category.

The expenditure on alcoholic beverage (NAR) is less in Sivaganga district for all household categories. But the share is much larger in Cuddalore district. LAL households in this

Table 9
Average Monthly Expenditure Pattern of Non-food Items in MF Households

(Rs.)

	Sivaganga District				*Cuddalore District*			
	V_1		V_2		V_1		V_2	
Items	*Mean*	%	*Mean*	%	*Mean*	%	*Mean*	%
VFL	252	34.1	226	36.7	213	27.6	192	28.5
	(13.7)		(15.5)		(16.5)		(15.6)	
VCC	273	36.9	232	37.7	248	32.2	229	34.0
	(27.6)		(21.2)		(23.1)		(18.6)	
VE	68	9.2	35.5	5.8	83	10.8	70	10.4
	(106.6)		(97.1)		(93.9)		(75.7)	
VME	21.5	2.9	17.5	2.9	34	4.4	20	3.0
	(34.4)		(36.2)		(64.9)		(42.0)	
VREC	8	1.1	5.5	0.9	2	0.2	1	0.2
	(174.7)		(161.0)		(315)		(310)	
VTR	33	4.5	18.5	3.0	36	4.7	19.5	2.9
	(36.3)		(25.6)		(55.4)		(38.9)	
HM	29	3.9	13	2.1	18	2.3	17.5	2.6
	(66.4)		(34.8)		(56.9)		(52.9)	
NAR	15	2.0	33	5.4	43	5.6	56	8.3
	(213)		(136.0)		(209.0)		(230)	
SRE	40.5	5.4	34	5.5	94	12.2	68	10.1
	(64.9)		(51.1)		(33.0)		(42.6)	
Total	740	100	615	100	771	100	673	100

Source: Computed.

(Figures in Parentheses denote co-efficient of variation = $\frac{\text{Standard Deviation}}{\text{Mean}} \times 100$)

district, surprisingly, are found to spend more (more than the amount spent on pulses and vegetables) on alcohol. Greatest inequality is also found among the households in that group in the quantum of amount they spend on alcohol. Recreation (VREC) causes insignificant amount of expenditure among the rural population. Except for VFL and VCC, the variability in the mean expenditure on all other non-food items among the households is seen to be subjective and highly inconsistent. Overall, the analysis shows that food expenditure was greater than non-food expenditure.

Table 10
Average Monthly Expenditure Pattern of Non-food Items in NFW Households

(Rs.)

	Sivaganga District				*Cuddalore District*			
	V_1		V_2		V_1		V_2	
Items	*Mean*	*%*	*Mean*	*%*	*Mean*	*%*	*Mean*	*%*
VFL	214	32.0	202	29.1	179	24.0	197	22.7
	(15.2)		(19.8)		(9.4)		(19.7)	
VCC	175	26.2	199	28.7	209	28.1	198	22.8
	(22.6)		(37.0)		(14.8)		(19.1)	
VE	43	6.4	51	7.35	73	9.8	69	7.9
	(102.2)		(64.3)		(43.2)		(102)	
VME	31	4.6	32.5	4.7	40	5.4	36.5	4.2
	(87.0)		(27.3)		(41.7)		(41.6)	
VREC	17	2.6	10.5	1.5	16	2.2	18.5	2.1
	(58.8)		(56.1)		(70.0)		(144.8)	
VTR	27	4.1	33	4.8	35.5	4.7	37.5	4.3
	(49.2)		(29.3)		(26.7)		(41.6)	
HM	56	8.4	51	7.35	54	7.3	103	11.8
	(58.9)		(32.5)		(36.1)		(58.2)	
NAR	56	8.4	38	5.5	40	5.4	135	15.5
	(126.0)		(181.0)		(177)		(203)	
SRE	49	7.3	76	11.0	97	13.1	76	8.7
	(36.5)		(16.5)		(35.9)		(21.5)	
Total	668	100	693	100	743	100	870	100

Source: Computed.

(Figures in Parentheses denote co-efficient of variation = $\frac{\text{Standard Deviation}}{\text{Mean}} \times 100$)

An informal interview which the researcher had with the respondents reveals that in almost all LAL households, expenditure always exceeds income and the deficit is met by debts. This has also been the finding of other researchers.[10]

Monthly Food Consumption Frequency

The village-wise monthly frequency for intake of selected food items like pulses, fruits, meat products and milk is given in Tables 12 and 13. Since rice and vegetables in some form (though the consumption is very low) are taken everyday, they are not included in the Tables. Pulses are one of the important

Table 11
Average Monthly Expenditure Pattern of Non-food Items in Lal Households

(Rs.)

	Sivaganga District				*Cuddalore District*			
	V_1		V_2		V_1		V_2	
Items	*Mean*	*%*	*Mean*	*%*	*Mean*	*%*	*Mean*	*%*
VFL	175	37.7	199	37.3	180	30.4	146	29.6
	(12.0)		(18.0)		(16.1)		(25.8)	
VCC	120	25.5	161	30.2	133	22.4	118	23.9
	(24.1)		(15.8)		(24.8)		(28.8)	
VE	49.5	10.6	56	10.5	48	8.1	51	10.3
	(61.2)		(78.5)		(62.5)		(61.0)	
VME	18	3.9	25	4.7	25.5	4.3	18	3.6
	(41.6)		(28.2)		(24.0)		(43.0)	
VREC	4.5	1.0	3.5	0.7	1	0.2	2.5	0.5
	(184.0)		(213.0)		(310)		(216)	
VTR	18	3.9	22	4.1	24.5	4.1	19	3.9
	(28.1)		(19.0)		(22.4)		(38.4)	
HM	15.5	3.4	22	4.1	64	10.7	28	5.7
	(31.6)		(44.0)		(27.0)		(51.7)	
NAR	25	5.4	12	2.2	86	14.4	79	16.0
	(137.2)		(191.0)		(133.0)		(112.0)	
SRE	38.5	8.3	33	6.2	32	5.4	32	6.5
	(49.3)		(39.3)		(24.3)		(50.0)	
Total	464	100	533	100	594	100	493	100

Source: Computed.

(Figures in Parentheses denote co-efficient of variation = $\frac{\text{Standard Deviation}}{\text{Mean}} \times 100$)

sources of nutrients, particularly protein. The frequency of pulse consumption recorded shows a minimum of 10 days for only one NFW household in V_1 of Sivaganga district and a maximum of all 30 days is recorded in three NFW households in V_1 in addition to two MF households in V_2. V_1 recorded an average number of 19 days and V_2 recorded an average of 20 days. In Cuddalore district, a minimum of 10 days is recorded for a few households belonging to LAL category whereas some MF households in both villages consume pulses for all the 30 days. V_1 recorded an average of 21 days of pulse consumption and V_2 recorded 18 days. Evidently, pulses, which are the main protein content food item consume by all households in the sample population, are not taken regularly by majority of the households thus indicating that the standard requirements set by nutritionists is not adequately met in these rural households.

Table 12
Food Consumption Frequency wise Percent Distribution of Sample Households

Sivaganga District

Frequency of consumption	*Pulses*	*Fruits* [a]	*Milk* [b]	*Meat products*
Once daily	38.6	-	45.4	-
Twice daily	-	-	15.3	-
Once-a-week	-	26.2	-	39.4
Twice-a-week	-	-	-	10.2
Three times a week	6.8	-	-	-
Five times a week	54.6	-	-	-
Occasionally	-	53.6	27.6	50.4

Cuddalore District

Frequency of consumption	*Pulses*	*Fruits* [c]	*Milk* [d]	*Meat products*
Once daily	35.4	-	39.6	-
Twice daily	-	-	13.4	-
Once-a-week	-	24.04	-	30.2
Twice-a-week	-	-	-	3.1
Three times a week	10.0	-	-	-
Five times a week	54.6	-	-	-
Occasionally	-	53.5	31.3	66.7

Source: Computed

(a) 20.2 per cent families do not consume any fruit in Sivaganga district.

(b) 11.7 per cent families do not get any milk in Sivaganga district.

(c) 22.5 per cent families do not consume any fruit in Cuddalore district.

(d) 15.7 per cent families do not get any milk in Cuddalore district.

Consumption of fruits is found to be occasional in the sample households. On an average, households in V_1 eat fruits for just three days in a month and V_2 villagers for only two days in a month. A good proportion of the surveyed households

Table 13
Average Monthly Food Consumption Frequency of Sample Households

Sivaganga District

		Pulses			*Fruits*			*Meat products*			*Milk*		
Category		*MIN*	*MAX*	*AV*	*MIN*	*MAX*	*AV*	*MIN*	*MAX*	*AV*	*MIN*	*MAX*	*AV*
V_1	MF	15	28	22.1	2	4	3.7	1	4	2.9	30	30	30
	NFW	10	30	18.2	0	4	1.9	2	10	4.7	0	30	21
	LAL	15	25	18.3	1	6	3.2	1	5	3.4	0	30	21
Overall		10	28	19.5	0	6	2.9	1	10	3.6	0	30	24
V_2	MF	20	30	22.8	2	5	3.6	2	4	2.5	0	30	21
	NFW	18	25	21.3	1	4	2.3	1	8	4.4	0	30	24
	LAL	15	20	18.4	0	4	1.8	2	4	2.5	0	30	15
Overall		15	30	20.8	0	5	2.5	1	8	3.1	0	30	20
Cuddalore District													
V_1	MF	15	30	23.1	1	8	2.8	1	10	4.2	0	30	21
	NFW	15	26	21.5	1	8	3.2	1	12	4.7	0	30	23
	LAL	15	25	20.2	0	4	2.9	2	6	3.5	0	30	24
Overall	15	30	21.6	0	8	2.9	1	12	4.1	0	30	22.6	
V_2	MF	12	30	20.0	1	8	2.4	2	6	3.4	0	30	18
	NFW	15	23	18.5	1	5	2.2	1	15	5.9	0	30	18
	LAL	10	25	17.3	0	5	1.8	1	6	3.1	0	30	18
Overall		10	30	18.6	0	5	2.1	1	15	4.1	0	30	18

Source: Computed
Note: AV – Average value

never consumes fruits at all. The percentage of households who do not consume fruits is worked out to be 20.2 per cent for Sivaganga district and 22.5 per cent for Cuddalore district. Surprisingly, LAL households in Sivaganga district recorded a maximum intake of fruits for six days in a month, the main reason being its availability in the home garden (see Table 12).

Likewise, the use of meat product is also occasional. For most of the households, food intake is much dependent on plant foods and the consumption pattern lack diversity. Meat products consumed mainly are poultry and fish. Fleshy foods, as they are quite expensive, are rarely taken. Some households consume eggs once a week in both the surveyed districts. On an average, meat products are taken for three days in a month by households in Sivaganga district and four days in Cuddalore district.

Milk consumption is also low for majority of the households. Though the frequency table shows all 30 days, the quantity they get is very low and they use it just as cream for making tea or coffee. Those who possess milch animals reserve a portion of the outflow for feeding children in the family. It is a universal truth that milk is the most balanced diet for health. But 11.7 per cent of families in Sivaganga district and 15.7 per cent of families in Cuddalore district do not take milk at all (see Table 12). Thus, households with adequate income are recorded to have encountered food inadequacy. The underlying cause is certainly the lack of knowledge about the nutritional value of foods.

Table 14 furnishes data on the minimum, maximum and average storage of food items like cereals (QSC), pulses (QSP) and oils (QSO). QSC is found to be the maximum for MF category in both the districts. The mean value of storage of cereals shows 404.0 kg and 317.0 kg for V_1 and V_2 of Sivaganga district and 440.0 kg and 292.0 kg for V_1 and V_2 of Cuddalore district. The mean value is higher for V_1 of Cuddalore district and the variability is at 36 per cent. Lower variability in the mean value is for V_1 of Sivaganga district at 21.8 per cent. The results reveal less inconsistency in the mean value among the MF households for that village Differing from the pattern

Table 14
Average Storage of Food Items of Sample Households

Sivaganga District

Category		QSC (in kg)			QSP (in kg)			QSO (in ltr)		
		MIN	MAX	MEAN	MIN	MAX	MEAN	MIN	MAX	MEAN
V_1	MF	260	500	404 (21.8)	0.5	2	0.98 (48.9)	0.2	1	0.720 (43)
	NFW	1	25	9.4 (97.8)	0	1	0.45 (81.7)	0	1	0.420 (88)
	LAL	1	8	4.8 (45.8)	0	0.5	0.31 (74.1)	0	0.5	0.270 (77)
V_2	MF	160	540	317 (39.5)	0.2	1	0.38 (78.9)	0.2	1	0.410 (61)
	NFW	5	20	13.1 (46.5)	0	1.5	0.90 (43.3)	0	1.5	0.770 (57)
	LAL	0	7	3.7 (64.8)	0	1	0.39 (82.1)	0	0.75	0.300 (70)

Contd...

Cuddalore District

Category		QSC (in kg)			QSP (in kg)			QSO (in ltr)		
		MIN	MAX	MEAN	MIN	MAX	MEAN	MIN	MAX	MEAN
V_1	MF	200	640	440 (36.9)	0.2	2	0.870 (64.3)	0.10	2	0.730 (71)
	NFW	3	15	8.4 (51.2)	0.5	2	0.950 (46.3)	0	1	0.720 (47)
	LAL	5	20	14.6 (35.4)	0	1	0.450 (95.5)	0	1	0.450 (68)
V_2	MF	120	520	292 (39.3)	0.2	2	0.920 (52.2)	0.25	1.5	0.515 (74)
	NFW	2	40	17.1 (80.3)	0.5	2	1.000 (45)	0	1.5	0.810 (50.6)
	LAL	0	15	4.4 (120.4)	0	1	0.350 (74)	0	1	0.295 (131)

Source: Computed

(Figures in Parentheses denote co-efficient of variation = $\frac{\text{Standard Deviation}}{\text{Mean}} \times 100$)

Note: QSC-Quantity Stored of Cereals, QSP-Quantity Stored of Pulses, QSO-Quantity Stored of Oils.

observed for MF category, the mean value of stored cereals is the lowest for LAL households and NFW households.

In the case of QSP, minimum storage is shown to be zero for NFW and LAL category in Sivaganga district and it is zero for LAL households in Cuddalore district. Mean values are also the lowest for LAL category in both the districts. This finding highlights the reality that daily wage earners with their low Income make their purchase of food items on a daily basis. Even some of the MF and NFW households do not store more than two kgs of pulses and oils. This is one of the reasons for the low consumption of pulses and oils by the majority of households in the study area.

Food Habits of the Households

The dietary lot of most Indians is meagre and monotonous. The households' food security status can also be measured by analysing the abrupt changes in food habits of households on the analysis of number of cooking sessions (CS), number of meals (NM), and food type (FT) during normal (period between post rainy and late summer) and lean seasons (late summer) through food habit matrix.

It is known from Table 15 that on an average 29 households in all the study villages have two cooking sessions and the proportion is found to be higher for MF category. Twenty-two households in Sivaganga district and 19 households in Cuddalore district have two cooking sessions in normal period and one session during the lean season. In lean and normal seasons cooking is done only once in the case of nine households in Sivaganga district and 12 households in Cuddalore district and the share of LAL households is higher in this regard. In most of these households, a portion of the food prepared on the previous day is kept and used as morning meal for the next day. With regard to meal pattern, 30 households in Sivaganga district and 29 in Cuddalore district have three square meals a day in both normal and lean seasons. Majority of these households belongs to MF category and a few to NFW category. Five households in Sivaganga district and eight in Cuddalore district eat just one square meal a day

Table 15
Shift in Food Habit Matrix of Sample Households

Category		*Lean*				*Sivaganga District*						*Cuddalore District*	
Normal		*CS*		*NM*		*FT*		*CS*		*NM*		*FT*	
V_1		*a=1*	*b=2*	*a=2*	*b=3*	*a=0*	*b=1*	*a=1*	*b=2*	*a=2*	*b=3*	*a=0*	*b=1*
MF (10)	a	-	-	-	-	-	-	-	-	1	-	1	-
	b	2	8	3	7	6	4	2	8	3	6	5	4
NFW (10)	a	2	-	1	-	-	-	-	-	2	-	-	-
	b	4	4	3	6	5	5	2	8	5	3	8	2
LAL (10)	a	2	-	4	-	4	-	4	-	3	-	4	-
	b	4	4	5	1	6	-	4	2	5	2	6	-
Overall (30)		14	16	16	14	21	9	12	18	19	11	24	6
V_2													
MF (10)	a	1	-	-	-	-	-	1	-	-	-	1	-
	b	3	6	6	4	4	6	1	8	2	8	6	3
NFW (10)	a	-	-	-	-	-	-	1	-	-	-	-	-
	b	5	5	3	7	7	3	6	3	3	7	6	4
LAL (10)	a	4	-	-	-	6	-	6	-	2	-	3	-
	b	4	2	5	5	4	-	4	-	5	3	6	1
Overall (30)		17	13	14	16	21	9	19	11	12	18	22	8
Grand Total (60)		31	29	30	30	42	18	31	29	31	29	46	14

Source: Computed.

Note: CS–Cooking Sessions per day (No.), NM–Number of Meals per day, FT–Food Type (a= Starchy food type : b= Protein content food type) .

(majority of them belong to LAL category) in both normal and lean seasons. The remaining households, 25 in Sivaganga district and 23 in Cuddalore district, most of them in LAL category, follow the pattern of three square meals during normal season and two square meals during the lean season.

Considering the food type, in Sivaganga district only 18 households, majority of them in MF category, eat protein rich food all year round while 10 LAL households take only starchy food round the year and 32 households eat protein content food during the normal time and starchy staple food during the lean season. Whereas in Cuddalore district 14 households, majority of them in MF category, take protein rich food all year round, while nine households (majority in LAL) take only starchy food throughout the year. Thirty-seven households take starchy staple food during the lean season and protein content food during the normal season. Ninety per cent of the households reported that during festival times their food consumption deviates considerably from the normal food habits.

Consumption of cereals too lack in variety. *Ragi* and wheat are consumed by very few households in Sivaganga district. No household is found to be using cereals other than rice in Cuddalore district. In Sivaganga district, the daily cuisine consists of a cereal (boiled rice) served with *Sambar* (a liquid gravy with pulses and vegetables) and a vegetable curry and the meal is whole at least once a day. In Cuddalore district rice is taken with *Sambar* alone for most of the days by households. Coarse cereals which were long back used by rural masses are not seen to be in use currently.

OPERATIONALIZING HOUSEHOLD FOOD SECURITY

While recognizing that food availability at the local level is not a sufficient condition for ensuring household food security, entitlement deficiency is often considered a critical impediment in this regard. The previous section on "Household Entitlements and Food System" analysed the ways in which rural households strove hard to ensure access to food, making it a continuous process through the best mix of procurement options (food entitlements). The notable variations in the exogenous variables in that section have made further statistical analysis necessary.

Household food security generally reflects three different dimensions: Past (Stability) food security, Current (Adequacy) food security and Future (Potentiality) food security.

To assess past food security, food usage pattern of households was obtained through a structured interview. The female members (mother) of the household were asked to recall frequency of 10 key foods acquired by the household during the previous one month from the interview date. The foods identified were cereals, pulses, roots and tubers, other vegetables, green leaves, fruits, meat (including fish and poultry products), sugar, oil and milk. Of these, frequency of pulse and frequency of meat were measured to record the dependent variable of past food security. To assess current food security, the respondents were asked to specify the quantity of food consumed with respect to cereals and pulses by the household for a 24 hour recall period. To predict future food security, the respondents were asked to catalogue the quantity of each food currently in storage limiting the list to storable food items such as rice, pulses and oil.

This stability, adequacy and potentiality of food security of households are expected to be determined by available resources in the sample household such as (i) Percentage Share of Income Generating and Liquid Assets against Total Assets (PSIGLA) (ii) Per Capita Annual Income of Households (PCI) (iii) Women's Access to Resources (ARES) (iv) Percentage Share of Home Production/Wage in Kind (HP/WIK). These are entitlements based on direct access to resources, which have particular focus on Sen's work on Entitlement and Deprivation.[11] Household Food Security is, thus, considered to be an outcome of various exchange entitlements. Other exogenous factors related to household food security and analysed here are: (v) Family Size (FS) and (vi) Earner Dependent Ratio (EDR). Further, the Multiple Linear Regression Model (MLRM) has been fitted Headship-wise to examine the hypothesised relation and to know the extent of contribution of selected predictor variables and the role of women in the three components of household food security. These variables are tested and verified for the absence of the problem of multi-collinearity. $\overline{R}^2$ tells the explanatory power of the fitted equations whose significance is tested with the F-value and, the estimated parameters are tested for their significance using the respective t-values.

Past Food Security: MLRM for Stability

A secured past food supply is reflected by the stable flow of food into the households and is associated with frequency of consumption of food items. Food frequency is taken as an indicator of stability of food supply. Since rice is a staple food used by all households all days, consideration of its frequency was deleted and so were the micro-nutrient content foods because of their low consumption. From the nutrition point of view, the monthly frequency of consumption of two important quality foods, pulses (Fpulse) and meat (Fmeat) were taken for analysis.

The MLRM predicting the important determinants of past food security in Sivaganga and Cuddalore districts are furnished in Table 16. In Sivaganga district it is seen that irrespective of the household headship, only two factors, PCI and FS, have made significant contribution to Fpulse. The regression co-efficient for PCI is positive and significant in FHH (0.758), JHH (0.419) and MHH (0.455) indicating that with increase in the PCI, there is greater increase in the frequency of pulse consumption. FS has a negative influence on the Fpulse indicating that with decrease in the size of the family, there would be an increase in the frequency of pulse consumption. The depressing impact of FS on Fpulse is relatively higher in FHH, showing that when family size increases by one person, the frequency of pulse consumption decreases by three. EDR has the expected negative relation but their co-efficient is insignificant. The adjusted $\overline{R}^2$ values show that the selected variables determine Fpulse significantly by 68 per cent for FHH, 75 per cent for JHH, and 65 per cent for MHH.

Table 16
Estimates of Past Food Security MLRM

Sivaganga District						
Household	*FHH (22)*		*JHH (25)*		*MHH (13)*	
Entitlements	*Fpulse (no.)*	*Fmeat (no.)*	*Fpulse (no.)*	*Fmeat (no.)*	*Fpulse (no.)*	*Fmeat (no.)*
PSIGLA (%)	-0.005^{NS}	-0.029^{NS}	0.057^{**}	0.026^{NS}	0.057^{NS}	-0.016^{NS}
	(0.101)	(0.813)	(1.793)	(1.057)	(0.618)	(0.176)
PCI (Rs.)	0.758^{***}	0.275^{**}	0.419^{***}	0.112^{*}	0.455^{**}	0.232^{NS}
	(3.515)	(1.941)	(3.865)	(1.338)	(2.802)	(1.372)
ARES (Score)	0.188^{NS}	0.310^{**}	0.217^{NS}	0.008^{NS}	1.10^{NS}	0.664^{NS}
	(0.796)	(1.992)	(1.232)	(0.393)	(1.136)	(0.657)
HP/WIK (%)	-0.010^{NS}	0.012^{NS}	0.002^{NS}	-0.005^{NS}	-0.013^{NS}	-0.012^{NS}
	(0.377)	(0.688)	(0.125)	(0.502)	(0.387)	(0.345)
EDR (Ratio)	-0.184^{NS}	-0.021^{NS}	-0.293^{NS}	-0.053^{NS}	-1.08^{NS}	-1.307^{NS}
	(0.155)	(0.027)	(0.304)	(0.007)	(0.204)	(0.237)
FS (No.)	-3.17^{***}	-1.18^{*}	-0.901^{**}	-0.044^{NS}	-2.53^{**}	1.121^{NS}
	(2.920)	(1.658)	(1.844)	(0.118)	(2.067)	(0.879)
$\overline{R}^2$	0.675^{***}	0.473^{***}	0.752^{***}	0.110^{NS}	0.643^{***}	0.152^{NS}
	(8.25)	(4.139)	(13.10)	(1.494)	(4.601)	(0.736)
Cuddalore District						
	FHH (13)		*JHH (21)*		*MHH (26)*	
PSIGLA (%)	-0.039^{NS}	-0.022^{NS}	0.074^{**}	0.002^{NS}	0.031^{*}	-0.013^{NS}
	(0.729)	(1.012)	(2.571)	(0.121)	(1.582)	(0.849)
PCI (Rs.)	0.897^{***}	0.532^{***}	0.915^{***}	0.480^{***}	1.007^{***}	0.441^{***}
	(3.993)	(5.809)	(7.274)	(4.468)	(6.462)	(3.495)
ARES (Score)	0.231^{NS}	0.032^{NS}	0.489^{**}	0.348^{*}	-0.310^{NS}	-0.139^{NS}
	(0.705)	(0.243)	(1.960)	(1.635)	(1.120)	(0.622)
HP/WIK (%)	0.034^{NS}	0.037^{**}	0.087^{***}	-0.029^{NS}	0.039^{**}	-0.011^{NS}
	(0.888)	(2.354)	(3.086)	(1.232)	(2.009)	(0.740)
EDR (Ratio)	0.327^{NS}	-0.540^{**}	-0.533^{***}	-0.131^{NS}	-1.318^{**}	-0.923^{**}
	(0.608)	(2.462)	(3.086)	(0.228)	(2.304)	(1.995)
FS (No.)	-1.14^{*}	-0.775^{**}	-1.76^{***}	-1.07^{**}	-2.22^{***}	-0.459^{**}
	(2.346)	(2.228)	(2.648)	(1.886)	(7.223)	(1.839)
$\overline{R}^2$	0.800^{***}	0.928^{***}	0.826^{***}	0.531^{***}	0.777^{***}	0.298^{**}
	(8.997)	(26.82)	(16.84)	(4.781)	(15.49)	(2.773)

Source: Computed (Figures in parentheses are t/F-values)

Note: For DF = 22-7=15 $t_{0.10}$ = 1.341 $t_{0.05}$ = 1.753 $t_{0.01}$ = 2.602, For DF = 25-7=18 $t_{0.10}$ = 1.330 $t_{0.05}$ = 1.734 $t_{0.01}$ = 2.552, For DF = 13-7=6 $t_{0.10}$ = 1.440 $t_{0.05}$ = 1.943 $t_{0.01}$ = 3.143 ,For DF = 21-7=14 $t_{0.10}$ = 1.345 $t_{0.05}$ = 1.761 $t_{0.01}$ = 2.624, For DF = 26-7=19 $t_{0.10}$ = 1.328 $t_{0.05}$ = 1.729 $t_{0.01}$ = 2.539

*** Significant at 1% level ** Significant at 5% level

* Significant at 10% level NS Not significant.

Fpulse–Frequency of Pulse Consumption. (No.)

Fmeat–Frequency of Meat Consumption.(No.)

With regard to Fmeat, it is interesting to note that no single intervening variable determines Fmeat significantly in JHH and MHH. But contrary to this, in FHH, Fmeat is significantly influenced positively by PCI and ARES, and influenced negatively by FS. The impact of ARES is relatively higher (0.310) and significant. The adjusted $\overline{R}^2$ value (0.473) is higher and significant in FHH whereas in JHH and MHH, these values are 11 per cent and 30 per cent respectively. Variations in Fmeat which could not be explained by the fitted MLRM may be due to the factors like consumption habit of the population in the study area, lack of functional knowledge of the nutritional requirements of the members and higher price of meat.

Contrary results are obtained for *Cuddalore district* with regard to the determinants of Fpulse and Fmeat. Surprisingly, all indicators show significant contribution for Fpulse in JHH and MHH. Of these, PSIGLA, PCI, ARES and HP/WIK have a positive influence on Fpulse and the co-efficient for PCI is significant. On the other hand FS and EDR have a significant negative influence on Fpulse, and FS has greater and significant impact in both JHH (-1.76) and MHH (-2.22). Contrary to these results, in the case of FHH, Fpulse is significantly determined by PCI and FS. The regression co-efficient for PCI is positive (0.897) and significant and for FS it is negative (-1.14) and significant. The selected variables explained 80 per cent, 83 per cent and 78 per cent variations in FHH, JHH and MHH respectively, which are indicated by $\overline{R}^2$ value.

With regard to Fmeat, the findings reveal that irrespective of the household headship, PCI and FS are the variables influencing it. Besides the above mentioned indicators, EDR is also found to influence Fmeat in FHH and MHH. Further, FS and EDR have negative influence on Fmeat. All these variables are highly contributing for Fmeat in FHH (92 per cent) and $\overline{R}^2$ account for 53 per cent in JHH and 29 per cent in MHH. It can be inferred from the fitted MLRM that PCI is the most important indicator, for this is significantly associated with the frequency of pulse and meat irrespective of the headship.

Current Food Security: MLRM for Adequacy

Present state of household food security refers to the adequacy of the households' present consumption of sufficient food to fulfil the immediate nutritional needs of the household members. Analysis of adequacy of food supply would include considerations of both quantity and quality of diet. So consumption of cereals and pulses per consumer unit is taken as an indication of current food security, these being the main food items used commonly by the rural households. The per unit cereal consumption (PUCC in gms.) and per unit pulse consumption (PUPC in gms.) is taken as indicators of the dependent variable "current food security".

Table 17 shows the functioning of the important determinants of current food security in both Sivaganga and Cuddalore districts in the fitted MLRM. The results show that in FHH in *Sivaganga district,* PUCC is influenced positively and significantly by ARES and HP/WIK. It means that per unit cereal consumption increases with increase in the access to resources. In JHH, the exchange entitlements ARES and PCI are more prominent and have significant positive relation with PUCC. In MHH, except PCI and EDR, all other factors are significantly contributing for PUCC. Among these, PSIGLA and HP/WIK are positively influencing, whereas the co-efficient for FS is found to be negative (-1.100). The co-efficient of determination $\overline{R}^2$ in FHH is 28 per cent which would mean that the selected variables explain for 28 per cent variation and the remaining 72 per cent variation should be attributed to other factors which are beyond the purview of this model. In JHH and MHH, these variables highly contribute for PUCC which are 66 per cent and 92 per cent respectively. This is an anticipated result as cereals constitute an important staple food in this region and are consumed daily in all households.

It is observed that PUPC is significantly influenced by PCI in all categories of households. The regression co-efficient for PCI is positive and relatively higher for FHH (1.352) when compared with that of JHH (0.532). The high $\overline{R}^2$ values confirm that all variables are statistically significant and highly

Table 17
Estimates of Current Food Security MLRM

Sivaganga District						
Household	*FHH (22)*		*JHH (25)*		*MHH (13)*	
Entitlements	*PUCC*	*PUPC*	*PUCC*	*PUPC*	*PUCC*	*PUPC*
PSIGLA (%)	0.049^{NS}	0.071^{NS}	- 0.0005^{NS}	0.008^{NS}	0.062***	0.020^{NS}
	(1.210)	(0.958)	(0.030)	(0.144)	(3.821)	(0.301)
PCI (Rs.)	0.141^{NS}	1.352***	0.184**	0.533***	0.019^{NS}	0.291**
	(0.874)	(4.651)	(3.114)	(2.756)	(0.649)	(2.380)
ARES (Score)	0.385**	- 0.176^{NS}	0.281***	0.651**	0.466**	0.880^{NS}
	(2.185)	(0.551)	(2.938)	(2.079)	(2.713)	(1.203)
HP/WIK (%)	0.471**	- 0.055*	- 0.007^{NS}	0.037^{NS}	0.019***	-0.031^{NS}
	(2.277)	(1.461)	(0.634)	(0.981)	(3.162)	(1.211)
EDR (Ratio)	- 0.396^{NS}	1.517^{NS}	- 0.868*	- 0.435^{NS}	0.766^{NS}	-5.808*
	(0.448)	(0.950)	(1.651)	(0.253)	(0.815)	(1.453)
FS (No.)	- 1.213*	0.269^{NS}	- 0.246^{NS}	- 0.506^{NS}	- 1.100***	1.302^{NS}
	(1.497)	(0.184)	(0.925)	(0.581)	(5.060)	(1.409)
$\overline{R}^2$	0.284*	0.834***	0.660***	0.557***	0.924***	0.835***
	(2.386)	(18.57)	(8.77)	(6.032)	(25.28)	(11.11)
Cuddalore District						
	FHH (13)		*JHH (21)*		*MHH (26)*	
PSIGLA (%)	0.035^{NS}	- 0.098^{NS}	0.023^{NS}	- 0.069*	0.010^{NS}	0.098**
	(1.014)	(1.378)	(0.869)	(1.172)	(0.675)	(2.173)
PCI (Rs.)	0.151^{NS}	1.151***	0.089^{NS}	0.917***	0.165*	0.593*
	(1.036)	(3.852)	(0.785)	(3.605)	(1.385)	(1.641)
ARES (Score)	0.170^{NS}	0.264^{NS}	0.455**	1.041**	- 0.175^{NS}	0.299^{NS}
	(0.799)	(0.607)	(2.010)	(2.065)	(0.825)	(0.465)
HP/WIK (%)	0.004^{NS}	0.049^{NS}	0.011^{NS}	0.038^{NS}	0.029**	- 0.058^{NS}
	(0.162)	(0.954)	(0.448)	(0.669)	(1.963)	(1.275)
EDR (Ratio)	- 0.308^{NS}	- 0.547^{NS}	0.569^{NS}	0.987^{NS}	- 0.770**	1.06^{NS}
	(0.882)	(0.766)	(0.931)	(0.726)	(1.759)	(0.802)
FS (No.)	- 0.420^{NS}	- 1.339*	1.637***	0.922^{NS}	- 0.110^{NS}	- 1.168*
	(1.181)	(1.181)	(2.709)	(0.686)	(0.468)	(1.634)
$\overline{R}^2$	0.600**	0.728***	0.508***	0.726***	0.403**	0.369**
	(4.005)	(6.360)	(4.44)	(9.81)	(3.810)	(3.436)

Source: Computed (Figures in Parentheses are t/F-values)

Note: For DF = 22-7=15 $t_{0.10}$ = 1.341 $t_{0.05}$ = 1.753 $t_{0.01}$ = 2.602
For DF = 25-7=18 $t_{0.10}$ = 1.330 $t_{0.05}$ = 1.734 $t_{0.01}$ = 2.552
For DF = 13-7=6 $t_{0.10}$ = 1.440 $t_{0.05}$ = 1.943 $t_{0.01}$ = 3.143
For DF = 21-7=14 $t_{0.10}$ = 1.345 $t_{0.05}$ = 1.761 $t_{0.01}$ = 2.624
For DF = 26-7=19 $t_{0.10}$ = 1.328 $t_{0.05}$ = 1.729 $t_{0.01}$ = 2.539
*** Significant at 1% level ** Significant at 5% level
* Significant at 10% level NS Not significant.
PUCC–Per Consumer Unit Cereals Consumption (gm);
PUPC-Per Consumer Unit Pulse Consumption (gm)

contributing for PUCC at 83 per cent, 55 per cent and 83 per cent respectively for FHH, JHH and MHH.

A contradictory observations is obtained from the analysis for *Cuddalore district*. The influence of all variables is insignificant for PUCC in the case of FHH. As reasoned earlier, this staple food is consumed daily and the consumption remains stable. But in JHH the regression co-efficient for ARES is found to be positive (0.455) and significant, whereas FS is found to be negatively and significantly correlated with PUCC. In MHH, HP/WIK and PCI are positively influencing the cereal consumption while EDR has depressing effect on PUCC. The adjusted co-efficient of multiple determination significantly contributing for PUCC are 60 per cent, 50 per cent and 40 per cent for FHH, JHH and MHH respectively.

PCI has a high significant positive correlation with PUPC in both FHH and MHH. In the case of MHH, the variable PSIGLA is shown to influence significantly the PUPC positively. The $\overline{R}^2$ values show that all indicators are highly contributing for PUPC at 72 per cent each in both FHH and JHH. In MHH, the adjusted $\overline{R}^2$ value (0.369) is low but significant. Evidently, means, the selected variables account for 36 per cent variation for PUPC and the remaining 64 per cent variation could be attributed to extraneous factors like truncated frequency of consumption of pulses, inadequate intake, women's illiteracy and low participation in decision-making in food related matters.

Future Food Security: MLRM for Potentiality

Future Food security refers to the reachability of households to essential food items for future use and it is measured by the storage potentiality of households for those essential and frequently used food items. This study obtained the storage position of households for two food items, Quantity of Stored Cereals (QSC in kg.) and Quantity of Stored Pulses (QSP in kg.), to measure their future food security achievement.

The results obtained from the analysis of the regression model for these two determinants of future food security are tabulated in Table 18. In *Sivaganga district,* it is found that HP/

Table 18
Estimates of Future Food Security MLRM

Sivaganga District						
Household	*FHH (22)*		*JHH (25)*		*MHH (13)*	
Entitlements	*QSC*	*QSP*	*QSC*	*QSP*	*QSC*	*QSP*
PSIGLA (%)	1.462^{NS}	0.005^{NS}	1.77**	0.010*	2.49*	0.018^{NS}
	(0.881)	(0.493)	(1.944)	(1.528)	(1.637)	(0.997)
PCI (Rs.)	8.309*	0.152^{NS}	12.81***	0.119***	2.48^{NS}	0.115***
	(1.382)	(3.492)	(4.159)	(5.237)	(0.929)	(3.487)
ARES (Score)	5.79^{NS}	0.050^{NS}	3.97^{NS}	0.013^{NS}	13.29^{NS}	0.016^{NS}
	(0.814)	(1.045)	(0.796)	(0.378)	(0.830)	(0.083)
HP/WIK (%)	3.526***	- 0.0001^{NS}	2.826***	0.0003^{NS}	3.69***	- 0.004^{NS}
	(4.198)	(0.21)	(4.645)	(0.080)	(6.588)	(0.691)
EDR (Ratio)	- 7.242^{NS}	- 0.033^{NS}	0.518^{NS}	- 0.126^{NS}	3.950^{NS}	- 0.128^{NS}
	(0.203)	(0.139)	(0.019)	(0.624)	(0.045)	(0.119)
FS (No.)	4.23*	0.592***	20.31*	0.340***	- 4.84^{NS}	0.116^{NS}
	(1.362)	(2.692)	(1.464)	(3.322)	(0.240)	(0.468)
$\overline{R}^2$	0.863***	0.772***	0.912***	0.785***	0.945***	0.761***
	(23.13)	(12.83)	(42.71)	(15.56)	(35.61)	(7.36)
Cuddalore District						
	FHH (13)		*JHH (21)*		*MHH (26)*	
PSIGLA (%)	0.005^{NS}	0.005^{NS}	2.13**	0.014*	1.181*	0.001^{NS}
	(0.003)	(0.740)	(2.448)	(1.728)	(1.426)	(0.342)
PCI (Rs.)	7.11^{NS}	0.137***	9.08**	0.206***	8.239^{NS}	0.191***
	(0.820)	(4.294)	(2.408)	(5.670)	(1.251)	(4.275)
ARES (Score)	15.10^{NS}	0.072*	1.37^{NS}	0.159**	0.786^{NS}	0.029^{NS}
	(1.194)	(1.559)	(0.184)	(2.214)	(0.067)	(0.378)
HP/WIK (%)	6.88***	- 0.011**	2.012**	0.017**	3.84***	- 0.005^{NS}
	(4.608)	(2.109)	(2.365)	(2.157)	(4.628)	(1.001)
EDR (Ratio)	16.8^{NS}	- 0.085^{NS}	3.53*	- 0.021^{NS}	- 6.08^{NS}	- 0.082^{NS}
	(0.811)	(1.126)	(1.514)	(0.110)	(0.251)	(0.500)
FS (No.)	12.42***	0.560***	12.03^{NS}	0.352**	62.45***	0.377***
	(3.771)	(4.623)	(0.604)	(1.833)	(4.792)	(4.265)
$\overline{R}^2$	0.851***	0.932***	0.884***	0.712***	0.823***	0.524***
	(12.49)	(28.61)	(26.41)	(9.242)	(20.40)	(5.58)

Source: Computed (Figures in Parentheses are t/F-values)

Note: For DF = 22-7=15 $t_{0.10}$ = 1.341 $t_{0.05}$ = 1.753 $t_{0.01}$ = 2.602
For DF = 25-7=18 $t_{0.10}$ = 1.330 $t_{0.05}$ = 1.734 $t_{0.01}$ = 2.552
For DF = 13-7=6 $t_{0.10}$ = 1.440 $t_{0.05}$ = 1.943 $t_{0.01}$ = 3.143
For DF = 21-7=14 $t_{0.10}$ = 1.345 $t_{0.05}$ = 1.761 $t_{0.01}$ = 2.624
For DF = 26-7=19 $t_{0.10}$ = 1.328 $t_{0.05}$ = 1.729 $t_{0.01}$ = 2.539
* Significant at 1% level , ** Significant at 5% level
* Significant at 10% level NS Not significant.
QSC–Quantity Stored of Cereals (kg) ; QSP–Quantity Stored of Pulses (kg)

WIK is significantly influencing positively QSC in all types of households (3.526 in FHH, 2.826 in JHH and 3.690 in MHH respectively) which means that the quantity of store cereals increases with the increase in the level of home production/ wage in kind. In FHH, PCI and FS are also seen to be influencing positively and significantly the households' cereal stores. In JHH, along with HP/WIK, PCI, FS and PSIGLA are also found to be influencing QSC. The adjusted $\overline{R}^2$ value shows that the selected indicators are most appropriate in determining QSC which is 86 per cent for FHH, 91 per cent for JHH and 94 per cent for MHH.

With regard to QSP, it is observed that the only variable significantly influencing QSP is FS. In JHH, QSP is significantly influenced by PCI and FS. FS has a relatively high impact on QSP, for the regression co-efficient is higher for FS (0.344) than PCI (0.119). In MHH, PCI alone is significantly influencing QSP. All the variables are seen to contribute highly for QSP at 77 per cent, 78 per cent and 76 per cent respectively for FHH, JHH and MHH households. The respective F-statistics values are significant at one per cent level.

In *Cuddalore district,* with reference to FHH households, HP/WIK and FS are significantly influencing QSC. In JHH, PSIGLA, PCI and HP/WIK have positive and significant association with QSC. In MHH, HP/WIK and FS have high positive and significant relation with QSC. The adjusted co-efficient () for QSC is 85 per cent, 88 per cent and 82 per cent for FHH, JHH and MHH households respectively.

For pulse storage (QSP), PCI and FS are the prominent variables positively and significantly influencing the storage of pulses. The adjusted $\overline{R}^2$ values show that these variables are highly contributing for QSP with 93 per cent for FHH, 71 per cent for JHH and 52 per cent for MHH. The cumulative findings show that QSC is positively and significantly influenced by HP/WIK and QSP is positively and significantly influenced by PCI in the sample households of both the districts.

ENTITLEMENTS AND DIMENSIONS OF FOOD SECURITY

(Testing of the First Hypothesis)

With the objective to operationalize food security of rural households and evaluate food insecurity risks and insurances, a hypothesis *"Exchange entitlements and Household food security move together"* is so framed. Testing of this hypothesis will disclose the relationship among the selected variables and help to identify the extent of influence of important exogenous features on the households surveyed.

Framework of Analysis

The earlier sections of this chapter tabulated and analysed the application of the multiple linear regression models on the respondent households to estimate the overall influence of the various indicators on the FHH, JHH and MHH households in both the districts. The cumulative findings given in Table 19 show that the exchange entitlements such as PSIGLA, PCI, ARES, HP/WIK, EDR and FS have influence and are highly contributing for Fpulse (71.7 per cent) QSC (90.2 per cent) and QSP (80.9 per cent), PUPC (60.6 per cent) and PUCC (52.6 per cent) in Sivaganga district, whereas in Cuddalore district these entitlements are contributing for Fpulse (73.7 per cent), QSC (80.7 per cent) QSP (70.9 per cent) PUCC (52.2 per cent) and Fmeat (57.7 per cent). Thus, comparing the two districts the variables are highly contributing for QSC and QSP and Fpulse and the observed F-values shows that the intervening variables included in the model are contributing significantly for the Past, Current and Future food security of the sample households.

It is observed that the estimated co-efficient of women's access to resources (ARES) is positive but not significant, possibly because of insufficient income and less control over income earned. It is observed that the regression co-efficient has expected sign for FS having negative effect with frequency of consumption (Fpulse and Fmeat) and PUCC and PUPC, but with positive effect for QSC and QSP. Households with higher dependency ratio are seen to be more vulnerable to food insecurity underscoring the importance of the size of the family

Table 19
Estimates of Multiple Linear Regression Model for Determinants of Past, Current and Future Food Security

Sivaganga District						
Household Entitlements	*Fpulse (no.)*	*Fmeat (no.)*	*PUCC (gm)*	*PUPC (gm)*	*QSC (kg)*	*QSP (kg)*
PSIGLA (%)	0.053***	0.002^{NS}	0.021*	0.059*	2.11***	0.012***
	(2.510)	(0.162)	(1.606)	(1.544)	(3.658)	(3.089)
PCI (Rs.)	0.511***	0.186***	0.060*	0.708***	7.75***	0.129***
	(6.806)	(3.149)	(1.308)	(5.241)	(3.832)	(8.913)
ARES (Score)	0.140^{NS}	0.136*	0.264***	0.097^{NS}	3.053^{NS}	0.003^{NS}
	(1.206)	(1.482)	(3.670)	(0.467)	(0.975)	(0.135)
HP/WIK (%)	- 0.010^{NS}	-0.001^{NS}	0.021***	- 0.016^{NS}	3.314***	- 0.001^{NS}
	(0.735)	(0.124)	(2.472)	(0.675)	(8.886)	(0.651)
EDR (Ratio)	- 0.066^{NS}	-0.361^{NS}	- 0.731**	0.185^{NS}	2.99^{NS}	- 0.153^{NS}
	(0.097)	(0.672)	(1.734)	(0.151)	(0.163)	(1.159)
FS (No.)	- 1.73***	- 0.451*	- 0.547**	- 0.364^{NS}	15.8*	0.341***
	(4.585)	(1.513)	(2.342)	(0.536)	(1.558)	(4.674)
$\overline{R}^2$	0.717***	0.264***	0.526***	0.606***	0.902***	0.809***
	(25.23)	(4.53)	(11.89)	(16.13)	(91.71)	(42.73)
Cuddalore District						
PSIGLA (%)	0.004^{NS}	- 0.007^{NS}	0.023**	0.044*	1.39***	0.005*
	(0.308)	(0.737)	(2.033)	(1.557)	(2.480)	(1.392)
PCI (Rs.)	0.764***	0.455***	0.165***	0.793***	3.206^{NS}	0.167***
	(9.523)	(8.224)	(2.734)	(5.281)	(1.079)	(8.787)
ARES (Score)	0.030^{NS}	- 0.117^{NS}	0.125^{NS}	0.108^{NS}	3.72^{NS}	0.013^{NS}
	(0.223)	(1.256)	(1.232)	(0.426)	(0.744)	(0.432)
HP/WIK (%)	0.004^{NS}	- 0.026***	0.002^{NS}	- 0.033*	4.035***	- 0.007**
	(0.379)	(2.912)	(0.296)	(1.347)	(8.262)	(2.369)
EDR (Ratio)	- 0.599**	- 0.124^{NS}	- 0.289*	- 0.489^{NS}	- 2.23^{NS}	0.040^{NS}
	(2.067)	(0.622)	(1.331)	(0.901)	(0.208)	(0.592)
FS (No.)	- 2.08***	- 0.789***	- 0.002^{NS}	- 1.09**	40.26***	0.416***
	(7.881)	(4.329)	(0.014)	(2.202)	(4.111)	(6.637)
$\overline{R}^2$	0.737***	0.577***	0.396***	0.522***	0.807***	0.709***
	(28.58)	(14.46)	(7.40)	(11.75)	(42.13)	(24.90)

Source: Computed.

Figures in Parentheses are t/F-values

Note: For DF = 53 $t_{0.10}$ = 1.299 $t_{0.05}$ = 1.678 $t_{0.01}$ = 2.406

*** Significant at 1% level ** Significant at 5% level

* Significant at 10% level NS Not significant.

for the purpose of food security targeting. These results confirm the findings of other studies (Swift, 1989[12], and Schiff and Valdes 1990[13]). It has thus been empirically proved that household income (PCI) has the highest explanatory power among various other exchange entitlements, to achieve household food security. The hypothesis interlinking exchange entitlements and household food security, consequently, is acceptable.

Key findings

- Income generating and liquid assets, and wage income are found to be the important means by which rural households acquired food for consumption.
- Very few MF households (<15 per cent) indulge in crop diversification to reduce the risk against food entitlement failure. The observed reasons are shortage of water and productive resources.
- Home production is the main source of food for majority of MF households; NFW households depend on the open market; LAL households purchase more from (PDS) as well as from open market. Majority of rural households is not satisfied with the working of Public Distribution System (PDS).
- Respondents gather secondary food from the fields and forests whose nutritive value is higher, with no or less time spent for procurement.
- Scarce productive assets are identified by most of the LAL respondents as one of the important reasons for food insecurity.
- Food expenditure is positively related to income. Expenditure on cereals occupied the highest priority and the lowest expenditure is made on fruits.
- Frequency of pulse consumption is greater than consumption of meat and fruits.
- Home production has exercised a favourable influence on storage of staple food.

- Proportion of households consuming starchy food type round the year is found to be higher in LAL and lesser in MF and NFW categories.
- Sharp variations are observed in the number of cooking sessions, number of meals and food type among the household categories.
- Operationalization of household food security for various exchange entitlements shows that PCI influences household food security positively and family size affects the frequency of food consumption.
- Women's access to resources has positive effect but is not strongly significant on food security.

NOTES AND REFERENCES

1. Swaminathan, M. (1997), "Dangers of Narrow Targeting", *Frontline*, October 31: 12-16.
2. Dev, S. Mahendra and M.H. Suryanarayana (1991), "Is PDS Urban Biased and Pro-Rich: An Evaluation", *Economic and Political Weekly*, Vol. 26, No. 4: 2357-66.
3. Parikh, K.S. (1993), "Who Get How Much from PDS. How Effectively Does it Reach the Poor?", *Sarvekshana*, Vol. 17, No. 3, January-March, 114- 117.
4. Food and Agriculture Organisation (1989), *Household Food Security and Forestry. An Analysis of Socio-economic Issues*. Forestry Paper No. 4413. Food and Agriculture Organisation of the United Nations, Rome.
5. Falconer, J. (1989), *Forestry and Nutrition: A Reference Manuel*, FAO, U.N.
6. Sen, A.K. (1981), *Hunger and Poverty, Essays on Entitlement and Deprivation*. The Clarendon Press, Oxford.
7. Haddad, Lawrence, Eileen Kennedy and Joan Sullivan (1994), "Choice of Indicators for Food security and Nutrition Monitoring", *Food Policy*, Vol. 19, No. 3: 329-43.
8. Sukhatme (1987), "Economics of Nutrition", *Indian Journal of Agricultural Economics*, Vol. 32, No. 3: 1-11.
9. For collecting household expenditure data the reference period is the last 30 days preceding the day of enquiry, the list of food

and non- food items largely conform to those used by NSSO and NNMB. For details see,

(i) National Sample Survey Organisation (NSSO), "Results of the Fourth Quinquennial Survey on Consumer Expenditure. 43rd Round July 1987 - June 1988." *Sarvekshana Journal of the NSSO*. Vol. 15. No.48, New Delhi.

(ii) National Nutrition Monitoring Bureau (NNMB) (1991), *Report of Repeated Survey*. NIN, Hyderabad.

10. Lalitha, K. and D. Sharada (1988), "Socio-economic and Living Conditions of Farm Labourers", *Journal of Rural Development*, Vol. 7, 343-349.

11. Sen, Amartya (1986), "The Causes of Famine, A Reply", *World Development*, Vol. 20, No.9, 1305-1312.

12. Swift, J.J. (1989), "Why Are Rural People Vulnerable to Famine?", *IDS Bulletin*, Vol. 20, No. 2, 8-15.

13. Schiff, M. and A. Valdes (1990), "Nutrition: Alternative Definitions and Policy Implications", *Economic Development and Cultural Change*, Vol. 38, 281-92.

6

Women's Role in the Food Chain

In the previous chapter, food security was conceptualized in terms of a set of variables linking household vulnerability to entitlement failures. In this chapter, an attempt is made to trailblaze the defensive role played by women within a household to overcome food insecurity.

In the rural areas, poor households often face scarcity of both time and material resources. Women's daily chores in rural areas often are centred around food chain and food security activities. A broad understanding of women's role in food and nutrition activities will help to realise the potential of women for improving food security and nutritional security of rural households.[1]

This chapter makes a three-level analysis of the role of women in food chain activities. The first is an analysis of various dimensions of women in terms of their task and time allocation, access to and control over resources, and decision-making in providing food to the family. The second section would test the hypothesis framed in the beginning of this study with reference to women empowerment and its ensuring adequate food consumption at the household level. The third section would evaluate the respondent households' nutrient intake by the two considerations of headship and women's food strategy. This three-phased framework is intended to highlight the elements acceptable to policy suggestions to improve household food security and the role of women.

MULTI DIMENSIONAL ROLE OF WOMEN IN FOOD SECURITY

Three problem areas emerged from the reviewed literature, and these are related to women's heavy workload, their low productivity and effectivity in the food chain. A framework incorporating all the problem-areas was evolved. The ensuing discussion, based on the evolved framework, includes observations on women's allocation of time, access to resources and decision-making with the limelight on their actual responsibilities in providing food to the family.

Task and Time Allocation

Women's food related activities should be understood in terms of women's total workload and the percentage share of their work. An elaborate time observation sheet was prepared to record the time utilization pattern of the respondents stating 'Time began' and 'Time ended' for various activities that rural women are likely to perform each day. Time spent in festivities and social activities was not considered. The observations are been tabulated in Tables 1 to 6.

Assessment of time allocation pattern of women in *MF households* of both the study districts, recorded in Table 1, shows their major role in rice production. Except ploughing, all other related work like mending the land, sowing, transplanting, weeding, harvesting and winnowing are all done by women. During the agricultural season, women in MF households are seen to spend more time on Farm Related Activities (FRA). The mean time spent on this task by the women of V_2 of Sivaganga district is shown to be 320 mins./ day followed by V_1 at 290 mins./day. In Cuddalore district, the mean time spent is 260 mins./day for V_1 and 250 mins./ day for V_2. It is seen that women in Sivaganga district spend more time on FRA.

Women belonging to MF households in the study villages are generally seen to spend considerable time in Dairy Work

Table 1
Time Allocation Pattern of Women in MF Households (Minutes Per Day)

	Sivaganga District						Cuddalore District					
	V_1			V_2			V_1			V_2		
Activities	*Min*	*Max*	*Mean*	*Min*	*Max*	*Mean*	*Min*	*Max*	*Mean*	*Min*	*Max*	*Mean*
FRA	180	360	290	180	360	320	120	360	260	60	300	260
NFA	0	120	40	0	0	0	0	0	0	0	0	0
DW	60	180	160	60	240	180	0	240	190	0	240	120
CC	0	180	130	0	180	60	0	240	130	0	540	140
CF	0	60	45	0	60	40	0	30	10	0	30	15
PF	0	0	0	0	60	45	0	30	10	0	30	15
FPP	60	60	60	60	60	60	30	60	55	30	60	75
CK	120	180	140	120	180	130	120	180	130	60	180	120
FLC	30	120	65	30	90	60	30	60	55	30	60	45
WC	30	90	70	30	110	65	30	90	50	30	60	45
FOR A	240	360	310	300	360	340	240	360	275	180	300	255
OA	60	120	80	60	120	85	60	60	60	60	60	60
TWT	840	960	930	600	960	850	720	960	860	420	960	760

Source: Computed.

FRA–Farm Related Activities, NFA–Non Farm Activities, DW - Dairy Work, CC–Child Care, CF - Collection of Food, PF - Purchase of Food, FPP–Food Processing and Preservation, CK- Cooking, FLC–Fuel Collection, WC–Water Collection, FORA–Food Related Activities, OA–Other Activities, TWT–Total Working Time.

(DW), barring some households in Cuddalore district which did not own any large livestock. Women in V_1 of Sivaganga district spend less time (160 mins./day) than V_1 of Cuddalore district (190 mins./day) on Dairy work. These women are also seen to spend a sizable amount of time on Food Related Activities (FORA), with women in V_1 and V_2 of Sivaganga district spending 310 mins./day and 340 mins./day respectively. But in Cuddalore district the mean time spent on this task is only 275 mins./day and 255 mins./day for V_1 and V_2 respectively.

Among the various Food Related Activities (FORA), they are observed to allocate for cooking (CK) more time, followed by "food supporting" activities such as Fuel Collection (FLC) and Water Collection (WC). Women in Sivaganga district are recorded to spend more time on Water Collection (WC). Accessibility and family size are seen to be the factors which govern time allocation for this task. Women in Cuddalore district had the advantage of the proximity of the public tap. Another added incentive to them is availability. Cuddalore district being a rain-fed district, water is abundant here, but scarce in Sivaganga district. In addition, the women of Sivaganga district also reported that the number of trips they had to go increased with the size of the family.

When the Total Working Time (TWT) of women of respondent of MF households is compared, it is astonishing to find that in V_2 of Cuddalore district the minimum total time worked (TWT) is only 420 mins./day (7 hours). It is interestingly discovered that in all the four study-villages the maximum TWT recorded is the same at 960 mins./day (16 hours). After a complete analysis of the data for time allocation pattern for women of MF households, it is generalised that women in Sivaganga district allocate more time for various household activities.

Analysis of percentage share of their work in various activities is given in Table 2. In V_1 of Sivaganga district the Percentage Share of Women's Farm Related Activities (PSFRA) varies between 30 per cent and 70 per cent and in V_2 the variation is between 30 per cent and 50 per cent. But in

Table 2
Per Cent Share of Women's Work in MF Households

	Sivaganga District						Cuddalore District					
	V_1			V_2			V_1			V_2		
Activities	*Min*	*Max*	*Mean*	*Min*	*Max*	*Mean*	*Min*	*Max*	*Mean*	*Min*	*Max*	*Mean*
PSFRA	30	70	43.6	30	50	46.0	12	80	40.1	12	80	41.1
PSNFA	0	60	14.0	0	0	0	0	0	0	0	0	0
PSDW	35	100	61.3	0	100	54.5	0	100	71.5	0	80	36.0
PSCC	0	100	38.5	0	100	22.5	0	100	65.5	0	90	43.0
PSCF	0	100	55.5	0	100	51.0	0	100	15.0	0	100	10.0
PSPF	0	0	0	0	90	29.5	0	40	8.0	0	50	12.0
PSFPP	90	100	99.0	60	100	93.0	70	100	94.5	100	100	100
PSCK	60	100	87.0	50	100	90.0	75	100	94.5	75	100	97.5
PSFLC	80	100	93.0	70	100	86.0	80	100	97.0	60	100	89.0
PSWC	60	100	89.0	20	100	67.0	30	100	93.0	50	100	86.0
PSFORA	85	100	92.8	80	100	92.3	90	100	97.5	80	100	92.5
PSOA	85	100	92.0	80	100	97.0	80	100	98.0	70	100	91.0

Source: Computed

Cuddalore district the range of variation is large between 12 per cent and 80 per cent in both the study-villages. Cumulatively, it may be inferred that women participated in FRA doing variety of tasks, but at a lesser degree than men.

Data for the Percentage Share of Dairy Work (PSDW) shows that women's share is less in three villages excepting V_2 of Cuddalore district. During the interview schedule with respondents it was gathered that in Sivaganga district men had a lesser degree of commitment in tending milch animals than women. Women's task included feeding the animals by preparing fodder at home, grazing them in the community field and milking. Women from both the districts felt that the extra-time they spent on the care of livestock gave them an upper hand in the households in decisions related to livestock.

Percentage Share of Child Care Activity (PSCC) is observed to be low for all the study villages. This might be perhaps because grown up children took care of themselves and the younger ones were taken care of by the older children or aged parents in the family.

With regard to Percentage Share of Food Related Activities (PSFORA), it is witnessed that more than 90 per cent of the work is done by women only. The various food supporting activities like Water Collection, Fuel Collection and Cooking are observed to be performed by women in all the study villages.

A household task which contributes to food security directly is Food Processing and Preservation (FPP). Women, in addition to performing time consuming tasks of grinding and pounding the staple grain, processed and preserved food for future use. In this task, MF category, women in V_1 of Cuddalore district are at an advantage. They had short access to roller flour and grinding mills in the near by town. Women in other study villages had to depend on their own labour performing these tasks in their homes. However, this gave them an added benefit, because home-processed food always had higher nutritive value.

Table 3 presents figures on time allocation of women in *NFW households*. Women in only a very few households in the

Table 3
Time Allocation Pattern of Women in NFW Households (Minutes per day)

	Sivaganga District						*Cuddalore District*					
	V_1			V_2			V_1			V_2		
Activities	*Min*	*Max*	*Mean*	*Min*	*Max*	*Mean*	*Min*	*Max*	*Mean*	*Min*	*Max*	*Mean*
FRA	0	240	50	0	0	0	0	240	70	0	300	130
NFA	0	420	240	180	420	300	60	360	130	0	420	90
DW	0	0	0	0	240	50	0	120	40	0	300	110
CC	0	180	100	60	180	130	60	360	180	60	300	180
CF	0	60	15	0	0	0	0	30	10	0	30	10
PF	30	60	40	30	60	30	0	30	15	0	60	25
FPP	30	60	45	30	60	40	30	60	40	60	60	60
CK	120	180	130	120	180	160	120	180	160	120	180	160
FLC	0	60	35	30	30	30	0	60	20	0	60	15
WC	30	80	55	30	85	50	30	60	35	30	60	35
FORA	300	420	340	240	360	310	240	360	300	180	360	290
OA	60	180	90	60	60	60	60	120	55	60	120	60
TWT	660	960	790	720	960	810	480	960	750	480	960	810

Source: Computed.

study area are seen to be engaged in Farm Related Activities (FRA). In the task of Non-Farm Activities (NFA), though a maximum of 420 mins./day is recorded for the three study villages, their mean values show great disparities at 300 mins./ day for V_{2} of Sivaganga district and a meagre 90 mins./day for V_2 of Cuddalore district. For Childcare Activities (CC) women of these households are seen to dedicate two to three hours per day.

Women belonging to this category spend maximum time for Food Related Activities (FORA). An interesting observation is that these women in the two study districts work for almost equal number of hours. The mean of their Total Working Time (TWT) is 790 mins./day. and 810 mins./day respectively for V_1 and V_2 of Sivaganga district, and 750 mins./day and 810 mins./day for V_1 and V_2 of Cuddalore district respectively. Thus, they are observed to work for 13 to 14 hours a day.

With regard to the percentage share of women's work (Table 4), it is the highest for Food Related Activities (PSFORA) at above 97 per cent for all the study villages. Unlike the women of MF households, the Percentage Share of Time spent for Purchase of Food (PSPF) is more for female of NFW households. The percentage range is between zero and 29.5 per cent for MF category, whereas the range is between 32 per cent and 72 per cent for the women of NFW category. Majority of women in V_2 of Sivaganga district complained of being away from the marketing centre and had to spend more time on this task as they had to purchase these stuffs on day to day basis because of resource constraints.

Table 5 furnishes data on the time allocation pattern of women in *LAL households*. These women are found to slot more time for Farm Related Activities (FRA) and the work-pressure, they told, was especially high in peak agricultural season. In V_1 and V_2 of Sivaganga district, on an average, women of LAL households spend 330 mins./day on this task whereas for V_1 and V_2 of Cuddalore district it is recorded at 310 mins./day and 320 mins./day respectively. Some women from Sivaganga district said that their low wages compelled them to work overtime in a nearby fields to supplement their income. Next

Table 4
Per Cent Share of Women's Work in NFW Households

	Sivaganga District						*Cuddalore District*					
	V_1			V_2			V_1			V_2		
Activities	*Min*	*Max*	*Mean*	*Min*	*Max*	*Mean*	*Min*	*Max*	*Mean*	*Min*	*Max*	*Mean*
PSFRA	0	100	35	0	0	0	0	100	30	0	100	60
PSNFA	0	90	38	40	80	51	20	50	15.5	0	100	20.0
PSDW	0	0	0	0	100	20.0	0	80.0	23.0	0	90	45.0
PSCC	0	100	87.0	20	100	62.0	20	90	65.0	20	100	81.0
PSCF	0	100	35.0	0	0	0	0	100	20.0	0	100	20.0
PSPF	40	100	72.0	40	100	62.0	0	60.0	33.0	0	100	59.0
PSFPP	100	100	72.0	40	100	62.0	0	60	33.0	0	100	59.0
PSCK	90	100	99.0	80	100	94.0	100	100	100	100	100	100
PSFLC	0	100	71.0	40	90	66.0	0	100	58.0	0	100	49.0
PSWC	80	100	96.0	60	100	88.00	100	100	100	100	100	100
PSFORA	95	100	99.5	90	100	98.5	90	100	97	90	100	98.5
PSOA	90	100	96.0	80	100	90.0	0	80.0	48.0	20	100	77.0

Source: Computed.

Table 5
Time Allocation Pattern of Women in Lal Households (Minutes Per Day)

	Sivaganga District						*Cuddalore District*					
	V_1			V_2			V_1			V_2		
Activities	*Min*	*Max*	*Mean*	*Min*	*Max*	*Mean*	*Min*	*Max*	*Mean*	*Min*	*Max*	*Mean*
FRA	300	390	330	180	360	330	180	360	310	120	360	320
NFA	0	120	70	0	120	70	0	180	25	0	120	70
DW	0	180	70	0	180	40	0	180	40	0	0	0
CC	0	120	80	0	360	120	0	300	190	0	360	120
CF	0	60	20	0	60	20	0	30	15	30	60	35
PF	0	60	20	0	60	40	0	30	15	0	30	20
FPP	30	60	40	0	40	25	30	30	30	0	30	15
CK	120	120	120	120	180	150	120	180	150	60	180	150
FLC	30	60	50	30	60	50	30	60	45	60	60	60
WC	30	60	45	60	90	65	30	60	40	30	60	40
FORA	240	360	300	300	360	310	240	360	300	240	300	280
OA	60	60	60	60	60	60	60	60	60	60	60	60
TWT	660	960	890	720	960	880	720	990	900	480	960	840

Source: Computed

to Farm Related Activities (FRA), these women are seen to spend more time on Food Related Activities (FORA). Majority of these women did not possess any large livestock, but some women who owned small livestock such as goat and poultry, spend time in maintaining them.

For Childcare Activity (CC), in V_2 of both the districts, a maximum of 360 mins./ day is spend. These women complaint that this caused monetary loss for them as they could not spend much time remunerative activities. Overall, like the women of NFW households, LAL women in Sivaganga district and Cuddalore district are also recorded to spend equal duration of time, as the Total Working Time (TWT) is configured at 890 mins., 880 mins., 900 mins., and 840 mins./day for V_1 and V_2 of Sivaganga and Cuddalore districts respectively.

Percentage share of women's work in LAL households (Table 6) shows that LAL women in only a very few households are engaged in Farm Related Activities (waged labour) at a higher time-level than men. This can be comprehended from the data for maximum percentage share of their work for almost all split-categories in all the four villages. In some households, it is found out that women had to work all day from dawn to dusk to provide food for the family. The Percentage Share of Work for Food Related Activities (PSFORA) is witnessed to be the highest ranging between 94 per cent and 98 per cent for the four sample villages.

Overall, the women belonging to all categories of rural households are seen to be overburdened with work but seasonal variations are noticed. The total time women allocate to work on a yearly basis is around 10-11 hours per day in Sivaganga district and 8-10 hours per day in Cuddalore district. In peak season, they work for as long as 14-16 hours per day in Sivganga district and 10-12 hours per day in Cuddalore district. This 'heaviness' of women's workload has also been reported in other Time Budget Studies.[2-4]

During interview schedules, it was observed that some women belonging to NFW and LAL households in Sivaganga district were found to spend leisure time in-between other household chores in profitable hobbies like weaving palm

Table 6
Per cent Share of Women's Work in Lal Households

	Sivaganga District						*Cuddalore District*					
	V_1			V_2			V_1			V_2		
Activities	*Min*	*Max*	*Mean*	*Min*	*Max*	*Mean*	*Min*	*Max*	*Mean*	*Min*	*Max*	*Mean*
PSFRA	45	70	50.5	30	60	50	30	50	45	25	100	55
PSNFA	38	100	55.8	0	80	40	0	100	15	0	100	44.5
PSDW	0	75	31	0	80	19.5	0	90	16.5	0	0	0
PSCC	0	100	74	0	100	55	0	90	71	0	100	77
PSCF	0	100	64	0	100	69	0	100	54	80	100	94
PSPF	0	100	34	0	100	52	0	80	27	0	100	83
PSFPP	90	100	99	100	100	100	100	100	100	100	100	100
PSCK	80	100	94.5	90	100	98	100	100	100	90	100	98
PSFLC	60	100	83	80	100	94	70	100	91	100	100	100
PSWC	80	100	93	90	100	98	100	100	100	80	100	98
PSFORA	90	100	94.8	90	100	96.5	90	100	94	95	100	98
PSOA	50	100	77	50	90	72	70	100	88	60	100	72

Source: Computed

leaves into thatches, straw mats and baskets and sold during off-season to meet livelihood expenditure.

Another time-related problem in women is nutritional stress. High energy output for work combined with low dietary intake is likely to end up in depletion of health. Women who returned home after heavy work preferred to forego food for rest. Logistic studies[5-6] on food habits of women have established that women readjusted their number of meals a day or the kind of food they cooked in the household based on workload. The women respondents in Sivaganga district narrated to the researcher the oral myth that in the past, women gathered and consumed variety of wild foods, but now due to environmental degradation, this has become extinct.

All households in the study-area are reported to be using the firewood as fuel for cooking. Time allocation for fuel collection is seen to vary depending on households' income, local availability of firewood and extent of deforestation of the neighbourhood. While conversing over Water Collection, some respondents in Sivaganga district explained that the water they potted from the pond was muddy and brown in colour and to purity it they used *"theithaan kottai"* (a seed variety). This purification process normally took about 20 minutes for a pot. Such region-specific time constraints too existed.

Women's Access to and Control over Resources

Participation of women in work is greatly dependent on their access to various resources. Thoughtfully, many erstwhile studies[7-8] have identified women's access to economic resources has a path-breaking variable in improving household welfare. Women in many of the NFW and LAL households were seen to be repeatedly reporting that factors limiting the achievement of food adequacy in their households were not only lack of an adequate asset base such as land and income but also lack of control over income earned, low access to credit, fuel and water and nutritional knowledge. Limited access to resources, in their case, is seen to be contrapositional with their capacity or ability to produce and provide food for the family.

In this study, using the Scaling Technique for various determinants like land, income, credit, fuel and water, health and sanitation and nutritional knowledge, category-wise analysis of women's access was made. The results are tabulated in Tables 7 to 9.

Table 7 shows women's access to resources in *MF households*. The over all mean total score value is shown to be maximum for V_1 of Sivaganga district at 17.5 followed by V_1 of Cuddalore district at 16.4. The mean score for V_2 of Cuddalore district is 16.3, and the lowest is for V_2 of Sivaganga district which is 15.6. In terms of total level of access to resources, Sivaganga district is seen to be marginally better placed. In access to land, the mean value is recorded higher for V_1 of Sivaganga district. Women's access to income in this category shows a mean score value of 3.3 in V_1 of both the districts, whereas it is 3.6 and 2.3 for V_2 of Sivaganga and Cuddalore districts respectively.

The mean score values and the variations in the mean values, while considering access to credit, is interpreted as low access to credit for women of MF households. In the case of access to fuel and water, the mean value is higher for V_1 of Cuddalore district. With regard to health and sanitation, the mean score is higher for V_1 of Sivaganga district at 4.7. Level of Access to Nutritional Knowledge shows a mean score of 3.3 for V_2 of Sivaganga district, relatively higher, as both the study-villages in Cuddalore district show a mean score value of 2.8 only.

Women's access to resources in *NFW households* is computed in Table 8. The highest access is witnessed in V_1 of Cuddalore district where the mean score value of access to all resources is 17.8, V_2 of Sivaganga district has a mean value of 17.0, V_1 of Cuddalore district has 16.7 and the least mean value is for V_1 of Sivaganga district at 15.6. However, in the level of access to income, the mean is higher for V_2 of Sivaganga district at 3.0 and lower for V_1 of Cuddalore district at 2.1. Access to credit is higher for V_1 of Cuddalore district at 3.4. In the level of access to water and fuel, NFW households in the two villages of Cuddalore district are seen to be better placed than their

Table 7

Women's Access to Resources in MF Households

Access to	*Sivaganga District*						*Cuddalore District*					
	V_1			V_2			V_1			V_2		
Resources (score)	*Min*	*Max*	*Mean*	*Min*	*Max*	*Mean*	*Min*	*Max*	*Mean*	*Min*	*Max*	*Mean*
Land (8)	0	7	2.2	0	6	1.7	0	6	1.5	0	5	1.7
Income (6)	2	5	3.3	2	4	3.6	3	4	3.3	2	3	2.3
Credit (8)	1	4	2.7	1	4	2.1	1	5	2.8	1	5	2.1
Water and Fuel (6)	1	3	2.2	1	2	1.9	2	5	2.7	2	4	2.6
Health and Sanitation (10)	2	7	4.7	2	6	3.4	2	7	3.5	3	5	4.1
Nutritional Knowledge (7)	1	5	2.7	1	6	3.3	1	5	2.8	1	6	2.8
All Resources (45)	11	25	17.5	12	22	15.6	11	29	16.4	10	21	16.3

Source: Computed.

Table 8
Women's Access To Resources in NFW Households

	Sivaganga District						*Cuddalore District*					
Access to	V_1			V_2			V_1			V_2		
Resources (score)	*Min*	*Max*	*Mean*	*Min*	*Max*	*Mean*	*Min*	*Max*	*Mean*	*Min*	*Max*	*Mean*
Land (8)	0	0	0	0	0	0	0	0	0	0	0	0
Income (6)	2	5	2.8	2	5	3.0	1	4	2.1	2	6	2.2
Credit (8)	1	4	2.8	1	4	2.4	1	4	3.4	0	4	2.6
Water and Fuel (6)	1	2	1.8	1	3	2.0	2	5	2.7	2	4	2.9
Health and Sanitation (10)	2	7	4.4	2	9	5.7	3	9	5.1	3	6	4.9
Nutritional Knowledge (7)	3	7	3.8	3	6	3.9	2	7	4.5	2	6	3.5
All Resources (45)	11	24	15.6	10	22	17	12	27	17.8	13	24	16.7

Source: Computed..

counterparts in Sivaganga districts. In the case of access to nutritional knowledge, the mean score value is the highest for V_1 of Cuddalore district at 4.5 and the lowest for V_2 of the same district at 3.5.

Table 9 showcases women's access to resources in *LAL Households.* The score value of access to all resources is the highest for V1 of Sivaganga district (18.4), followed by V_1 of Cuddalore district (16.6), then by V_2 of Sivaganga district (15.0), and the least score value for V_2 of Cuddalore district (12.0).

With regard to the level of women's access to income in LAL households the study villages in Sivaganga district have better access. In the level of access to credit, V_2 of Cuddalore district is seen to have alarmingly poor access with its mean value incredibly low at 1.3. Access to fuel and water is recorded to be low in both the study villages of Sivaganga district. Level of access to health and sanitation is higher for the women folk of LAL households in V_1 of Sivaganga district with the corresponding mean score value at 4.4. The level of access nutritional knowledge id higher for V_1 of Sivaganga district with the mean value at 4.5 followed by V_1 of Cuddalore district with the mean value at 3:9. Overall, it is comprehended that women of LAL households of V_2 of Cuddalore district have awfully low access to various resources.

Table 10 presents cross-sectional data on category-wise, headship-wise distribution of sample households according to level of access to resources. It is observed that in Sivaganga district, out of the 60 households surveyed, 22 households are seen to have 'Low' access to resources, 28 households have 'Low Moderate' access and only 10 households have 'High Moderate' access to resources. It is also interesting to observe that among the 10 'High Moderate' households eight belong to FHH category. Another cross-sectional observation is that none of these household belong to LAL category. In V_1 of the district, majority of FHH and JHH households is seen to have 'Low Moderate' access to resources. In V_2 of the district, for FHH and JHH households, the level of access to resources is shown to be 'High Moderate' whereas in MHH households, level of access to resources is only 'Low Moderate'.

Table 9
Women's Access to Resources in Lal Households

Access to	*Sivaganga District*						*Cuddalore District*					
	V_1			V_2			V_1			V_2		
Resources (score)	*Min*	*Max*	*Mean*	*Min*	*Max*	*Mean*	*Min*	*Max*	*Mean*	*Min*	*Max*	*Mean*
Land (8)	0	0	0	0	0	0	0	0	0	0	0	0
Income (6)	2	6	3.8	2	6	3.2	2	5	3.1	1	3	2.2
Credit (8)	1	4	2.6	1	3	2	2	4	2.7	1	2	1.3
Water and Fuel (6)	2	3	2.1	2	2	2	2	3	2.5	2	3	2.3
Health and Sanitation(10)	3	7	5.4	3	5	4	3	5	4.4	2	5	3.8
Nutritional Knowledge (7)	2	6	4.5	3	6	3.8	2	6	3.9	1	6	2.4
All Resources (45)	11	24	18.4	12	20	15	13	23	16.6	9	19	12

Source: Computed

Table 10
Headship wise Distribution of Sample Households According to Level of Access to Resources

Category		FHH				JHH				MHH				
		Low	*LM*	*HM*	*Total*	*Low*	*LM*	*HM*	*Total*	*Low*	*LM*	*HM*	*Total*	*Total*
Sivaganga District														
V_1	MF	-	2	2	4	1	2	1	4	0	1	1	2	10
	NFW	1	1	2	4	2	1	0	3	2	1	0	3	10
	LAL	1	3	0	4	1	3	-	4	2	0	-	2	10
	Overall	2	6	4	12	4	6	1	11	4	2	1	7	30
V_2	MF	-	1	2	3	2	2	-	4	1	2	-	3	10
	NFW	1	0	2	3	2	3	0	5	0	2	0	2	10
	LAL	2	2	0	4	3	2	-	5	1	-	-	1	10
Overall		3	3	4	10	7	7	0	14	2	4	0	6	30
Grand Total		5	9	8	22	11	13	1	25	6	6	1	13	60
Cuddalore District														
V_1	MF	0	0	2	2	1	1	1	3	2	1	2	5	10
	NFW	0	0	1	1	1	2	1	4	2	3	0	5	10
	LAL	0	1	0	1	1	2	1	4	3	2	0	5	10
	Overall	0	1	3	4	3	5	3	11	7	6	2	15	30
V_2	MF	0	2	0	2	1	2	1	4	2	2	0	4	10
	NFW	1	2	1	4	0	3	0	3	2	1	0	3	10
	LAL	2	1	0	3	2	1	0	3	4	0	0	4	10
Overall		3	5	1	9	3	6	1	10	8	3	0	11	30
Grand Total		3	6	4	13	6	11	4	21	15	9	2	26	60

Source: Computed.
LM–Low Moderate.
HM–High Moderate.

In Cuddalore district, out of 60 households surveyed, 24 households are found to be slotted under 'Low' access, 26 households under 'Low Moderate' , and 10 households under high moderate level of access. Village-wise break-up shows that in V_1 a majority of FHH households have 'High Moderate' access, a majority of JHH households have 'Low Moderate', access and MHH households have 'Low' level of access to resources. This village can be the most fitting example for the sliding level in access from 'High Moderate' to 'Low Moderate' to 'Low' as the headship shifts from FHH to JHH to MHH. In V_2 of Cuddalore district, majority of women in FHH and JHH households are seen to have 'Low Moderate' level of access and the women belonging to MHH are found to have only 'Low' level of access to resources. Conclusively, most of the women with less access to resources are identified to belong to the poor households of LAL category.

The problems faced by women in rural areas varied according to the intensity of access to various resources. the interview sessions which the researcher had with the women in the surveyed villages brought to the fore many issues of socio-economic validity. Women in Cuddalore district complained that their lands were under their husband's control. They were not consulted in matters related to choice of crops to be grown and quantum of amount to be retained for household's consumption. In Sivaganga district, women in FHH who owned land near their house grew leafy vegetables and sold them in the nearby town bus-stand and raised money. They said that it gave them power to control the income earned by them. Women belonging to NFW and LAL categories in both districts were of the opinion that landlessness was the major cause for their low status and argued that working on own farm could be more remunerative than working on alien farms. Such arguments, one might think, would have been the forerunner for IFAD's proverbial statement, 'Giving women land means Giving them power'.[9] Research studies have shown that giving women more control over non labour income would have remarkable impact on child anthropometric measures and nutritional intake than when men had control over this income.[10]

In JHH, women were often consulted when food expenditures were made. They could also spend the amount in consultation with their husbands. In terms of access to and control over income, female headed households were better off. In FHH, income was most often pooled and spent by women. In MHH, a portion of the non-pooled income of the male members some of the households were spent on alcohol and cigarettes. In households where women contributed more than 50 per cent of the household wage income, they had decision-making powers in household matters. However they sought the succour of support services such as training and credit facilities.

Women's access to credit was generally limited particularly from formal sources such as banks. They experienced difficulties in getting loans mainly because of problems in producing security in banks and heavy rate of interest with private money-lenders who waived security. Women in two MF households of Cuddalore district reported that they were forced by their husbands to seek credit by mortgaging the land owned by them to meet their daughter's marriage expenses. LAL households often borrowed money from relatives and neighbours at a low rate of interest to provide for food expenditure and the borrowed money was repaid through their earnings on easy instalments.

Low access to fuel and water made rural women's life miserable. Women spent more time on these activities which otherwise would have been spent on income generating activities.

Health services were accessed through Primary Health Centres (PHC) and private clinics in the nearby town area. Unlike in Sivaganga district, women in Cuddalore district were satisfied with the functioning of PHCs. A very low proportion of households in the study areas had shown preference for private dispensaries. 15 per cent of households in Sivaganga district and 9 per cent in Cuddalore district chose self-medication based on their traditional knowledge of health. About 80 per cent of women in Sivaganga district and 85 per cent in Cuddalore district had their last delivery in the hospitals. Around 60 per cent of women in the middle age group in both the districts had undergone tubectomy. Sample population ailing from jaundice, tuberculosis, asthma was very less in numbers. Awareness about vaccination and immunization was found in the women of both the study areas through health workers, from radio, television programmes and other voluntary organizations. Almost all children in the age group 0-10 years in both the districts were immunized. Chewing of pan, tobacco and alcohol consumption was high among illiterates. They did not know that not only nutritional factors but environmental factors also affected the health of persons. Occasionally insanitary conditions had depleted the health of household members, especially children.

When asked about the relative importance of qualitative and quantitative diet, 61 per cent of the women in Sivaganga district and 40 per cent of the women in Cuddalore district said that both were important. Rest of the respondents said that only quantitative diet was important. Even though women in 70 per cent of the households in Sivaganga district and 45 per cent of the households in Cuddalore district were aware that sprouting and fermination enhanced the nutritive value of pulses, only some households in Sivaganga district practiced it. When asked about their food selection priorities, out of 120 households, 60 respondents said that their first choice was to 'satisfy hunger', 50 respondents told that their food households, food selection was based on 'energy needs' and for 10 households it was based on the 'cost of the food'. Almost all women in the age group of 20-45 years expressed that their children should be encouraged to adopt good nutritional practice. Educated women among the respondents were found to have some functional knowledge of nutrition.

Women in Decision-Making

Since decisions that affect the well-being of individuals are made within the households, women's access to decision-making is considered to be one of the important intra-household dynamics of food security.

Table 11 presents computed data on the extent of participation of women in decision-making in matters related

Table 11
Participation of Women in Decision Making

Sivaganga District										
		WDFORA (12)			*WDFAD (14)*			*WDCCH (10)*		
Category		*Min*	*Max*	*Mean*	*Min*	*Max*	*Mean*	*Min*	*Max*	*Mean*
V_1	MF	7	10	9.2	3	8	5.9	1	9	6.6
	NFW	6	12	8.5	4	14	7.2	2	8	5.0
	LAL	4	10	6.8	4	9	6.5	4	10	7.4
Overall		4	12	8.2	3	14	6.5	1	10	6.3
V_2	MF	6	12	8.0	1	14	6.5	0	10	5
	NFW	6	12	8.7	5	10	6.9	2	6	4.6
	LAL	4	8	6.2	4	12	6.6	6	9	7
Overall		4	12	7.6	1	14	6.6	2	10	5.5
Cuddalore District										
V_1	MF	5	12	7.5	2	8	5.4	2	6	4
	NFW	5	10	7.1	2	8	5.2	2	10	4.6
	LAL	6	10	8.3	2	10	4.4	2	8	3.3
Overall		5	12	7.6	2	8	5	2	10	3.9
V_2	MF	4	12	7.0	2	8	4.9	2	6	4.9
	NFW	6	12	8.6	3	12	6.4	2	7	5.2
	LAL	3	8	6.1	2	10	5.1	2	10	5.3
Overall		3	12	7.2	2	8	5.4	2	10	5.1

Source: Computed.
WDFORA–Women Decision-Making in Food Related Activities.
WDFAD–Women Decision-Making in Family Administration.
WDCCH–Women Decision-Making in Caring of Children and Health.

to Food Related Activities (FORA), Family Administration (FAD) and Caring of Children and Health (CC) for the sample households. The following observation is made for women's participation in decision-making for Food Related Activities (WDFORA): the maximum is recorded for V_1 of Sivaganga district with the mean score value at 8.2, followed by V_1 of Cuddalore district and V_2 of Sivaganga district with an equal mean score value of 7.6 and the lowest for V_2 Cuddalore district at 7.2. Category-wise analysis shows that in V_1 of Sivaganga district, the mean score value is higher for women of MF households (9.2), but in V_2, the mean score value is higher for NFW households (8.7) followed by MF category (8.0) and the lowest mean score is for LAL households (6.2). In V_1 of Cuddalore district, the highest mean score value is shown for women of LAL category (8.3). In V_2 of Cuddalore district, the mean score value reading shows higher level of participation for the women of NFW category (8.6).

A comparative analysis of level of participation of women in affairs related to Family Administration (WDFAD) of both the districts, show that women in Sivaganga district take active participation with the mean score value for V_1 at 6.5 and that of V_2 at 6.6. The corresponding mean values for the villages of Cuddalore district show poor participation rate at only 5.0 and 5.4. This mean value might reliably lead us to conclude that rural women in Sivaganga district are better empowered than their counterparts in Cuddalore district with reference family administration decision-making.

Regarding Caring of Children and Health (WDCCH). Women in Sivaganga district are seen to be more participative in decision-making with the average of the mean values for V_1 and V_2 at 5.9. The average mean value for this activity in Cuddalore district for V_1 and V_2 is only 4.5. Category-wise data show that in Sivaganga district, it is the women in LAL households who participate, rather hyperactively, hitting a mean value of 7.4 and 7.00 respectively for V_1 and V_2 villages. This is a remarkable position when compared to the overall average mean value of 5.9 for the two villages in Sivaganga district and the overall average mean value of all the four villages in the study-area is only 5.3. The figures and the cross-sectional analysis of data for tasks and categories will convince any analyst to conclude that women in Sivaganga district are more participative and more empowered to take decisions.

Table 12 provides headship-wise, category-wise, cross-sectional, zig-zag analysis of the level of participation of women in decision-making. Data was analysed for three calibrated levels of decision-making: High, Moderate, Low level. It is seen that 'High' level of participation of found only in female headed households (FHH) of both districts. The participation of women in majority of JHH and MHH in both the districts show only 'Low' or 'Moderate' level of participation in decision-making. The gender-divide is more glaringly visible in this analysis, because among 39 Male Headed Households (MHH) in the study-villages of both the districts only in a lone household 'High' level of participation in decision-making is recorded.

Apart from family headship, other factors like age, education and women's access to resources are also seen to be influencing women's participative role in decision-making. Table 13 provides info-data on Age, Education and Access to Resources for women in the sample households category-wise. Among women under 30 years of age and between 31-40 years of age, the level of participation is only 'Moderate'. 'High' level of participation is recorded for these age groups only for six per cent and 22 per cent respectively. For the age group 41-50, 'Moderate' level of participation is reported for 38 per cent and 'High' level of participation for 31 per cent. But women in the 50 plus slot show 'High' level with 41 per cent of them effectively participating in decision-making. A noticeable corollary observation is that the percentage of women with 'Moderate' level of participation is seen to decrease with the increase in age, whereas the percentage of women with 'High' level of participation is seen to increase with the increase in age. This may be due to the fact that when women advances in age she gains ability and experience to command reverence and respect from other members of the household. Senile

Table 12
Headship wise Participation of Women in Decision Making

Sivaganga District														
		FHH				*MHH*				*JHH*				*Grand*
Category		*L*	*M*	*H*	*Total*	*L*	*M*	*H*	*Total*	*L*	*M*	*H*	*Total*	*Total*
V_1	MF	0	1	3	4	1	1	0	2	0	4	0	4	10
	NFW	0	2	2	4	2	1	0	3	0	3	0	3	10
	LAL	0	2	2	4	0	2	0	2	1	3	0	4	10
Overall		0	5	7	12	3	4	0	7	1	10	0	11	30
V_2	MF	0	1	2	3	1	2	0	3	1	3	0	4	10
	NFW	0	1	2	3	0	2	0	2	1	4	0	5	10
	LAL	0	2	2	4	1	0	0	1	0	5	0	5	10
Overall		0	4	6	10	2	4	0	6	2	12	0	14	30
Grand Total		0	9	13	22	5	8	0	13	3	22	0	25	60
Cuddalore District														
V_1	MF	0	1	1	2	3	2	0	5	0	3	0	3	10
	NFW	0	1	0	1	2	3	0	5	3	0	1	4	10
	LAL	0	0	1	1	3	1	1	5	1	3	0	4	10
Overall	0	2	2	4	8	6	1	15	4	6	1	11	30	
V_2	MF	0	0	2	2	3	1	0	4	1	3	0	4	10
	NFW	0	2	2	4	1	2	0	3	2	1	0	3	10
	LAL	0	0	3	3	4	0	0	4	0	3	0	3	10
Overall		0	2	7	9	8	3	0	11	3	7	0	10	30
Grand Total		0	4	9	13	16	9	1	26	7	13	1	21	60

Source: Computed.

Table 13
Factors Affecting Participation of Women in Decision Making of the Sample Households

	Level of Participation			
Particulars	*Low*	*Moderate*	*High*	*Total*
Age (in Years)	(13)	(19)	(3)	
Upto 30	5	10	1	16
	(31)	(63)	(6)	(100)
	(38)	(48)	(36)	
31 - 40	14	25	11	50
	(28)	(50)	(22)	(100)
	(27)	(23)	(32)	
41 - 50	10	12	10	32
	(31)	(38)	(31)	(100)
	(22)	(10)	(29)	
Above 50	8	5	9	22
	(36)	(23)	(41)	(100)
Over All	(100) 37	(100) 52	(100) 31	120
Level of Education				
	(54)	(17)	(32)	
Illiterate	20	9	10	39
	(52)	(23)	(25]	(100)
	(46)	(48)	(39)	
Primary (1-5)	17	25	12	54
	(31)	(45)	(24)	(100)
	(0)	(25)	(16)	
Middle (6-8)	0	13	5	18
	(0)	(72)	(28)	(100)
	(0)	(10)	(13)	
High School (9+)	0	5	4	9
	(0)	(56)	(44)	(100)
Over All	(100) 37	(100) 52	(100) 31	120
Access to Resources				
	(68)	(50)	(23)	
Low	25	26	7	58
	(43)	(45)	(12)	(100)
	(32)	(44)	(58)	
Low Moderate	12	23	18	53
	(23)	(43)	(34)	(100)
	(0)	(6)	(19)	
High Moderate	0	3	6	9
	(0)	(33)	(67)	(100)
Over All	(100) 37	(100) 52	(100) 31	120

Source: Computed.

Figures in the (i.) Left Parentheses denote percentages to column total (ii) Right Parentheses denote percentages to Row total.

women with increased participation in decision-making have been the source of other studies also.[11]

Apart from age, education is yet another variable which influenced the involvement of women in decision-making. Twenty out of 39 women belonging to the 'Illiterate' category, about 52 per cent of the total, are able to command only 'Low' level of participation in decision-making. On the other hand, none of the literate women is found to be neglected with 'Low' participation level. This single observation is enough to convince that literacy leads to recognition, and recognition leads to empowerment. Studies have proved that education of women has led to kaleidoscopic readjustments in household decision-making.[12-13] Wisdom and self confidence are inseparable.

Another important factor which has influenced decision-making levels in women is their access to resources. When the level of access to resources is seen to increase from 'Low' to 'High Moderate' the participation level in decision-making is also recorded to increase. Women with 'High Moderate' level of access to resources, about 67 per cent of the total, are found to actively participate in the decision-making process. When added access to resources is made available to women, their level of participation in household related decisions is seen to increase sizably.[14]

WOMEN EMPOWERMENT AND HOUSEHOLD FOOD SECURITY

(Testing of Second Hypothesis)

Participation of women in decision-making and their access to and control over resources are critical indicators in the process of empowerment.[15-16] It was also found in the foregone analysis of surveyed data that increase in the level of women's literacy and enhanced access to resources increased the level of participation of women in decision-making.

The purpose of this section is to measure the level of women empowerment in the study-area and relate it to household food security. Based on total score values for level of access to resources and level of access to decision-making, the households are pigeonholed into three empowerment categories. Low Empowered Households (LEMPH), Moderately Empowered Households (MEMPH) and Highly Empowered Households (HEMPH). Further, the level of empowerment is linked with food adequacy status of households and the intensity and invulnerability of the household's welfare is measured.

An attempt is also made in this section to quantify the variations in households' food consumption by women empowerment group. The per capita figures for each household are computed using consumer units. The household size is measured in terms of adult equivalent consumption unit in the household. The procedure of assigning the number of consumer units is based on the method adopted by the Indian National Sample Survey.[17] The per day per unit food intake is compared with the Recommended Daily Allowance of ICMR (RDA).[18] Dietary Adequacy Ratio (DAR) is computed as (Actual Intake/RDA) x 100.

It may be observed from the relevant figures given for the above computations in Table 14 that the pattern of food consumption varied sharply between families with different levels of women empowerment. In *Sivaganga district*, the mean intake of cereals (rice) is 368.9 gm. for LEMPH, 396.2 gm. for MEMPH and 400.0 gm. for HEMPH. This is the only food-item with DAR of 80 per cent. In the case of pulses, the intake is negligible with only 19.3 gm. for LEMPH, 20.18 gm. for MEMPH and slightly higher for HEMPH with 28.56 gm., recording a short-fall of 51.7 per cent 49.6 per cent and 28.6 per cent respectively from the standard requirements.

The intake of green leafy Vegetables and Roots and Tubers is very low for all empowerment groups despite relatively higher DAR for MEMPH and HEMPH. The low consumption of roots and tubers is due to non-availability. Except for potato and raddish other tubers like beet-root and carrot are rare commodities for the a women of the study-villages. Some households manage to purchase these things once in a way from the nearby wakly market. Interestingly enough, in Sivaganga district, carrot, beet-root and cauliflower are

Table 14
Women Empowerment and Adequacy of Dietary Intake (Gm/Cu/Day) of Various Foods

Sivaganga District

	LEMPH (20)		*MEMPH (22)*		*HEMPH (18)*		
Foods	*Mean Intake*	*DAR*	*Mean Intake*	*DAR*	*Mean Intake*	*DAR*	*R.D.A*
Cereals *(FG_1)*	368.9	80.2	396.2	86.14	400.0	86.96	460
Pulses *(FG_2)*	19.34	48.35	20.18	50.47	28.56	71.4	40
Vegetables							
(i) Green leafy *(FG_3)*	16.2	40.52	18.8	47.18	22.5	56.43	40
(ii) Roots and Tubers *(FG_4)*	7.8	15.6	11.11	22.23	13.25	26.50	50
(iii) Others *(FG_5)*	30.8	50.13	49.18	81.97	51.18	85.3	60
Fruits *(FG_6)*	3.18	10.6	6.13	20.45	10.36	34.56	30
Fish, Meat, Poultry products *(FG_7)*	9.7	32.36	14.04	46.74	14.53	48.44	30
Milk and Milk Products *(FG_8)*	49.9	33.3	100.2	66.8	107.61	71.74	150
Fats and Edible oils *(FG_9)*	12.34	61.70	14.7	73.5	20.20	101.82	20
Sugar and Jaggery *(FG_{10})*	12.67	42.26	20.02	66.74	26.0	86.69	30

Contd...

Cuddalore District							
Foods	*LEMPH (31)*		*MEMPH (15)*		*HEMPH (14)*		*R.D.A*
Cereals *(FG_1)*	371.22	80.7	416.2	90.48	397.4	86.4	460
Pulses *(FG_2)*	16.88	42.21	19.76	49.4	26.69	66.73	40
Vegetables							
(i) Green leafy *(FG_3)*	20.56	51.4	18.4	46	24.1	60.4	40
(ii) Roots and Tubers *(FG_4)*	7.15	14.30	8.60	17.20	8.17	16.35	50
(iii) Others *(FG_5)*	38.1	63.5	39.78	66.3	47.5	79.18	60
Fruits *(FG_6)*	2.85	9.5	4.17	13.9	9.0	30.0	30
Fish, Meat, Poultry products *(FG_7)*	12.21	40.7	14.8	49.62	13.35	44.5	30
Milk and Milk Products *(FG_8)*	59.46	39.64	59.13	39.42	89.6	59.76	150
Fats and Edible oils *(FG_9)*	11.6	58.1	14.08	70.4	17.2	86.4	20
Sugar and Jaggery *(FG_{10})*	9.21	30.72	12.03	40.12	19.08	63.62	30

Source: Computed R.D.A. - Recommended Daily Allowance (per cu/gm)
LEMPH-Low Empowered Households MEMPH-Moderately Empowered Households
HEMPH-Highly Empowered Households .

considered to be status edibles, consumed only by the affluent people. They are also popularly known as 'English Vegetables'. In HEMPH, Fats and Edible Oil is the only food-group seen to be consumed more than the required minimum (101.82 per cent). Fruit consumption is the lowest for LEMPH with the DAR depressively low at 10.6 per cent, followed by MEMPH at 20.45 per cent and HEMPH at 34.56 per cent. The intake of milk and meat is also less for all empowerment groups compared to ICMR standards.

In *Cuddalore district* cereal consumption is maximum for MEMPH (416.2 gm.) when compared to that of LEMPH (371.2 gm.) and HEMPH (397.4 gm.). In the case of mat, fish and poultry food items, the mean intake is higher for MEMPH. The consumption of all other food items, except cereals, the staple food, is lower for all empowerment groups. In spite of higher consumption of oils and vegetables in juxtaposition with other nutritious food, its intake is inadequate to meat ICMR prescribed standards.

The empowerment level-wise assessment of consumption of various food items for both the study districts gives us the impression that the intake of essential and quality food improved simultaneously from the Low Empowered Households (LEMPH) to the Highly Empowered Households (HEMPH). Poor control over income and food expenditure, low level of access to resources, lack of knowledge about important nutrients in food items might be the reasons for low DAR and variations among women empowerment groups.

Gopalan[19] identifies, within developing countries, striking variations in food consumption pattern and attributes it to gross inequality in income. But related studies propagate that apart from income, food consumption level could be influenced through women's access to and control over resources and higher participation in decision-making in activities related to food and childcare. As an axiomatic corollary to this, the hypothesis, *Women empowerment contributes to household food security,* is framed and put to evaluation.

As part of the evalutory procedure of the framed hypothesis, the mean difference in Dietary Adequacy Ratio (DAR) is tested between women empowerment groups using the Fisher's Two-way Analysis of Variance (ANOVA). The calculated F-statistic shows significant difference at one per cent level (Table 15). Further, the critical difference is also worked out and compared with the mean difference in DAR between various foods groups for each of the three empowerment groups.

Mean difference in DAR between empowerment groups is analysed and recorded in Table 16. This shows that in *Sivaganga district* the differences in DAR for FG_1, FG_3 and FG_4 are significant at 5 per cent level between low empowerment and moderate empowerment groups. For pulses (FG_2), the variation is not significant. This is due to the reason that pulses, being a source of nutrition, are consumed equally and balancedly with vegetables and rice. Households in both the empowerment groups might consume this in equal amount. Considerable variations are found for food groups FG_5, FG_6, Fg_7, FG_8, FG_9, and FG_{10} because the mean differences are significant at one per cent. Greater variation is found for FG_8 (Milk and Milk Products). The consumption of high quality food by MEMPH might be the reason for greater variations.

Between MEMPH and HEMPH, except for food groups, FG_1, FG_4, FG_5 and FG_7 all others are seen to be significant at five per cent level and only FG_8 has one per cent level of significance. It could be inferred that per unit consumption of cereals, roots and tubers, vegetables and egg, fish and poultry products is almost the same for both the groups. Between LEMPH and HEMPH, the variations are significant for all food groups.

In *Cuddalore district*, greater variations are seen to exist between LEMPH and MEMPH groups even in the consumption of cereals. Family size is seen to have negatively influenced DAR here. For food groups FG_2, FG_9 and FG_{10}, the mean differences are significant at five per cent level, but for food groups FG_4, FG_5, FG_6 and FG_8 variations are insignificant. Between MEMPH and HEMPH empowerment groups, insignificant difference is found in cereals (FG_1), roots and tubers (FG_4) and meat products (FG_7), for all other food groups mean variations are significant at one per cent level. Between

Table 15
Anova Two-way Classification Table

Source of Variation	*Sum of Squares*	*df*	*Mean Sum of Squares*	*F-Statistic*	*F-critical value for 1%*
Sivaganga District					
Between Food Groups	12865.41	9	1429.490	21.756**	3.598
Between Women EmpowermentGroups	3272.77	2	1636.386	24.905**	6.097
Error	1182.65	18	65.702		
Cuddalore District					
Between Food Groups	13255.15	9	1472.794	37.935**	3.598
Between Women Empowerment Groups	1337.51	2	668.759	17.225**	6.097
Error	698.83	18	38.823		

Source: Computed.
Note: ** Significant at 1% level

Critical Mean Difference for Empowerment Group $t_a \sqrt{\frac{2}{r} MSE}$

Critical Mean Difference for Food Group $t_a \sqrt{\frac{2}{c} MSE}$

r = Number of rows c = Number of coloumns
For 18 D.F

$t_{0.05} = 1.734$ $t_{0.01} = 2.552$

Between groups	*5% CMD*	*1% CMD*
WEMP	4.832	7.107
Food	8.821	12.982

LEMPH and HEMPH empowerment groups, insignificant variation is noticed only for vegetables (FG_4) and Meat Products (FG_7), all others have significant variation in DAR.

Table 16
Mean Difference in Dietary Adequacy Ratio: Between Women Empowerment Groups

	Sivaganga			*Cuddalore*		
Food Group	*L→M*	*M→H*	*L→H*	*L→M*	*M→H*	*L→H*
FG_1	5.94*	0.82^{NS}	6.76*	9.10**	-3.40^{NS}	5.70*
FG_2	2.12^{NS}	20.93**	23.05**	7.19**	17.33**	24.52**
FG_3	6.66*	9.25**	15.91**	-5.40*	14.40**	9.00**
FG_4	6.63*	4.27^{NS}	10.90**	2.90^{NS}	-0.85^{NS}	2.05^{NS}
FG_5	31.84**	3.33^{NS}	35.17**	2.80^{NS}	12.88**	15.68**
FG_6	9.85**	14.11**	23.96**	4.40^{NS}	16.10**	20.50**
FG_7	14.38**	1.7^{NS}	16.08**	5.92*	-2.12^{NS}	3.80^{NS}
FG_8	33.5**	4.94*	38.44**	0.22^{NS}	20.34**	20.12**
FG_9	11.8**	28.32**	40.12**	12.30**	16.00**	28.30**
FG_{10}	24.48**	19.95**	44.43**	9.40**	23.50**	32.90**

Source: Computed.
Note: $CD_{0.05} = 4.832$ $CD_{0.01} = 7.107$
* Significant at 5% level
** Significant at 1% level
L→ M -Between LEMPH and MEMPH
M→ H -Between MEMPH and HEMPH
L→ H -Between LEMPH and HEMPH.

The obtained results uphold the second hypothesis. It can be generalised that women's access to income and control over the income earned and their effective involvement in matters related to food expenditure and nutrition knowledge will help improve DAR in rural areas. Katone Apte [20] and Tinker [21] have also established that women's control over income and decision-making influence positively the provision of basic food to the family-members.

The absolute mean difference in DAR between various food groups was computed for the households in each of the empowerment groups. Table 17 presents data on mean difference of DAR between food groups for *Low Empowered Households* (LEMPH) in the study-villages. In Sivaganga district, difference in DAR of cereals (FG_1) is found to be statistically

Table 17

Absolute Mean Difference in Dietary Adequacy Ratio Between Food Items in Lemp Households

Sivaganga District										
	FG_1	FG_2	FG_3	FG_4	FG_5	FG_6	FG_7	FG_8	FG_9	FG_{10}
FG_1										
FG_2	31.85**									
FG_3	39.68**	7.83^{NS}								
FG_4	64.60**	32.75**	24.92**							
FG_5	30.07**	1.78^{NS}	9.61*	34.53**						
FG_6	69.60**	37.75**	29.92**	5.00^{NS}	39.53**					
FG_7	47.84**	15.99**	8.16^{NS}	16.76**	17.77**	21.76**				
FG_8	46.90**	15.05**	7.22^{NS}	17.70**	16.83**	22.7**	0.94^{NS}			
FG_9	18.50**	13.35**	21.18**	46.10**	11.57*	51.10**	29.34**	28.40**		
FG_{10}	37.94**	6.09^{NS}	1.74^{NS}	26.66**	7.87^{NS}	31.66**	9.90*	8.96*	19.44**	
Cuddalore District										
	FG_1	FG_2	FG_3	FG_4	FG_5	FG_6	FG_7	FG_8	FG_9	FG_{10}
FG_1										
FG_2	38.49**									
FG_3	29.30**	9.19*								
FG_4	66.40**	27.91**	37.10**							
FG_5	17.20**	21.29**	12.10**	49.20**						
FG_6	7.12^{NS}	32.71**	41.90**	4.80^{NS}	54.00**					
FG_7	40.00**	1.51^{NS}	10.70*	26.40**	22.80**	31.20**				
FG_8	41.06**	2.57^{NS}	11.76*	25.34**	23.86**	30.14**	1.06^{NS}			
FG_9	22.60**	15.89**	6.70^{NS}	43.80**	5.40^{NS}	48.60**	17.40**	18.50**		
FG_{10}	49.98**	11.49**	20.68**	16.42**	32.78**	21.22**	10.06*	8.92*	27.38**	

Source: Computed. Note : $CD_{0.05} = 8.821$ $CD_{0.01} = 12.982$ * Significant at 5% level ** Significant at 1% level

significant at one per cent level with all the food groups. This implies that the intensity of cereal consumption is more than that of other food items for the LEMPH group. Greatest variations is found in the case of Fruits (FG_6) which is measured at 69.6 and the lowest variation is found form Fats and Edible Oils (FG_9) at 18.5. In Cuddalore district, while measuring the DAR of cereals (FG_1) in relation to other food groups, significant variation is identified in all the food groups. A wide variation is seen with Fruits (FG_6) and low variation is seen with Vegetables (FG_5). This implies that consumption of vegetables is the second dietary content for the LEMPH group.

The difference in DAR of Pulses (FG_2) for the LEMPH empowerment group is found to be insignificant with food groups FG_3, FG_5 and FG_{10}. For other groups, in relation to pulses, the variation is statistically significant. In Cuddalore district, contrarily, FG_2 has insignificant variation with FG_7 and FG_8 and all other food groups are significant at one per cent level. DAR of Pulses (FG_2) is seen to show great variation with that of Fruits (FG_6) irrespective of the district. In the case of FG_3, in Sivaganga district, except FG_7, FG_8 and FG_{10}, all others have significant variations; in Cuddalore district, except FG_9, all others have significant variations at five per cent and one per cent level. In the case of FG_4, in Sivaganga district except FG_6, all others are significant; almost similar results are obtained for FG_4, in Cuddalore district also. Considering FG_5, in Sivaganga district, except FG_{10}, all other are significant; but in Cuddalore district, insignificant differences is found in FG_9. The absolute mean differences in DAR of FG_6 and FG_7 are found to be statistically significant with all other food groups in both the districts. In the case of FG_8, other food groups are statistically significant at one per cent and five per cent. In the case of FG_9, it is seen to be statistically significant with FG_{10}.

Table 18 presents configurations of absolute mean difference in DAR between various food groups in *Moderately Empowered Households* (MEMPH) for both the districts. For Sivaganga district, the mean difference in DAR of cereals (FG_1) is found to be statistically significant with all the food groups, except Vegetables (FG_5). This implies that the intake of Vegetables

Table 18

Absolute Mean Difference in Dietary Adequacy Ratiobetween Food Items in Memp Households

Sivaganga District

	FG_1	FG_2	FG_3	FG_4	FG_5	FG_6	FG_7	FG_8	FG_9	FG_{10}
FG_1										
FG_2	35.67**									
FG_3	38.96**	3.29^{NS}								
FG_4	63.91**	29.24**	24.95**							
FG_5	4.17^{NS}	31.50**	34.79**	59.74**						
FG_6	65.69**	30.02**	26.73**	1.78^{NS}	61.52**					
FG_7	39.40**	3.73^{NS}	0.44^{NS}	24.51**	35.23**	26.29**				
FG_8	19.34**	16.33**	19.62**	44.57**	15.17**	46.35**	20.06**			
FG_9	12.64*	23.03**	26.32**	51.27**	8.47^{NS}	53.05**	26.76**	6.70^{NS}		
FG_{10}	19.40**	16.27**	19.56**	44.51**	15.23**	46.29**	20.00**	0.06^{NS}	6.76^{NS}	

Cuddalore District

	FG_1	FG_2	FG_3	FG_4	FG_5	FG_6	FG_7	FG_8	FG_9	FG_{10}
FG_1										
FG_2	40.40**									
FG_3	43.80**	3.40^{NS}								
FG_4	72.60**	32.20**	28.80**							
FG_5	23.50**	16.90**	20.30**	49.10**						
FG_6	87.90**	35.50**	32.10**	3.30^{NS}	52.40**					
FG_7	43.18**	2.78^{NS}	0.62^{NS}	29.42**	19.68**	32.72**				
FG_8	50.38**	12.98**	6.58^{NS}	22.22**	26.88**	25.52**	7.20^{NS}			
FG_9	19.40**	21.00**	24.40**	53.20**	4.10^{NS}	56.50**	23.78**	30.98**		
FG_{10}	49.68**	9.28**	5.88^{NS}	22.92**	26.18**	26.22**	6.50^{NS}	0.70^{NS}	30.28**	

Source: Computed, *Note:* $CD_{0.05} = 8.821$ $CD_{0.01} = 12.982$ * Significant at 5% level ** Significant at 1% level

in overmuch: FG_1, does not find much variation with FG_5. In relation to FG_1 the maximum mean difference is in FG_6 at 65.6. In the case of FG_2, except FG_3 and FG_7 significant variation at one per cent level is seen for all other food groups. The difference in DAR of FG_3 is found to be significant for all food groups except FG_7 in the case of FG_4, all food groups except FG_6 are recorded to have significant variation in DAR at one per cent. For FG_5, except FG_9, all other groups are significant at one per cent level. The difference in DAR of FG_6 and FG_7 with other food groups is found to be statistically significant at one per cent level. The difference in DAR of FG_8 is recorded to be statistically insignificant with FG_9 and FG_{10}. The difference in DAR between FG_9 and FG_{10} is statistically insignificant.

Corresponding data for Cuddalore district for the MEMPH group shows the mean difference in the DAR of cereals (FG_1) with all the remaining food groups. In the case of FG_2, except FG_3 and FG_7, all the other food groups are significant. While juxtaposing the mean difference of FG_3 with other groups, FG_7, FG_8 and FG_{10} are observed to be insignificant, all other food groups are seen to be significant at one per cent level. In the case of FG_4, except FG_7, all other food groups are significant. In the case of FG_5, except FG_9, all others show great variation.

The difference in DAR of FG_6 is seen to be significant with all other food groups. In the case of FG_7, it is in insignificant variation with FG_8 and FG_{10}; but with FG_9 it has remarkably significant variation. For FG_8, the mean difference is significant with FG_9 and insignificant with FG_{10}. The mean difference of DAR of FG_9 has significant variation with FG_{10}.

Table 19 presents absolute mean difference data for DAR of various food groups for *High Empowered Households* (HEMPH). In Sivaganga district, the DAR of cereals (FG_1) is in proximity with FG_5 and FG_{10}. In relation to FG_1 the variation in mean difference is insignificant for these food items. For all other remaining food groups, FG_1 has significant difference at one per cent level, but the variation is greatly significant between FG_1 and FG_4. But in Cuddalore district, the mean difference between food groups FG_1 and FG_9 is observed to be zero with nil variation. For all other groups, except FG_5, the

Table 19

Absolute Mean Difference in Dietary Adequacy Ratio Between Food Items in Hemp Households

Sivaganga District

	FG_1	FG_2	FG_3	FG_4	FG_5	FG_6	FG_7	FG_8	FG_9	FG_{10}
FG_1										
FG_2	15.56**									
FG_3	30.53**	14.97**								
FG_4	60.46**	44.90**	29.93**							
FG_5	1.66^{NS}	13.90**	28.87**	58.80**						
FG_6	52.40**	36.84**	21.87**	8.06^{NS}	50.74**					
FG_7	38.52**	22.96**	7.99^{NS}	21.94**	36.86**	13.88**				
FG_8	15.22**	0.34^{NS}	15.31**	45.24**	13.56**	37.18**	23.30**			
FG_9	14.86**	30.42**	45.39**	75.32**	16.52**	67.26**	53.38**	30.08**		
FG_{10}	0.27^{NS}	15.29**	30.26**	60.19**	1.39^{NS}	52.13**	38.25**	14.95**	15.13**	

Cuddalore District

	FG_1	FG_2	FG_3	FG_4	FG_5	FG_6	FG_7	FG_8	FG_9	FG_{10}
FG_1										
FG_2	19.67**									
FG_3	26.00**	6.33^{NS}								
FG_4	70.05**	50.38**	44.05**							
FG_5	7.22^{NS}	12.45**	18.78**	62.83**						
FG_6	56.40**	36.73**	30.40**	13.65**	49.18**					
FG_7	41.90**	22.23**	15.90**	28.15**	34.68**	14.50**				
FG_8	26.64**	6.97^{NS}	0.64^{NS}	43.41**	19.42**	29.76**	15.26**			
FG_9	0	19.67**	26.00**	70.05**	7.22^{NS}	56.40**	41.90**	26.64**		
FG_{10}	22.78**	3.11^{NS}	3.22^{NS}	47.27**	15.56**	33.62**	19.12**	3.86^{NS}	22.78**	

Source: Computed, *Note:* $CD_{0.05} = 8.821$ $CD_{0.01} = 12.982$, * Significant at 5% level ** Significant at 1% level

variations are significant at one per cent level; among these, a very highly significant variation at 70.5 is found for Roots and Tubers (FG_4). Irrespective of the level of empowerment, the consumption of this food groups is seen to be very low and very inadequate to reach the Recommended Level. With FG_5 the DAR of FG_1 shows insignificant variation.

In the case of FG_2, in Sivaganga district, all food groups except FG_8 have significant difference at one per cent level; with FG_2, greatest variations is found in FG_4 at 44.9. But data for Cuddalore district shows that the mean difference in DAR of FG_2 is insignificant with food groups FG_3, FG_8 and FG_{10}. For other groups, the variation is significant at one per cent level. In Sivaganga district, FG_3 is in significant variation with all food groups except FG_7; but in Cuddalore district it shows insignificant difference with FG_8 and FG_{10}. In Sivaganga district, in the case of FG_4, all food groups except FG_6 are seen to exhibit significant variation at one per cent level; but in Cuddalore district FG_4 has significant difference at one per cent level with all other food groups. Greatest variation is found for FG_4 with FG_9, the impression is that in Cuddalore district, the DAR of Oils and Fats (FG_9) is more when compared with Roots and Tubers (FG_4). With reference to the DAR of (FG_5), all other food groups except FG_9 are shown to be significant with it one per cent level in Sivaganga district; whereas in Cuddalore district, FG_5 is in significant variation with all food groups except FG_9. For food groups FG_6 and FG_7, their mean differences in DAR with other food groups are found to be significant at one per cent level in both the districts. In the case of FG_8, FG_9 and FG_{10} are found to be significant in Sivaganga district; but in Cuddalore district FG_8 has insignificant difference with FG_{10}. The mean difference in DAR between FG_9 and FG_{10} is significant at one per cent level in both the districts.

WOMEN AND FOOD STRATEGIES

The previous analysis focussed on the food adequacy status of households in quantitative terms of per day per capita intake of various food stuffs. A connected food security problem faced by the households is the consumption and utilization of foods which give a qualitative dimension to food security in the form of nutritional security. Achievement of nutritional security depends on adequate intake of energy, protein and other micronutrients by all household members. In the following analysis an evaluation of the nutrient adequacy status of households surveyed with the objective to arrive at an estimate of food secured households based on the nutrients intake such as calorie and protein consumption, and strategies adopted by women to achieve it.

Energy is measured in term of calories. It is most necessary for body maintenance[22] and deficiency in calorie is described as 'under-nourishment'.[23] In addition to calories, proteins are the chief substances in the cells of body. They supply the essential building material for the body and make good the wear and tear of tissues, thus enabling a person to lead a healthy active life. The level of protein intake measures the extent of 'malnutrition'.

The poor in India are sometimes identified on the basis of consumption levels of nutrition. Much of the earlier works have widely recognised the importance of the nutrition components, calorie intake level has been the single most important criterion for measuring the nutrition gap.[24-25] In the context of emerging knowledge about the critical importance of nutrients for both physical and mental development, it is now recognised that increased calorie consumption alone may not necessarily ensure an adequate intake of other nutrients. So, the spectrum of measurement of food security is broadened in this study to include the intake of protein, in addition to the usual concern with dietary energy.

Adequacy of Calorie and Protein Intake

The estimates relate directly to the actual calorie and protein consumption information using the food weighment method and Nutritive Value of Indian Foods (see Appendix-1). The analysis is carried out in terms of per consumer unit (CU) by dividing the total nutrient intake by the number of consumer units in the household. This would be a reliable strategy to measure households' nutritional adequacy.

The level of 2400 calories for energy and 42gm for protein, is taken as the mean requirement.[26] If in a given household the average daily intake of calorie/protein (per CU) is found to be equal or above this 'mean' level, then the household would be considered to be food secured.

Tables 20 and 21 present respectively calorie and protein intake composition of MF, NFW and LAL households classified by headships. These enable comparisons to establish relationship between headship of the household's and nutrient intake. The data for V_1 and V_2 of Sivaganga district shows that the mean *calorie intake* is the maximum for FHH. In MF households, the highest consumption is made by FHH (2315 kcal. in V_1 and 2251 kcal. in V_2). In the NFW category in, V_1 the mean calorie consumption is higher for MHH (2327 kcal) than JHH (2263 kcal.) and in V_2, MHH calorie consumption is higher. Among the LAL households in both the study villages of Sivaganga district female-headed households are found to be better than JHH and MHH, in terms of calorie consumption.

The data for V_1 of Cuddalore district also records the over all mean consumption higher for FHH. In V_2 also the mean intake is higher for FHH. A study made by Basiotis et al. (1983)[27] also found the energy and other nutrient intakes significantly greater in FHH and JHH than MHH.

A comparative analysis of calorie intake by different household categories shows that it is higher for MF and NFW categories than LAL category. This is also confirmed by comparing further the question of actual intake of the households with the mean requirement set (2400 Kcal). In Sivaganga District, of the 60 households, 24 are food secured households (13 in V_1 and 11 in V_2) aggregating 46 per cent. Category-wise analysis shows that 45 per cent of the MF households, 50 per cent of the NFW category, and 25 per cent of the LAL category are food secured with respect to calorie intake. But in Cuddalore district, only 22 households (12 in V_1 and 10 in V_2) are found to be food secured aggregating 37 per cent. Only two LAL households are found to be consuming in excess of the mean requirement. Category-wise, the food

Table 20
Headship wise Calorie Intake of Sample Households

Category		FHH			JHH			MHH		
		Min	*Max*	*Mean*	*Min*	*Max*	*Mean*	*Min*	*Max*	*Mean*
Sivaganga District										
V_1	MF 5	2228	2460	2315	1936	2448	2268	2044	2253	2149
	NFW 5	2020	2590	2307	2130	2570	2263	2160	2583	2327
	LAL 3	2120	2532	2253	1920	2490	2262	1870	1950	1910
Overall	13	2020	2590	2291	1920	2570	2264	1870	2583	2128
V_2	MF 4	2037	2531	2286	1794	2477	2082	1794	2343	2023
	NFW 5	1846	2545	2284	2096	2430	2279	2360	2420	2390
	LAL 2	2050	2440	2205	1780	2530	2114	1890	1890	1890
Overall	11	1846	2545	2251	1780	2530	2163	1794	2420	2104
Cuddalore District										
V_1	MF 6	2034	2578	2289	1833	2562	2143	1676	2521	2022
	NFW 5	2470	2470	2470	2330	2520	2407	1860	2480	2108
	LAL 1	2310	2310	2310	1940	2490	2245	1630	1990	1834
Overall	12	2034	2578	2293	1833	2562	2276	1630	2521	1955
V_2	MF 5	2084	2400	2242	1846	2482	2116	1643	2420	2041
	NFW 4	2160	2590	2405	2300	2450	2366	2200	2290	2231
	LAL 1	1430	2420	1800	1810	1980	1883	1470	2170	1762
Overall	10	1430	2590	2156	1810	2482	2121	1470	2420	2014

Source: Computed

Figures in bold letters denote number of food secured households.
FHH-Female Headed Household JHH- Joint Headed Household.
MHH-Male Headed Household.

Table 21
Headship wise Protein Intake of Sample Households

Sivaganga District										
		FHH			*JHH*			*MHH*		
Category		*Min*	*Max*	*Mean*	*Min*	*Max*	*Mean*	*Min*	*Max*	*Mean*
V_1	MF 7	44.6	60.9	48.8	41.2	47.8	46.1	41.1	55.6	48.1
NFW7	50.0	60.8	53.8	38.8	55.0	47.6	33.5	55.7	42.0	
	LAL 5	35.4	50.8	47.1	40.0	51.8	44.1	36.7	41.0	38.8
Overall	19	35.4	60.8	49.9	38.8	57.8	46.5	33.5	55.7	42.8
V_2	MF 7	45.7	51.8	48.2	33.4	50.0	44.3	39.1	47.7	43.4
	NFW 7	40.0	57.0	50.9	41.0	55.0	49.4	47.5	51.4	49.4
	LAL 4	42.2	51.4	45.2	34.1	52.0	43.2	40.0	40.0	40.0
Overall	18	40.0	57.0	46.6	33.4	55.0	45.7	39.1	51.4	44.6
Cuddalore District										
V_1	MF 6	44.1	48.2	46.1	39.3	55.3	45.7	35.1	45.2	41.2
	NFW 7	55.6	55.6	55.6	44.6	58.8	53.5	41.0	49.6	45.3
	LAL 5	46.0	50.0	46.0	31.5	47.5	40.7	32.0	44.7	37.5
Overall	18	43.1	55.6	48.2	31.5	58.8	46.4	32.0	49.6	41.3
V_2	MF 6	45.6	53.5	49.5	41.7	51.8	46.6	31.8	49.6	42.3
	NFW 7	40.0	64.0	55.1	49.7	52.9	51.7	41.0	56.8	51.2
	LAL 3	30.2	41.5	34.3	35.1	43.1	38.6	30.1	41.7	35.8
Overall	16	30.2	64.0	47.3	35.1	52.9	45.7	30.1	56.8	42.3

Source: Computed.
Figures in bold letters denote number of food secured households.
FHH-Female Headed Household JHH- Joint Headed Household.
MHH-Male Headed Household.

secured households are 55 per cent, 45 per cent and 10 per cent respectively for MF, NFW and LAL households.

While studying protein intake computations, it is known that most of the households manage to consume the mean protein requirement of 42 gm per consumption unit and achieve protein adequacy. In Sivaganga district, the over all picture for V_1 shows that the mean *protein intake* is higher for FHH (49.9gm) followed by JHH (46.5gm). In the case of FHH of NFW category, protein consumption is found to be in excess of the mean requirement. In V_2 of Sivaganga district the higher mean intake of protein is by FHH (46.6 gm). It is interesting to note that in NFW category households MHH are much better in protein consumption for their mean intake is shown to be 49.4 gm.

Households in Cuddalore district exhibit consistently higher intake of proteins irrespective of category and headship. The minimum consumption is 55.6 gm. in the FHH of NFW category in V_1; even in the JHH of the same category the mean intake is 53.5 gm. The mean intake of is seen to show protein lower co-efficient of variation, especially for JHH, in all categories of households showing higher mean intake along with consistency.

The nutritionally secured households in terms of protein consumption are found in 37 households (19 in V_1 and 18 in V_2) of Sivaganga district, accounting for 62 per cent of the sample population. Category-wise data shows that 70 per cent of the MF and NFW households and 45 per cent in LAL households are nutritionally secured. In Cuddalore District a total of 34 households (18in V_1 -and 16 in V_2) are considered secured which account for 57 per cent of the total respondents. Category-wise, 60 per cent in MF category, 70 per cent in NFW and 40 per cent in LAL category are secured in protein intake.

Analysis of nutrition adequacy status of households reveal that majority of households are insecure with regard to calorie intake rather than protein intake. A comparison of mean per capita consumption with household headship leads to the affirmed conclusion that female headed households are much better than male headed households in terms in nutrient consumption (Calorie/Protein). Majority of LAL households is recorded to be deficient in nutrition adequacy status both in terms of calorie and protein intake. This deficiency is mainly due to their lower economic status and this finding confirms the results of Thimmayamma's study.[28] The extent of deficits in calorie/protein is an endorsement of the leading manifestation of malnutrition.

Proximate Variables for Food Security

The observed variability in the intake of nutrients among all households in different categories and household pattern prompted this researcher to focus on the important socio-economic factors determining the nutrient-intake. Headship-wise information for proximate variables such as per day per capita Income (PPCI), per day per capita expenditure (PPCE), per day per capita expenditure on food (PPCEF) were computed and are reported in Tables 22, 23 and 24. Family size and mother's education and nutrient intake are laid out as they are seen to allow causal analysis for identifying follow-up steps to reduce food insecurity. Average propensity to consume (APC) is also found out for the sample households dividing their average annual total income of households by total expenditure.

The findings show the existence of a positive relationship between PPCI and PPCEF. Empirical literatures provide conclusive evidence that income is a major determinant of household food expenditure,[29-30] and expenditure greatly influencing calorie intake.[31] The consumption expenditure is maximum for MF households followed by NFW households. It is minimum in LAL households. It could also be seen that for increased income, the food expenditure level also rises but the proportion of income spent on food is seen to decline.

Analysis shows that there are households with adequate expenditure but with depleted level of nutrition, while there are also households with comparatively lower expenditure showing higher level of nutrition. These discrepancies are seen to persist irrespective of household headship. What is really intriguing is that, despite being characterized as MF landholders,

Table 22
Proximate Variables and Nutrient Intake Levels-FHH

Category		*PPCI*	*PPCE*	*APC*	*PPCEF*	*PCCI*	*PCPI*
Sivaganga District							
V_1	MF	19.1	21.4	1.13	12.3 (64.3)	2315	48.8
	NFW	13.7	16.1	1.17	8.6 (63.4)	2307	53.8
	LAL	12.0	13.4	1.11	7.9 (66.6)	2253	47.1
V_2	MF	21.4	23.1	1.10	15.1 (70.0)	2286	48.2
	NFW	11.3	14.8	1.28	8.9 (79.0)	2284	50.9
	LAL	10.4	13.2	1.27	7.7 (74.0)	2205	45.2
Cuddalore District							
V_1	MF	17.1	18.2	1.09	11.4 (66.6)	2289	46.1
	NFW	16.9	18.0	1.00	9.8 (58.0)	2470	55.6
	LAL	16.1	17.4	1.11	10.9 (67.7)	2310	46.0
V_2	MF	13.8	16.8	1.24	10.7 (77.5)	2242	49.5
	NFW	17.1	15.5	0.97	10.0 (58.8)	2405	55.1
	LAL	9.5	11.8	1.26	8.5 (89.4)	1800	34.3

Source: Computed.
Figure in parentheses denote % of income on food
PPCI–Per day Per Capita Income (Rs)
PPCE–Per day Per Capita Expenditure (Rs)
APC–Average Propensity to Consume
PCEF–Per day Per Capita Expenditure on Food (Rs)
PCCI–Per Capita Calorie Intake (kcal per day)
PCPI–Per Capita Protein Intake (gm per day)

having comparatively high PPCI, these respondents are often calorie deficient. NFW households with comparatively low PPCI than MF category households are nutrition efficient (managing the household with better priority). The underlying assumption is the inappropriate allocation of expenditure on

Table 23
Proximate Variables and Nutrient Intake Levels-JHH

Sivaganga District

Category		*PPCI*	*PPCE*	*APC*	*PPCEF*	*PCCI*	*PCPI*
V_1	MF	20.5	21.2	1.05	13.5 (65.8)	2268	46.1
	NFW	11.6	12.6	1.10	7.9 (68.1)	2263	47.6
	LAL	11.4	13.0	1.15	8.0 (70.1)	2262	44.1
V_2	MF	15.4	15.8	1.01	9.3 (63.6)	2082	44.3
	NFW	12.0	14.9	1.24	8.5 (71.6)	2279	45.4
	LAL	8.7	10.7	1.24	6.5 (75.8)	2114	43.2
Cuddalore District							
V_1	MF	20.0	20.6	1.04	13.8 (68.8)	2143.3	45.7
	NFW	13.4	15.5	1.16	9.5 (70.8)	2407.5	50.5
	LAL	11.4	13.6	1.21	8.8 (77.1)	2245	40.7
V_2	MF	14.2	16.8	1.20	10.7 (75.3)	2116.5	46.6
	NFW	10.8	13.2	1.23	8.8 (82.1)	2366	51.7
	LAL	9.3	11.7	1.27	7.8 (83.8)	1883.3	38.6

Source: Computed.
Figure in parentheses denote % of income on food
PPCI–Per day Per Capita Income (Rs)
PPCE–Per day Per Capita Expenditure (Rs)
APC–Average Propensity to Consume
PCEF–Per day Per Capita Expenditure on Food (Rs)
PCCI–Per Capita Calorie Intake (kcal per day)
PCPI–Per Capita Protein Intake (gm per day)

items of consumption, thus depriving a balanced diet although the over all expenditure level of these households can afford and ensure such a diet. A similar observation is that the food expenditure (PPCEF) made by LAL category of V_1 and V_2 of Sivaganga district is shown to be lower than that of their

Table 24
Proximate Variables and Nutrient Intake Levels-MHH

Category		*PPCI*	*PPCE*	*APC*	*PPCEF*	*PCCI*	*PCPI*
Sivaganga District							
V_1	MF	28.4	23.0	0.81	14.5 (51.7)	2149	48.1
	NFW	11.3	13.9	1.24	8.7 (76.9)	2327	42.0
	LAL	8.4	11.0	1.32	7.6 (90.4)	1910	38.8
V_2	MF	10.0	12.4	1.26	8.9 (89.0)	2023	43.4
	NFW	13.0	14.6	1.13	9.0 (69.2)	2390	49.4
	LAL	8.2	9.8	1.20	7.9 (96.0)	1890	40.0
Cuddalore District							
V_1	MF	12.7	15.0	1.19	10.1 (79.5)	2022	41.2
	NFW	11.6	14.7	1.28	8.61 (74.0)	2108	45.3
	LAL	9.7	12.1	1.27	8.0 (82.4)	1834	37.52
V_2	MF	15.9	18.2	1.16	12.0 (75.4)	2041	42.3
	NFW	12.6	16.1	1.27	10.6 (84.0)	2231	51.2
	LAL	8.2	11.3	1.38	7.7 (93.9)	1762	35.8

Source: Computed.
Figure in parentheses denote % of income on food
PPCI–Per day Per Capita Income (Rs)
PPCE–Per day Per Capita Expenditure (Rs)
APC–Average Propensity to Consume
PCEF–Per day Per Capita Expenditure on Food (Rs)
PCCI–Per Capita Calorie Intake (kcal per day)
PCPI–Per Capita Protein Intake (gm per day)

counterparts in V_1 and V_2 of Cuddalore district but with better nutrition intake. In this context it has to be the pointed out that there are other factors which influence the level and consumption of food intake, and so one cannot make the generalisation that income and expenditure alone promote intake of nutrients.

However, prevalence of under nutrition is acute in LAL households mainly due to their low access to food. Low level of income causing ineffective consumption of nutrition is confirmed in another study.[32] The phenomenon of deficit income and excess expenditure is shown by APC. Except for NFW households with FHH (in V_2 of Cuddalore district) and MF households with MHH (in V_I of Sivaganga district) the APC ratio for all others is shown to be less than one (0.97 and 0.87 respectively). Borrowed money is mostly directed to consumption expenditure. Women explained the troubles they faced to balanced price-wise and income and the resultant nutrient deficiencies or borrowing is inevitable for their survival. APC is seen to be very high in Cuddalore district and it is the maximum for LAL households. Another example of in probable expenditure is that some households spend more on non–food items of consumption for instance, pan and alcohol and consequently on medicine, and less on nutritious food.

The evaluation on the relationship of family size with nutrient intake (Table 25) reveals that family size is closely but negatively correlated with nutrient intake. Economy of family size in food consumption is found to be substantial. Family size is an important explanatory variable of food consumption and its negative correlation with current food security (food adequacy) was empirically proved in the previous section. Findings show that in Cuddalore district, the mean intake of calorie and protein is found to be low for LAL households belonging to medium and large family. More than the absolute size of the family, women respondents said, the high dependency ratio (one or two earning members and many dependents) put the households to a high degree of exposure to risk and susceptibility to food insecurity. From the field survey, it is also found out that in some extended medium size families, the number of earners are also more, providing additional income which is sufficient enough spend on food and this minimizes the risk of food insecurity in these households. It correlates well with the findings of Shama (1992).[33]

Table 25
Family Size wise Mean Nutrient Intake of Sample Households

Sivaganga District							
		Small <4		*Medium 5-7*		*Large 8+*	
Category		*PCCI*	*PCPI*	*PCCI*	*PCPI*	*PCCI*	*PCPI*
V_1	MF	2344	54.9	2090	45.1	-	-
	NFW	2478	57.2	2220	44.7	-	-
	LAL	2290	47.1	2217	39.4	-	-
V_2	MF	2283	46.9	2005	41.4	-	-
	NFW	2377	51.5	2215	48.7	-	-
	LAL	2423	49.2	1990	42.5	-	-
Cuddalore District							
V_1	MF	2372	47.0	2022	41.4	1809	38.75
	NFW	2317	51.5	2241	48.0	-	-
	LAL	2188	46.3	1936	39.7	-	-
V_2	MF	2222	46.8	2166	45.9	-	-
	NFW	2360	52.1	2337	53.7	-	-
	LAL	2000	38.0	1683	34.9	-	-

Source: Computed.
PCCI–Per Capita Calorie Intake (kcal per day)
PCPI–Per Capita Protein Intake (gm per day).

Women's Coping strategies

During food shortage, it is only the females of the households who often strengthen the coping mechanism. Women's Ex–anti coping includes strategies for maintaining consumption such as saving grains (SG), Livestock Rearing (LR) and Home Garden (HG). With regard to their Ex–Post coping, strategies such as Borrowing (SB), Gathering of Food (GF), Selling of Livestock (SL) and Selling of other Articles (SoA). Table 26 explains the main food chain strategies adopted by women in the study villages in order to secure food for their families in the lean season.

The data shows that almost all MF households in both the districts, make effort to save grains since it is produced by them in their own lands. Though LAL households use this strategy to cope with food insecurity, they reported that, very often,

Table 26
Women's Coping Strategies for Food Shortage

Sivaganga District

						Ex-post Coping Strategy				
		Village 1					*Village 2*			
Category	*Ex-Anti CS*	*SB*	*GF*	*SL*	*SOA*	*Ex-Anti CS*	*SB*	*GF*	*SL*	*SOA*
MF	SG (10)	6	10	2	2	SG (10)	8	7	4	0
	LR (8)	5	8	2	2	LR (9)	7	6	9	0
	HG (4)	2	4	1	1	HG (4)	1	3	3	0
NFW	SG (1)	1	0	0	0	SG (5)	5	1	2	1
	LR (7)	7	5	6	1	LR (7)	7	3	5	1
	HG (4)	1	2	1	0	HG (4)	5	3	1	1
LAL	SG (4)	4	4	4	1	SG (5)	5	5	5	0
	LR (10)	10	10	7	2	LR (10)	10	9	7	0
	HG (4)	4	4	1	1	HG (2)	2	2	0	0
Over all	SG (15)	11	14	6	3	SG (20)	18	13	11	0
	LR (25)	22	23	15	5	LR (26)	24	18	21	3
	HG (12)	7	10	3	2	HG (10)	8	8	4	2

Contd...

Cuddalore District										
MF	SG (10)	9	1	4	4	SG (9)	9	4	5	5
	LR (9)	7	1	4	6	LR (5)	5	2	5	3
	HG (4)	1	0	1	1	HG (2)	2	1	2	1
NFW	SG (2)	2	0	2	0	SG (4)	4	0	3	0
	LR (7)	7	2	6	0	LR (7)	7	2	3	0
	HG (4)	4	0	3	0	HG (3)	3	3	1	0
LAL	SG (4)	4	4	4	1	SG (5)	5	5	3	1
	LR (10)	8	5	5	1	LR (5)	5	5	3	1
	HG (1)	1	1	1	1	HG (2)	2	2	2	1
Over All	SG (16)	15	5	10	5	SG (18)	18	9	11	6
	LR (26)	25	8	15	7	LR (17)	17	9	11	4
	HG (9)	6	1	5	2	HG (7)	7	6	5	2

Source: Computed.
SG–Saving grains, LR–Live stock rearing HG–Home garden.
SB-Sources of Borrowing SL–Sale of live stock, SOA–Sale of other articles.

when presented with a hypothetical scenario of entitlement failure, saved grain would be sold off for some reason. Some few NFW households are found to use this ex-anti coping strategy. In Sivaganga district, 35 households (58 per cent) and in Cuddalore 34 household (56 per cent) use this ex-anti strategy.

Livestock rearing is identified as the most important *Ex-anti coping* strategy to overcome food insecurity by many of the households. During the interview it was found out that households who owned large livestock like milching animals and small livestock like goats were less vulnerable to food insecurity. In case of poultry, they were slaughtered for food in times of hardship. Livestock rearing as an ex-anti coping strategy is seen to adopted by 51 households (85 per cent) and 43 (71 per cent) in both villages of Sivaganga and Cuddalore districts respectively. Of these, less than half of the households had large livestock. Women respondents reported that the potential contribution of livestock to food security was great. Because in few households, these livestock contributed to food security through increased output of livestock and income generated on that might assure access to food. Home garden as an ex-anti coping strategy is adopted by 20 household (33 per cent) in Sivaganga district and only 16 households (26 per cent) in Cuddalore district.

A comparative analysis shows that livestock rearing is a prominent Ex-anti coping strategy in the study area followed by saving grains and home garden. Number of households using these strategies is found to be more in Sivaganga district than in Cuddalore district.

With regard to *Ex-post coping strategies,* the majority of women respondents reported that borrowing from neighbours or relatives is used as a strategy to avoid food shortage at least on a temporary basis. Some LAL women respondents in both the study areas reported that membership in the Self-help Group helped them to borrow money easily to meet their food needs during lean season. Gathering of food is one of the most important ex-post coping strategy for people in Sivaganga district. This strategy is used by only a very few households in Cuddalore district selling of small livestock is also used as an important ex–post coping strategy. Selling of other articles and assets is a very rarely used strategy for households who possess it. It is seen as the last resort to try and cope with food insecurity. The data also shows that in Sivaganga district, out of 35 households use Saving Grains as an ex–anti coping strategy, 29 households use borrowing as an ex–post coping strategy, 27 households adopt gathering of food, 17 households resort to selling of livestock and only three households use selling of articles as an ex–post coping strategy. Out of 51 households, which rear livestock as an ex–anti coping strategy, 46 of them use borrowing as an important coping mechanism followed by gathering of food (41 households) and selling of livestock (36 households). Among households which have home garden (22 households) as an important ex-anti coping strategy, 15 of them use gathered food for home consumption or convert them into cash to purchase food.

In Cuddalore district, borrowing and selling of livestock is considered an important ex–post coping strategy by majority of the households. Some households also make use of selling of articles an important coping mechanism. Women reported that the unplanned responses to coping with unexpected crisis initially involve reduction in their food intake and this might have a negative impact on their health. Livestock, as an important strategy enhancing risk management, and also as an important means of food security is noted by Campbell (1990).[34]

The pay off of women's education in improved welfare is solidly established.[35] The fact that mother's education contributes more than men's education to family nutrition is also proved in an earlier study by Schultz (1989).[36] Table 26 shows that nutrients intake varies by the level of female literacy status. While it is interesting to observe a close positive relation between the variables, a closer look at the data reveals, that in some cases, particularly that of the MF category in V_2 of Sivaganga district, though the level of female literacy increases, it is not accompanied with an increase in the nutrient intake. And this is mainly due to the insufficient per capita income over lapping female literacy causing reduction in food intake.

Table 27

Mean Nutrient Intake of Sample Households According to Mother's Education

Category		Illiterate			Primary			Middle			High school		
		PPCI	PCCI	PCPI	PPCI	PCCI	PCPI	PPCI	PCCI	PCPI	PPCI	PCCI	PCPI
Sivaganga District													
V_1	MF	20.6	2278	47.6	22.5	2090	47.0	18.5	2300	48.5	18.4	2350	60.1
	NFW	13.7	2199	44.0	15.3	2358	50.1	17.1	2543	55.8	-	-	-
	LAL	10.6	2032	42.6	10.2	2180	42.9	13.2	2500	51.3	-	-	-
V_2	MF	19.1	2261	45.4	13.5	2026	45.7	11.6	2281	50.0	-	-	-
	NFW	7.2	1971	43.0	13.1	2325	51.9	14.0	2340	49.8	13.2	2416	53.3
	LAL	10.7	1993	40.1	8.6	2000	42.2	9.8	2500	45.4	-	-	-
Cuddalore District													
V_1	MF	12.8	1884	40.2	16.2	2020	43.5	12.4	2015	42.4	20.7	2485	50.6
	NFW	10.7	1974	43.0	12.1	2345	48.7	15.4	2480	50.8	17.3	2490	58.8
	LAL	10.0	2050	40.1	11.3	1985	38.8	9.9	2400	47.5	-	-	-
V_2	MF	15.0	1936	40.2	13.3	2163	47.3	15.3	2300	51.2	21.4	2360	50.6
	NFW	17.1	2281	53.7	9.5	2274	49.6	15.5	2480	57.7	-	-	-
	LAL	9.7	1878	37.3	6.7	1610	31.8	10.8	2080	43.1	-	-	-

Source: Computed.
PPCI–Per day Per Capita Income (Rs), PCCI–Per Capita Calorie Intake (kcal per day).
PCPI–Per Capita Protein Intake (gm per day).

This explains the reason for why food security is often considered as an issue related to income. In the case of LAL households of the same village, it is seen that even when the PPCI is found to be comparatively low, the nutrient intake is seen to improve as the level of literacy increases. This confirms the assumption that income is a necessary but not a sufficient condition for food security as factors like education of mother certainly contributes to food security. At the same time, minimum level of income is necessary to ensure better nutritional status. The findings of an earlier study by Alderman and Garcia (1995)[37] identify that mother's education has a vital role in the intake of nutrition and balanced diet.

KEY FINDINGS

- Women in Sivaganga district allocate relatively more time in household chores and remunerative activities than Cuddalore district.
- Percentage Share of women's work is the greatest for Food Related Activities (PSFORA) in both the districts.
- Women's access to various resources is limited in both districts. Among them, women in FHH are seen to have better access when the level of resources by score value is compared.
- Awareness about vaccination and immunization is found in women of both study areas. Educated women are found to have some functional knowledge on nutrition.
- Women in Sivaganga district take higher level of participation in decision- making. Women's age, education and their level of access to resources influence positively the level of decision-making in various household matters.
- The Dietary Adequacy Ratio improves as the level of women empowerment increases.
- Over all mean calorie consumption is comparatively higher for FHH. Occupation-wise, calorie consumption is comparatively higher for MF and NFW categories than LAL category.

- When income increases, the food expenditure level also rises but the proportion of income spent on food declines.
- Saving grains is found to be an important ex-anti coping strategy for majority of MF households. Livestock rearing is identified as the most important ex-anti coping strategy of women whereas borrowing is by far the most important ex-post coping strategy for majority of the households in both districts.
- Maternal education contributes to food security.

NOTES AND REFERENCES

1. Safilios-Rotschild, Constantina (1980), "The Role of the Family: A Neglected Aspect of Poverty", *World Bank Staff Working Paper.* No. 403, Washington, D.C., 372.
2. Desai, Sonalde and Devaki Jain (1994), "Maternal Employment and Changes in Family Dynamics: The Social Context of Women's Work in Rural South India", *Population and Development Review,* Vol. 20, No. 1, 115-136.
3. Palmer, Ingrid (1981), "Seasonal Dimensions of Women's Roles", *in Seasonal Dimensions to Rural Poverty.* Institute of Development Studies. Frances Pinter Publication, London: 195-201.
4. B'eiro, Ann-Jacqueline (1984), "The Use of Time Allocation Data in Developing Countries: from Influencing Development Policies to Estimate Energy Requirements", Paper Delivered at the International Research Group on Time Budgets and Social Activities, Helsinki, FAO, Rome, August, 35.
5. Hamilton, Sahni, Barry Popkin and Deborah Spicer (1984), *Women and Nutrition in Third World Countries,* Praeger Press, USA: 143.
6. Prehm, M.S. (1991), "Developing Integrative Methods for Describing Food Production and Consumption Linkages", *Ecology of Food and Nutrition,* Vol. 25, 193-207.
7. Holmboe-Ottensen, Gerd and Margareta Wandel (1985), "The Intra-household Dimension: Opportunities and Limitations for Strategies to Ensure Access to Food." Introducing Nutritional Considerations into Rural Development Programmes with Focus on Agriculture. Report No. 1. A. Theoretical Contribution. Institute of Nutrition Research, University of Oslo: 36.

8. Agarwal, Bina (1994), "Gender and World Development. Command Over Properties: A Critical Gap in Economic Analysis and Policy in South Asia." *World Development*, Vol. 22, No. 10: 1455-78.

9. IFAD (2001). *Rural Poverty Report 2001. The Challenge of Ending Rural Poverty*. Oxford University Press, New Delhi..

10. Duncan, Thomas (1993), "The Distribution of Income and Expenditure Within Household", *Annals of Economics and Statistics*,Vol. 29, 109-35.

11. Cheater, Angela (1981), *Women and Their Participation in Commercial Agricultural Production: The Case of Medium-Scale Freehold in Zimbabwe*. Development and Change, Sage Publications, London.

12. D'Souza, S. and A. L. Bhuia (1982), "Socio-economic Mortality Differentials in a Rural Area of Bangladesh", *Population and Development Review*, Vol. 8, 753-759.

13. Mwanasa, D.M. (1995), "Perspectives on Literacy, Gender and Change, A Case for and Zambia", *British Journal of Sociology of Education*, Vol. 16, No. 4, 495-516.

14. Folbre, Nancy (1986), "Cleaning Home: New Perspectives on Households and Economic Development", *Journal of Development Economics*, Vol. 22: 5-40.

15. Reddy, G. N. (1999), "Social Mobilisation and Empowerment of Women: A Case of Peddamamangataram Village. Multi Country Study", Mission Report, Asian Productivity Organisation, Japan.

16. Reddy, G. N. (2002), *Building Capacities for Sustainable Development*, Krishna Publishers, New Delhi.

17. National Sample Survey Organisation (NSSO), (1996), *Sarvekshana*, Vol. 19, No. 3, 66th Issue January-March. Department of Statistics, Ministry of Planning and Programme Implementation, Government of India, New Delhi.

Consumer units for Age in Complete Years

Age	*0-1*	*1-3*	*4-6*	*7-9*	*10-12*	*13-15*	*16-19*	*20-39*	*40-49*	*50-59*	*60-69*	*≥ 70*
Male	.43	.54	.72	.87	1.03	.97	1.02	1.0	.95	.90	.80	.70
Female	.43	.54	.72	.87	.93	.80	.75	.71	.68	.64	.51	.50

18. Indian Council of Medical Research (1981), *Recommended Dietary Intake for Indians*. I.C.M.R., New Delhi: 58-59.

19. Gopalan, C. (1993), "Variation in Food Consumption Pattern of Population. Towards Better Nutrition: Problems and Policies", N.F.I., Special Report Series, 9: 131-135.

20. Katona–Apte, Judith (1983), "A Socio-cultural Perspective on the Significance of Sex Roles in Agriculture." in *Nutritional Impact of Agricultural Projects*. Papers and Proceedings of a Workshop Held by the UN ACC/Sub-committee on Nutrition: 28-43.

21. Tinker, Irene (1979), "New Technologies for Food Chain Activities: The Imperative of Equity for Women", Office of Women in Development, AID, Washington, D.C.

22. Indian Council of Medical Research (2002), *Nutrient Requirements and Recommended Dietary Allowance for Indians: A Report of the Indian Council of Medical Research*. National Institute of Nutrition, Hyderabad: 11.

23. Shah, C.H., S.D. Savant, B. Sangvi (1983), *Nutrition Gap: An Economic Analysis*, Himalaya Publishing House, Bombay.

24. World Bank (1986), *Poverty and Hunger*. A World Bank Poverty Study, Washington, D.C.

25. Broca, Sumiter and Peter Oram (1991), *Study on the Location of the Poor*. IFPRI, Washington, D.C., Mimeo.

26. Indian Council of Medical Research (1981), *Recommended Dietary Intakes for Indians*. ICMR, New Delhi.

    See also, K.R. Venugopal (1995), "Poor Strategies", *Frontline*, July 28: 15.

27. Basiotis, P.M. Brown, S.R. Johnson, and K.J. Morgan (1983), "Nutrient Availability. Food Cost and Food Stamps", *American Journal of Agricultural Economics*, Vol. 65, 685-93.

28. Thimmayamma, B.V.S, Parvathi Rao and Visweswara Rao (1982), *Socio-economics Status, Diet and Nutrients Adequacies of Different Population Groups in Urban and Rural*. Hyderabad.

29. Brown, M., S. R. Johnson, and R.L. Rizek (1983), "Food Stamps: Program Parameters and Standard of Living for Low Income Households." *Southern Journal of Agricultural Economics*, Vol. 15, No. 4: 43-49.

30. Bunch, K. and L. Hall (1983), "Factors Affecting Nutrient Consumption." Cornel University Agricultural Express Statistical Research Report. No. 83, June 22.

31. Gray, C.W. (1982), "Food Consumption Parameter for Brazil and Their Application to Food Policy", Research Report 32. IFPRI, Washington, D.C.

32. Davis, C.G. (1982), "Linkages between Socio-economic Characteristics, Food Expenditure Patterns and Nutritional Status of Low Income Households: A Critical Review", *American Journal of Agricultural Economics,* Vol. 64, 1017-25.

33. Shama, R.P. (1992), "Monitoring Access to Food and Household Security", *Food, Nutrition and Agriculture,* Vol. 2, No. 4.

34. Campbell, D. J. (1990), "Strategies for Coping with Severe Food Deficits in Rural Africa: A Review of Literature", *Food and Food Ways,* Vol. 4, No. 2, 143-162.

35. Caldwell, J.C. (1979), "Education as a Factor in Mortality Decline", Population Studies, 33.

36. Schultz, T.P. (1989), "Women in Development: Objectives, Framework and Policy Intervention", *Working Paper* No. 200, World Bank PPR, Washington, D.C.

37. Alderman, H. and M. Garcia (1995), "Food Security and Health Security. Explaining the Levels of Nutrition in Pakistan", *Policy Research Working Paper,* No. 865.

7

Perspectives of Individual Food Security

Exchange entitlements and women empowerment were seen in the earlier chapters, to be synergising rural household food security and influencing the coping strategies. Further, household nutritional security is seen to be the interface of individual food and nutrition security. An assessment of individual nutrition security is needed to identify appropriate policies for nutritional security of rural households. Of the several indicators[1] for the assessment of individual nutritional status, the researcher found the Dietary Intake and Anthropometric Indicators as the most efficient, highly reliable and best suited approach to the present study.

In this chapter, the analysis of individual nutritional status is presented under three divisions. First, *'adequacy'* of nutrition in terms of nutrients intake (Calorie and Protein) of individuals is assessed to compare the relative positions of individuals according to age and sex and to explore the causes for nutritional poverty. Second, the empirical work based on *'equity'* dimension of nutrition which is one of the determinants of intra-household food allocation is discussed. Last, *'efficiency'* of nutrition (individual's growth status) through the 'incidence' of malnutrition arising from nutritional deficiency is analysed by Anthropometric Measurements. Growth "faltering" is clearly identified as a phenomenon associated with the perils of "weaning" (insufficient nutrients intake).

ADEQUACY PERSPECTIVE OF INDIVIDUAL FOOD SECURITY

Diet surveys are helpful to assess whether people eat quantitatively and qualitatively. Diet quality can be assessed directly (units of nutrients consumed) or indirectly (expenditure level on food). A more reliable test of nutritional discrimination between the sexes can be performed by using the calorie and protein share in place of the food share.[2] The reason for this is that an assessment of calorie and protein consumption is a more precise indicator of nutritional attainment than an assessment of food expenditures. Assessments of nutritional attainment by food expenditures would embody price information that may not be welfare relevant because higher costing foods do not necessarily convey nutritional value than lower costing food [3]; level of expenditure cannot capture the full and true picture of the way resources are allocated within households. So, it is thought that direct assessment is the reliable method to find out the inadequacies in the nutrient intake of individuals.

Ensuring nutrition security is a step ahead to food security, while the latter can be achieved through an intake of a single staple cereal like rice or wheat in a bolus, the former will demand besides cereals, an adequate supply of other foods such as pulses, vegetables, fruits and milk.

Measurement of Nutritional Adequacy

Nutritional Adequacy is defined as the level of intake that will balance energy requirements, and it ensures that an individual has a body size and composition and level of physical activity consistent with long-term good health and the performance of economically necessary and socially desirable tasks.[4] This definition will form the basis of many of the calculations presented here and the computations are performed in accordance with accepted ICMR standards to derive all values.

A key element in this survey was the direct measurement of individuals' food intake of all household members. They numbered 574. Because of the measurement errors involved in the recall and expenditure methods[5], the researcher used the weighment method, i.e., foods consumed over 24 hours are weighed.[6] For a sample of 120 households, individual food consumption data for a twenty-four hour period was collected using a food-weighing method for each of all the household members (279 individuals in Sivaganga district and 295 individuals in Cuddalore district). Documenting the ingredients of every dish prepared also was done. In addition, household members were asked to provide information about food they ate outside the household. The calorie and protein content of each individual's diet were calculated using the food value tables available for India for the various food items consumed (see Appendix-1).

The categorization of individuals into protein and calorie adequacy was done with respect to variations in average consumption. An individual is considered as consuming adequate calories (Kcal) if the intakes are equal to or above the Recommended Dietary Allowance (RDA) for the corresponding age, weight, sex and activity (see Appendix-2 and Appendix-3), and this is marked by positive (+) sign. If the intake is below the requirement level negative (-) sign is marked. Protein adequacy is assessed in the following method. Requirements for protein upto 18 years are derived by a two-step process as indicated by ICMR.[7] First, the level of requirement according to age is chosen and next, the actual amount is calculated by multiplying with the ratio of the actual body weight to the standard body weight. For adults the standard requirements are used (see Appendix-4).

Protein-Calorie Adequacy Status

By using these cut-off levels, the protein-calorie adequacy of the individuals is assessed more accurately by the distribution of individuals and their categorization into the following groups:

P^+C^+: Protein Adequacy and Calorie Adequacy

P^+C^-: Protein Adequacy and Calorie Inadequacy

$P^- C^+$: Protein Inadequacy and Calorie Adequacy

$P^- C^-$: Protein Inadequacy and Calorie Inadequacy

The Protein-Calorie Adequacy status in *Sivaganga district* (Table 1) shows that 30.7 per cent of females and 34.0 per cent of males have adequate calorie and protein intake ($P^+ C^+$), while 20.0 per cent of females and 24.0 per cent of males have inadequacy in both protein and calories ($P^- C^-$). 29.3 per cent of females and 20.0 per cent of males are adequate in protein and inadequate in calories ($P^+ C^-$), whereas 20.0 per cent of females and 22.0 per cent of males are inadequate in protein and adequate in calorie ($P^- C^+$). In the female population, the percentage of deficiency in calories is seen to be greater (49.3 per cent) than their male counterparts (38.0 per cent). But the difference is less significant. It can be comprehended that a little less than half of the sample population in Sivaganga district suffers from calorie deficiency. Protein deficiency is seen in 52.0 per cent of males whereas this is only 40.0 per cent in females. Protein adequacy status appears to be better than calorie adequacy status for females. It should be taken into account that when calories are deficient, the body will use protein to compensate and produce energy which is necessary for body maintenance.[8] This continuum will end in greater calorie gap leading to under-nutrition and ultimately resulting in weight loss.

Age-wise comparison shows that children in the age group 16-18 are relatively better off in terms of nutrient adequacy status, for in this age group, only 9.1 per cent of females and 10.0 per cent of males are found to be inadequate in protein and calorie intake ($P^- C^-$). This may be due to the reason that with increasing age, the children are provided with relatively more food. And it is also observed in some of the households, girls take over cooking responsibilities and their nibbling while preparing food is also found to be one of the reasons for their better-off position in term of nutritional adequacy status. The observation made in this table does not support the contention that rural Indian women are more undernourished than men. Men are equally malnourished and this finding agrees well with the findings of NNMB data for rural Indians.[9]

Table 1
Protein–Calorie Adequacy Status in Sivaganga District

Age (in years)	*No.*	*Percentage of Sample Female Population* P^+C^+	P^+C^-	P^-C^+	P^-C^-	P^-	C^-
1-3	2	50.0	50.0	-	-	-	50.0
		(1)	(1)				(1)
4-6	6	33.3	50.0	-	16.7	16.7	66.7
		(2)	(3)		(1)	(1)	(4)
7-9	7	14.3	42.8	14.2	28.6	42.8	71.4
		(1)	(3)	(1)	(2)	(3)	(5)
10-12	14	21.4	21.4	21.4	35.8	57.2	57.2
		(3)	(3)	(3)	(5)	(8)	(8)
13-15	15	20.0	6.6	33.4	40.0	73.0	47.6
		(3)	(1)	(5)	(6)	(11)	(7)
16-18	11	54.5	9.1	27.3	9.1	36.4	18.2
		(6)	(1)	(3)	(1)	(4)	(2)
Adults	95	31.5	33.7	19.0	15.8	34.8	49.5
(Moderate)		(30)	(32)	(18)	(15)	(33)	(47)
Overall	150	30.7	29.3	20.0	20.0	40.0	49.3
		(46)	(44)	(30)	(30)	(60)	(74)
Age (in years)		*Percentage of Sample Male Population*					
1-3	6	33.3	33.3	-	33.3	33.3	66.6
		(2)	(2)		(2)	(2)	(4)
4-6	3	33.3	-	33.3	33.3	66.6	33.3
		(1)		(1)	(1)	(2)	(1)
7-9	6	33.3	-	33.3	33.3	66.6	33.3
		(2)		(2)	(2)	(4)	(2)
10-12	9	33.3	11.1	22.2	33.3	55.5	44.4
		(3)	(1)	(2)	(3)	(5)	(4)
13-15	9	11.3	11.0	33.3	44.4	77.7	55.5
		(1)	(1)	(3)	(4)	(7)	(5)
16-18	10	40.0	20.0	30.0	10.0	40.0	30.0
		(4)	(2)	(3)	(1)	(4)	(3)
Adults	86	36.0	14.0	29.0	21.0	50.0	35.0
(Moderate)		(31)	(12)	(25)	(18)	(43)	(30)
Overall	129	34.0	14.0	28.0	24.0	52.0	38.0
		(44)	(18)	(36)	(31)	(67)	(49)

Source: Computed (Figures in parentheses denote number of persons).

The Protein-Calorie adequacy status in *Cuddalore district* (Table 2) records that 29.0 per cent of females and 29.8 per cent of males have adequate nutrient intake (P^+C^+). The inadequacy status (P^-C^-) shows higher percentage for females (30.0 per cent) than males (22.9 per cent). Protein adequacy and calorie inadequacy (P^+C^-) is noticed in 22.0 per cent in females and 19.3 per cent in males. Protein inadequacy and calorie adequacy (P^-C^+) is found in 19.0 per cent of females and 28.0 per cent of males. Age-wise comparison of females and males shows that adult population is better off in their nutritional status than children. The age-group 16-18 suffers from nutritional deficiency because majority of them belong to low income households and LAL category, where the dietary diversity is lacking. Nutritional status is found to be inadequate to a greater extent for females than male in this districts.

A comparative analysis of both the districts shows females in Sivaganga district are better-off than the females in Cuddalore district in terms of nutritional status. Status of women in the household or their empowerment at the household level is seen to be an indirect determinant of nutritional well-being of women in the family.

From the analysis, it is found that people in the study area suffer from calorie gap to a greater extent than protein gap. It is in confirmation with the earlier findings in this study that majority of the households are secured in terms of mean protein requirement rather than mean calorie requirement. In India the bottleneck in the diets of poor economic groups is calories and not proteins.[10] Dietary habits of LAL households are traditional and poor. The calorie gap observed in them may be due to the low calorie density of their diets consisting of inadequate fats and oils. In the previous chapter also (Chapter 6, Table 14), surveyed data showed low dietary adequacy for majority of households and food consumption frequency data also indicated that in most of the households intake of protein-rich, fat-rich food (derived from animal sources) are very low. The restricting factor, of course, is the matter of price, for their economic conditions would not allow them to purchase these items. Concerns about the nutritional quality of foods are

Table 2
Protein–Calorie Adequacy Status in Cuddalore District

Age (in years)	*No.*	*Percentage of Sample Female Population* P^+C^+	P^+C^-	P^-C^+	P^-C^-	P^-	C^-
1-3	5	-	20.0	20.0	60.0	80.0	80.0
			(1)	*(1)*	*(3)*	*(4)*	*(4)*
4-6	10	20.0	30.0	-	50.0	50.0	80.0
		(2)	*(3)*		*(5)*	*(5)*	*(8)*
7-9	8	25.0	37.5	12.5	25.0	37.5	62.5
		(2)	*(3)*	*(1)*	*(2)*	*(3)*	*(5)*
10-12	13	30.7	7.7	15.4	46.2	61.5	53.8
		(4)	*(1)*	*(2)*	*(6)*	*(8)*	*(7)*
13-15	10	30.0	20.0	20.0	30.0	50.0	50.0
		(3)	*(2)*	*(2)*	*(3)*	*(5)*	*(5)*
16-18	7	-	28.5	28.5	43.0	71.5	71.5
			(2)	*(2)*	*(3)*	*(5)*	*(5)*
Adults	81	35.0	21.0	22.0	22.0	44.0	43.0
(Moderate)		*(28)*	*(17)*	*(18)*	*(18)*	*(36)*	*(35)*
Overall	134	29.0	22	19.0	30.0	49.2	51.4
		(39)	*(29)*	*(26)*	*(40)*	*(66)*	*(69)*
Age (in years)		*Percentage of Sample Male Population*					
1-3	8	12.5	12.5	25	50.0	75	62.5
		(1)	*(1)*	*(2)*	*(4)*	*(6)*	*(5)*
4-6	11	18.0	46.0	18.0	18.0	36.0	64.0
		(2)	*(5)*	*(2)*	*(2)*	*(4)*	*(7)*
7-9	5	-	40.0	-	60.0	60.0	100
			(2)		*(3)*	*(3)*	*(5)*
10-12	13	38.4	15.4	23.1	23.1	46.0	38.0
		(5)	*(2)*	*(3)*	*(3)*	*(6)*	*(5)*
13-15	13	23.1	15.4	30.7	30.7	62.0	46.0
		(3)	*(2)*	*(4)*	*(4)*	*(8)*	*(6)*
16-18	17	23.5	11.8	52.9	11.8	64.7	23.6
		(4)	*(2)*	*(9)*	*(2)*	*(11)*	*(4)*
Adults	94	35.0	18.0	27.0	20.0	47.0	38.0
(Moderate)		*(33)*	*(17)*	*(25)*	*(19)*	*(44)*	*(36)*
Overall	161	29.8	19.3	28.0	22.9	50.9	42.2
		(48)	*(31)*	*(45)*	*(37)*	*(82)*	*(68)*

Source: Computed.
Figures in parentheses denote number of persons.

secondary to them than the more basic issue of "having something to eat".

EQUITY PERSPECTIVE OF INDIVIDUAL FOOD SECURITY

(Testing of Third Hypothesis)

The foregone 'Adequacy' analysis confirmed the prevalence of inadequate nutrient intake among individuals in the sample population discriminatively in age and gender. The existence of these gender and age bias needs to be examined in terms of the intra-household allocation of food.

Studies on sample South Asian population (Carloni 1981; Leslie 1991)[11-12] found that the allocation of food among the family members of the household is unequal disfavouring the females (Sex-bias) and disfavouring the children (Age-bias), is also noted in the studies made by Sen 1981[13] and Abdulla et al. 1985.[14] Though superficially this may seem a specific problem of less endowed households, at deeper levels, it has been found that discrimination against females is not necessarily a response to resource-scarce situation. Even in privileged families, some girls are malnourished because of the distribution of food within the households.[15] This malnutrition is an outcome of maldistribution of food among family members.

Contradictory studies that women and children receive equitable share of household food are also available from other regions of the world.[16]

Studies carried out in developing countries indicate that women take direct and major responsibilities for the allocation of food to household members, particularly for infants and small children than do males.[17] In this context, in the present study, using the spot observation method and an in-depth interview, women respondents were asked a series of questions with regard to the criteria used in the food distribution within households. In all surveyed households, it was found that food distribution is done by females only. In 75 per cent of the households, food was cooked and distributed by wives and in 22 per cent of households the daughter or daughter-in-law performed the chores and 5 per cent of the households reported that it was done by mother-in-law. All members in the household were reported to have received the same food.

Measurement of Intra-household Food Allocation

In the interview with the respondents it was understood that in Sivaganga district, parents in general never exercise any partial treatment while distributing food. They do not engage in selective underfeeding of particular child even though 10 per cent of the households in Sivaganga district and 40 per cent in Cuddalore district expressed their preferences for having male child in the family, which is just a reflection of embedded cultural preference only. It should never be understood as a trend towards discriminatory allocation of food to household members. Usually when girls are in charge of cooking responsibility, they are able to consume more share (eating while cooking) and this helps them to improve their nutritional status. This was, as reported earlier, observed in the villages of Sivaganga district.

In Cuddalore district, men in MF and NFW households were favoured with large proportion of available food especially the quality food. The women respondents from the households justified this preferential treatment saying that men are the major contributors of household income. Whenever protein rich food like meat, fish and milk are bought, a considerable portion is given to men and male children. This observation shows that discrimination, though small, is not driven entirely by cultural factors, on the other hand, it was also on their potential economic roles.[18]

Traditional meal habits such as separation of males and females, the order of serving were not found in the study area. But using a common pot is reported in some LAL households in Cuddalore district which may cause age-bias against small children. In majority of households it was women who eat last and least. Enquiry was also made to the respondents about the skipped meals if any in the previous week from the day of interview. Women in LAL households affirmed that they skipped meals in times of shortage of cooked food. They control their hunger by reducing their own consumption but not the consumption of other members. None of the respondents admitted allowing their children to go hungry. Such sacrificing roles by women explain that the imbalanced distribution sometimes is self-imposed due to economic reasons, leading to scarcity and poverty. Another factor contributing to an individuals uneven intake within a family is the taste and preference of individuals towards certain food types.

The specific indicator the researcher uses to analyse the age and gender bias is the 'Relative Nutrient Allocation' (RNA) of individuals within the family. The basic dependent variable, Relative Nutrient Allocation (RNA) is derived by dividing the Individual's Nutritional Adequacy Ratio (INAR) by the over all Nutritional Adequacy Ratio for the entire Household (HNAR) as is done by Sanauer *et al.*[19]

The Individual's Nutrient (calorie/protein) Adequacy Ratio (INAR) is derived by dividing the Individual's Nutrient Intake (INI) by his or her Recommended Daily Allowance (IRDA) for the nutrient and multiplying by 100.

$$\text{INAR} = \frac{\text{INI}}{\text{IRDA}} \times 100$$

The household's nutrient (calorie/protein) adequacy ratio (HNAR) in the denominator of RNA, is derived by summing the nutrient intake (HNI) of all the family members, then dividing the quantity by the total Recommended Daily Nutrient Allowance (HRNA) for the entire household (Sum of RDA of the family members) and multiplying by 100.

$$\text{HNAR} = \frac{\text{HNI}}{\text{HRDA}} \times 100$$

Relative Calorie/Protein Allocation (RCA/RPA) is used in order to get the Individuals Calorie/Protein Adequacy Ratio in relation to that of the average of the entire household (Household Calorie/Protein Adequacy Ratio) and RNA is derived for calorie and protein by dividing the ICAR/IPAR by the HCAR/HPAR respectively. A model is given to compute the Relative Nutrient Allocation.[20]

$$RCA = \frac{ICAR}{HCAR} = \text{and } RPA = \frac{IPAR}{HPAR}$$

If the ratio is greater than or less than one it implies that there is an inequitable allocation of calories/protein among family members. Further (RCA/RPA)>1 implies favouritism and (RCA/RPA)<1 shows nepotism among family members. If it is equal to one, it indicates that there is an equitable allocation of calorie/protein among family members.

Testing of Third Hypothesis: RCA/RPA

In the previous chapter, the empirical findings confirmed the existence of positive relationship between women empowerment and household food security and the analysis of the association of headship to nutrient intake also confirmed that the nutrition consumption of family members are better under female headship. Conclusively, women's decision-making power is an important determinant of family nutrition.[21] In the foregone section of this chapter, while analysing the equity concept, it was observed that though differences in intake existed among male and female population and children in the food sufficient households, this pattern did not necessarily imply purposeful discrimination. The disparity is only because of the failure to perceive the importance of the required nutrient needs. Nutrition knowledge is observed to be lacking in most of the respondents. To scientifically ascertain the views expressed by the surveyed households and recognising female headship as an important variable, the hypothesis *Female headship reduces age and gender bias in individual food security* is so framed for empirical verification. This may help to find out the existence and extent of age and sex discrimination, if any, in the study villages and this may also help to project whether female headship will improve the position of females vis-a-vis males in the household.

Table 3 shows the age-wise *Relative Calorie Allocation* of males and females for different categories of households in the study-villages by household headship. Mean difference in RCA between males and females is computed to identify the

Table 3
Age and Sex-wise Relative Calorie Allocation

Sivaganga District							
		FHH		*JHH*		*MHH*	
Category		*M*	*F*	*M*	*F*	*M*	*F*
MF	0-5	0.96	1.01	0.95	1.00	NA	0.99
	6-18	0.97	1.01	0.97	0.95	0.95	1.01
	18 +	1.01	1.00	1.03	0.99	1.01	1.00
OVERALL		0.99	1.01	1.02	0.98	0.99	1.00
NFW	0-5	1.03	NA	0.99	0.97	0.93	NA
	6-18	0.98	0.99	0.98	1.0	0.98	1.01
	18 +	1.01	0.99	1.03	0.99	1.02	0.99
OVERALL		1.00	0.99	1.01	0.99	1.00	0.99
LAL	0-5	0.87	NA	0.95	0.95	NA	NA
	6-18	0.99	1.02	1.00	1.01	0.96	0.98
	18+	0.99	1.00	1.00	0.99	1.04	1.01
OVERALL		0.98	1.00	0.99	1.0	1.01	1.00
Cuddalore District							
MF	0-5	NA	1.02	0.88	NA	0.89	0.93
	6-18	0.97	1.03	1.04	0.98	1.04	0.96
	18 +	1.00	0.99	1.03	0.97	1.04	0.96
OVERALL		0.99	1.00	1.01	0.97	1.03	0.95
NFW	0-5	1.02	NA	0.91	1.00	1.00	0.95
	6-18	0.97	1.00	0.99	1.01	1.00	0.97
	18 +	0.97	1.03	0.99	0.98	1.01	0.98
OVERALL		0.98	1.01	0.98	0.99	1.00	0.96
LAL	0-5	NA	0.94	0.86	1.00	0.96	NA
	6-18	1.00	1.06	1.05	1.01	1.00	1.01
	18 +	0.98	0.97	1.01	1.00	0.99	1.00
OVERALL		0.99	1.00	0.98	1.00	0.99	1.00

Source: Computed.

extent of the sex-bias and age-bias of the intra familial food allocation and is statistically tested for variations using the 't' statistics.

The analysis of data for *sex-wise disparity* indicates that under female headship, the Relative Calorie Allocation (RCA) for females in almost all age groups is slightly higher than calorie allocation for males and only in the adult category of NFW households in Sivaganga district and LAL households in Cuddalore district the RCA is lower than that of the males.

Though females are better placed in terms of allocation, the comparison of the 't' value (Table 4) does not show any significant favouritism (towards females) and nepotism (towards males). Food and nutrition distribution is found to be more or less equitable because the variation shown in relative nutrient allocation between males and females is statistically insignificant. In the case of MF category of both the districts, JHH households reveal the existence of sex-bias, for the RCA of female members in these households are lower than that of their male counterparts. The over all mean value shows the difference to be significant at five per cent level.

For MHH, the data shows that in Sivaganga district, the females are relatively better off than males in terms of their calorie allocation (Table 3), but the difference in the mean value shows (Table 4) insignificant effect. A glaring sex-bias is observed in the MF category of Cuddalore district. Though mean difference is observed in the relative calorie allocation between males and females of NFW category, the statistical verification shows insignificant variation. Whereas for the MF category, sex-bias in the allocation of food (favouring males) is shown to be significant at one per cent level.

Age-wise disparity is also analysed and it could be observed from Table 5 that in most cases, there is a gradual increase in relative calorie allocation from children to adults. Under JHH, the NSG children (0-5 years) in MF and NFW households of both the districts are seen to be better off in terms of RCA but the difference is insignificant. For LAL households in Sivaganga and Cuddalore districts, the food allocation favours adult children and adults showing the significance at one per cent and five per cent levels respectively. The reduced relative calorie intake of NSG children is observed and this is attributed to the fact that young children are less able to make their needs known and are also more vulnerable to the effects of poor parenting. Here again, a literacy and knowledge level of the parents is the constraining factor. Another observed fact in Cuddalore district is, children belonging to some LAL households eat from a common pot, young children often face fierce competition for a share of the food in the cartel.

Table 4
Testing for Sex-bias in Relative Calorie Allocation

Sivaganga District

		FHH			*JHH*			*MHH*		
Category		*M.D*	*'t'*	$t_{0.05}$	*M.D*	*'t'*	$t_{0.05}$	*M.D*	*'t'*	$t_{0.05}$
MF	0-5	-0.05	0.79	2.92	NA	NA	NA	NA	NA	NA
	6-18	-0.04	0.80	2.01	-0.03	0.73	1.86	-0.06	0.84	2.92
	18 +	0.01	0.30	1.74	0.04	1.08	1.71	0.01	0.22	1.77
Overall		-0.02	0.32	1.70	0.04	1.19	1.69	-0.01	0.16	1.73
NFW	0-5	NA	NA	NA	0.02	0.75	2.35	NA	NA	NA
	6-18	-0.01	0.95	1.83	-0.02	1.11	1.86	-0.03	1.85	1.94
	18 +	0.02	1.15	1.72	0.04	1.44	1.71	0.03	1.81	1.75
Overall		0.01	1.31	1.70	0.02	1.24	1.68	0.01	0.21	1.71
LAL	6-18	-0.03	1.63	1.94	-0.01	0.41	1.76	-0.02	0.72	2.01
	18 +	-0.01	0.29	1.71	0.01	0.39	1.71	0.03	0.20	2.01
Overall		-0.02	1.11	1.69	-0.01	0.12	1.68	0.01	0.53	1.78

Contd...

		FHH			JHH			MHH		
Category		*M.D*	*'t'*	$t_{0.05}$	*M.D*	*'t'*	$t_{0.05}$	*M.D*	*'t'*	$t_{0.05}$
Cuddalore District										
MF	0-5	NA	NA	NA	NA	NA	NA	-0.04	1.04	2.01
	6-18	-0.06	0.85	2.92	0.06**	3.36	2.82[a]	0.08*	1.96	1.94
	18 +	0.01	0.11	1.78	0.06*	1.91	1.74	0.08**	4.36	2.45[a]
Overall		-0.01	0.33	1.73	0.04*	1.78	1.69	0.08**	4.33	2.42[a]
NFW	0-5	NA	NA	NA	NA	NA	NA	0.05	1.20	1.94
	6-18	-0.03	1.06	1.81	-0.02	0.27	1.83	0.03	0.38	1.89
	18 +	-0.06	1.05	1.79	0.01	0.12	1.72	0.03	1.06	1.71
Overall		-0.03	1.47	1.71	-0.01	0.53	1.69	0.04	1.40	1.68
LAL	0-5	NA	NA	NA	-0.14*	3.25	2.35	NA	NA	NA
	6-18	-0.06	1.90	2.13	0.04	1.43	1.89	-0.01	0.89	1.76
	18 +	0.01	0.46	2.01	0.01	0.48	1.75	-0.01	0.34	1.71
Overall		-0.01	0.27	1.78	-0.02	0.93	1.69	-0.02	1.19	1.68

Source: Computed

Note: NA – ' t' cannot be computed either because at least one of the group is empty or the data is not sufficient to compute ' t' value.

* Significant at 5% level

** Significant at 1% level

[a] ' t' value for 1% level of significance.

Table 5
Testing for Age-bias in Relative Calorie Allocation

Sivaganga District

	FHH			*JHH*			*MHH*		
Category	*M.D*	*'t'*	$t_{0.05}$	*M.D*	*'t'*	$t_{0.05}$	*M.D*	*'t'*	$t_{0.05}$
MF NSGC-SGC	0.001	0.04	1.83	0.02	0.65	1.81	-0.005	0.06	2.35
NSGC-AD	-0.03	0.58	1.72	-0.04	1.34	1.70	-0.007	0.11	1.76
SGC-AD	-0.02	0.82	1.71	-0.06*	2.32	1.69	-0.002	0.06	1.74
NFW NSGC-SGC	0.04	1.40	1.81	-0.014	0.91	1.77	-0.06	1.59	1.89
NSGC-AD	0.03	0.92	1.71	-0.03	1.80	1.70	-0.07*	1.93	1.74
SGC-AD	-0.01	0.77	1.69	-0.018	1.12	1.69	-0.014	0.87	1.71
LAL NSGC-SGC	-0.14**	6.14	2.99[a]	-0.05**	4.99	2.58[a]	NA	NA	NA
NSGC-AD	-0.12*	2.04	1.71	-0.03**	3.95	2.48[a]	NA	NA	NA
SGC-AD	0.02	1.12	1.69	0.018	1.23	1.68	-0.044	1.03	1.78

Contd...

	FHH			JHH			MHH		
Category	*M.D*	*'t'*	$t_{0.05}$	*M.D*	*'t'*	$t_{0.05}$	*M.D*	*'t'*	$t_{0.05}$
Cuddalore District									
MF NSGC-SGC	0.03	0.53	2.13	-0.12**	4.23	2.72[a]	-0.09*	3.08	1.77
NSGC-AD	0.028	0.41	1.76	-0.12**	3.93	2.55[a]	-0.09**	4.24	2.42[a]
SGC-AD	-0.008	0.24	1.74	0.01	0.31	1.70	-0.001	0.07	1.68
NFW NSGC-SGC	0.03	0.71	1.80	-0.05	0.64	1.78	-0.003	0.12	1.75
NSGC-AD	0.01	0.18	1.78	-0.04	0.46	1.71	-0.025	0.97	1.69
SGC-AD	-0.02	0.61	1.71	0.015	0.65	1.69	-0.02	0.91	1.69
LAL NSGC-SGC	-0.09	1.74	2.01	-0.11**	2.71	2.68[a]	-0.04	1.65	1.72
NSGC-AD	-0.03	0.84	1.94	-0.08*	2.17	1.72	-0.035	1.26	1.70
SGC-AD	0.055*	2.29	1.79	0.025	1.36	1.71	-0.009	0.68	1.68

Source: Computed.
NSGC–Non-School Going Children SGC–School Going Children AD–Adult

Note: NA– 't' cannot be computed either because at least one of the group is empty or the data is not sufficient to compute 't' value.
* Significant at 5% level
** Significant at 1% level
[a] 't' value for 1% level of significance.

In JHH, adults in MF and LAL categories enjoy a higher allocation and statistical verification also ascertains this. Though age-bias is observed in the NFW category the variation is insignificant. In MHH of both the districts age-bias (favouring adult children and adults) is found in all occupational categories but a significant difference in the mean value is observed only for NFW households in Sivaganga district and MF households in Cuddalore district.

Table 6 presents the data on *Relative Protein Allocation* (RPA) showing that under FHH, females are shown to be favoured, for their RPA is higher than that of males in both

Table 6
Age and Sex-wise Relative Protein Allocation

Sivaganga District							
		FHH		*JHH*		*MHH*	
Category		*M*	*F*	*M*	*F*	*M*	*F*
MF	0-5	1.00	0.99	1.0	0.96	NA	1.28
	6-18	0.93	0.95	0.87	0.96	0.98	0.90
	18 +	0.99	1.02	1.0	1.06	0.95	1.01
OVERALL		0.97	0.99	0.97	1.02	0.95	1.01
NFW	0-5	0.93	NA	0.93	0.86	1.01	NA
	6-18	0.99	0.95	0.97	0.91	0.94	0.96
	18 +	0.99	1.05	1.07	1.02	0.99	1.04
OVERALL		0.99	1.0	1.02	0.97	0.97	1.02
LAL	0-5	1.12	NA	1.01	1.00	NA	NA
	6-18	0.88	1.00	0.93	0.99	0.94	0.96
	18+	0.98	1.02	0.98	1.00	1.05	1.01
OVERALL		0.97	1.01	0.97	1.00	1.00	0.98
Cuddalore District							
MF	0-5	NA	1.0	1.01	NA	1.02	0.89
	6-18	0.96	0.96	1.02	0.92	0.89	1.02
	18 +	1.02	1.09	1.03	0.99	1.03	1.02
OVERALL		1.00	1.06	1.02	0.96	0.98	1.00
NFW	0-5	1.09	NA	0.96	0.99	0.95	0.98
	6-18	0.93	1.02	1.03	0.92	0.95	0.93
	18 +	0.97	1.02	1.07	0.99	1.05	1.03
OVERALL		0.96	1.02	1.04	0.97	1.02	1.00
LAL	0-5	NA	1.15	1.04	0.93	1.03	NA
	6-18	0.99	1.01	1.00	0.91	0.91	0.97
	18 +	0.93	1.01	0.96	1.03	1.02	1.02
OVERALL		0.96	1.03	0.98	0.95	0.99	1.00

Source: Computed.

the districts but the variations shown in Table 7 are found to be statistically significant at one per cent for NFW category in Cuddalore district. Under JHH, in Sivaganga district, the allocation is more for females in MF and LAL category whereas it is more for males in NFW category. But the mean difference, except for 6-18 years in MF category is shown to be statistically insignificant. In Cuddalore district the results show a reverse trend. Favouritism is recorded for males and the statistical verification also confirms the existence of sex-bias in the RPA which shows five per cent and one per cent level of significance for MF and NFW category respectively. Under MHH, relative protein allocation is seen to be more for females in MF and NFW category and five per cent significant level is observed in NFW households. Testing for age-bias (Table 8) again shows adults are in an advantageous position in their relative protein allocation. In Cuddalore district, the relative allocation is more for male children in the age group 0-5 whereas it is more for female children in the age group 6-18 years where the extent of variation for the 't' value is highly significant at 1% level.

A comparative analysis of both the study districts shows that in Sivaganga district there is no sex-bias against females in terms of relative calorie and protein consumption within the household. The result corroborates with the findings of NNMB Report for Indians[22] and in a study in Vietnam.[23] In Cuddalore district the existence of sex-bias is observed favouring males. The sex-bias is seen to be significant for MF and NFW households coming under JHH and MHH.

Age shows a positive effect in relative CA/PA favouring adults and adult children but the effect is significant only for those households which come under JHH and MHH. The significant level is less pronounced in the female headed households.

The findings show that female headship has a positive effect on the equitable relative nutritional allocation to its members. This could be attributed to the monochromatic fact that their meaningful participation in the allocation process is enhanced by their empowered decision-making level. The

Table 7
Testing for Sex-bias in Relative Protein Allocation

Sivaganga District

		FHH			*JHH*			*MHH*		
Category		*M.D*	*'t'*	$t_{0.05}$	*M.D*	*'t'*	$t_{0.05}$	*M.D*	*'t'*	$t_{0.05}$
MF	0-5	0.001	0.06	2.92	NA	NA	NA	NA	NA	NA
	6-18	-0.02	0.46	2.01	-0.09*	2.03	1.86	0.08	1.23	2.92
	18 +	-0.03	1.04	1.74	-0.06	1.61	1.71	-0.06	1.36	1.77
Overall		-0.02	0.92	1.70	-0.05	1.55	1.70	-0.06	1.20	1.73
NFW	0-5	NA	NA	NA	0.07	0.61	2.35	NA	NA	NA
	6-18	0.04	0.52	1.83	0.06	0.12	1.86	-0.02	0.30	1.94
	18 +	-0.06*	2.17	1.72	0.05	1.70	1.71	-0.05*	2.13	1.75
Overall		-0.01	0.61	1.70	0.05	1.57	1.68	-0.05*	1.95	1.71
LAL	6-18	-0.12*	2.49	1.94	-0.06	1.09	1.76	-0.02	0.21	2.01
	18 +	-0.04	0.99	1.71	-0.02	0.49	1.71	0.04	0.78	2.01
Total		-0.04	1.36	1.70	-0.03	1.21	1.68	0.02	0.28	1.78

Contd...

Cuddalore District										
		FHH			*JHH*			*MHH*		
Category		*M.D*	*'t'*	$t_{0.05}$	*M.D*	*'t'*	$t_{0.05}$	*M.D*	*'t'*	$t_{0.05}$
MF	0-5	NA	NA	NA	NA	NA	NA	0.13**	3.70	3.36[a]
	6-18	-0.001	0.06	2.92	0.10	1.34	1.83	-0.13**	3.31	3.14[a]
	18 +	-0.07	1.29	1.78	0.04	0.96	1.75	0.01	0.54	1.70
Overall		-0.06	1.29	1.73	0.06*	1.77	1.70	0.02	0.54	1.68
NFW	0-5	NA	NA	NA	NA	NA	NA	-0.03	0.62	1.94
	6-18	-0.09**	3.03	2.76[a]	0.11*	2.12	1.83	0.02	0.06	1.89
	18 +	-0.05	1.33	1.80	0.08*	2.28	1.721	0.02	0.50	1.72
Overall		-0.06**	2.50	2.06[a]	0.07**	2.74	2.45[a]	0.02	0.62	1.68
LAL	0-5	NA	NA	NA	0.11*	2.88	2.35	NA	NA	NA
	6-18	-0.02	0.44	2.13	0.09	0.96	1.89	-0.06	1.60	1.76
	18 +	-0.08	1.24	2.01	-0.07*	2.50	1.75	0.001	0.01	1.71
Overall		-0.07	1.68	1.78	-0.03	0.53	1.69	-0.01	0.17	1.68

Source: Computed.

Note: NA– 't' cannot be computed either because at least one of the group is empty or the data is not sufficient to compute 't' value.

* Significant at 5% level

** Significant at 1% level

[a] 't' value for 1% level of significance.

Table 8
Testing for Age-bias in Relative Protein Allocation

Sivaganga District									
	FHH			*JHH*			*MHH*		
Category	*M.D*	'*t*'	$t_{0.05}$	*M.D*	'*t*'	$t_{0.05}$	*M.D*	'*t*'	$t_{0.05}$
MF NSGC-SGC	0.04	1.09	1.83	0.05	1.72	1.81	0.35**	4.97	4.54[a]
NSGC-AD	-0.018	0.50	1.72	-0.04	1.58	1.71	0.29**	3.02	2.62[a]
SGC-AD	-0.06**	2.54	2.49[a]	-0.09**	3.23	2.46[a]	-0.055	1.37	1.74
NFW NSGC-SGC	-0.028	0.35	1.81	-0.014	0.25	1.77	0.06	0.92	1.89
NSGC-AD	-0.09	1.39	1.72	-0.14**	2.85	2.46[a]	-0.01	0.15	1.74
SGC-AD	-0.06*	2.38	1.69	-0.13**	4.61	2.45[a]	-0.07**	2.58	2.50[a]
LAL NSGC-SGC	0.16	1.52	1.89	0.08	1.64	1.74	NA	NA	NA
NSGC-AD	0.11	1.31	1.61	0.06	1.31	1.70	NA	NA	NA
SGC-AD	-0.05	1.39	1.69	-0.02	0.77	1.68	-0.08*	2.28	1.78

Contd...

Cuddalore District									
	FHH			*JHH*			*MHH*		
Category	*M.D*	't'	$t_{0.05}$	*M.D*	't'	$t_{0.05}$	*M.D*	't'	$t_{0.05}$
MF NSGC-SGC	0.047	0.98	2.13	0.04	0.37	1.79	-0.005	0.11	1.77
NSGC-AD	-0.049	0.93	1.76	0.001	0.01	1.73	-0.09*	2.45	1.68
SGC-AD	-0.096**	2.87	2.58[a]	-0.039	0.94	1.70	-0.095*	2.58	1.68
NFW NSGC-SGC	0.11	1.48	1.79	-0.01	0.20	1.78	-0.013	0.36	1.75
NSGC-AD	0.08	1.17	1.78	-0.04	0.87	1.71	-0.07*	2.37	1.69
SGC-AD	-0.02	0.93	1.71	-0.05	1.45	1.69	-0.08*	2.74	1.69
LAL NSGC-SGC	0.15*	2.72	2.01	0.098	0.85	1.78	0.09	1.40	1.73
NSGC-AD	0.17	1.65	1.94	0.003	0.09	1.72	0.013	0.21	1.70
SGC-AD	0.02	0.57	1.79	0.09	0.84	1.71	-0.08**	2.90	2.42[a]

Source: Computed.
NSGC–Non-School Going Children SGC–School Going Children AD–Adult

Note: NA – ' t' cannot be computed either because at least one of the group is empty or the data is not sufficient to compute ' t' value.
* Significant at 5% level
** Significant at 1% level
[a] 't' value for 1% level of significance.

obtained result confirms the third hypothesis that female headship reduced age and gender prejudice in individual food security.

EFFICIENCY PERSPECTIVE OF INDIVIDUAL FOOD SECURITY

(Testing of Fourth Hypothesis)

The incidence of adequate and equitable allocation of food has to be encouraged to reach the efficiency level of individual food security, which is referred to as nutritional status or nutritional security of individuals. The results based on dietary characteristics have shown that the main nutritional problem faced by many individuals, which deserves special mention, is *Protein-Calorie Malnutrition* (PCM). PCM is primarily due to an inadequate intake of food both in quantity and quality (referred to as food gap). The diet must provide adequate calorie and protein and help in prevention of *stunting* and *wasting*. Inadequate diet results in under nutrition (hollow hunger) caused by inadequacy in the quantity of food calories and malnutrition (hidden hunger) which results from insufficient amount of protective foods (quality foods) like protein, vitamins and minerals.[24] So, better nutrition is the prime entry point to stop the malnutrition maelstrom.

Low income and poverty are the main contributory factors to a wide prevalence of malnutrition. The root cause of poor nutritious diet is in the socio-economic variables associated with households, where factors such as ignorance, lack of nutritional knowledge, inadequate sanitary environment, faulty feeding habits, frequent infections, large families and poor health care are often operating synergistically to hasten the rapid decline from malnutrition to under-nutrition. Identifying variables which operate to affect diet and nutritional status of individuals are particularly important 'efficiency' for policy options. This section examines the important determinants at household level and the maternal factors which bear most directly on the quality of life and may be the true determinants of malnutrition in rural households.

Measurement of Nutritional Status

Dietary assessment is not indicative of malnutrition by itself. For a comprehensive assessment of nutritional status of the sample population, anthropometric parameters are used, as this is considered to be the convenient and reliable technique whereby the changes in the status of nutrition in a person can be evaluated easily.[25]

Anthropometric measurements are often used as proxies for assessing the eventual extent and severity of malnutrition. As the cardinal indicators in this respect are connected to the physical growth, the two indices used for children are (i) Height-for-Age and (ii) Weight-for-Height. The indicator used for measuring the body composition of adults is Body Mass Index (BMI).

Height-for-Age Index: This calibrates height in relation to chronological age. Low height for age is called *stunting malnutrition*. This index is an indicator of past under-nutrition. It is associated with a number of long-term factors like insufficient food intake (protein/energy), frequent infections and poverty. A given deficit in height may represent a short period of growth failure at an early age or a longer period of growth failure at a later stage. This is generally considered a measure of long-term malnutrition or *chronic malnutrition*. At a very young age children's height-for-age is a strong predictor of mortality.[26]

Weight-for-Height Index: This calibrates body mass in relation to height. Low weight for height, called as *wasting malnutrition*, indicates in most cases a recent and severe process of weight loss. It is appropriate for examining short-term maladies. This as a measure of current malnutrition may be a sensitive indicator of the prevalence of PCM in children and adults. Even mild form of malnutrition shows signs of slowing rate of growth and physical activity.[27]

In this analysis of nutritional security of individuals, these indices are used to identify two nutritional conditions 'stunting' and 'wasting'. For children, height-for-age and weight-for-height are reasonably reliable indicators of long term cumulative and short term health. When either measure is very low the risk of mortality increases incredibly.[28] Interpretation of anthropometric data requires the use of scientific norm and appropriate classification for interpretation. The heights and weights of children aged between 0-18 years, according to ICMR recommended standards (See Appendix-5), are used as reference population for analysis. The nutritional status of children in the sample population, according to these two measures is calculated, and compared with the standard reference population.

Children's Nutritional Status

Data on children's growth status is obtained by measuring weight and height. The height and weight measurements are converted into height for age index and weight for height index and put them in percentage of standards for all individuals using Waterlow's method.[29] These classifications are widely used in developing countries for quantifying the extent and severity of malnutrition prior to administering nutrition interventions.

$$\text{Height-for-Age Index (HAI)} = \frac{\text{Height of the child}}{\text{Height of a normal child at the same age}} \times 100$$

$$\text{Weight-for-Height Index (WHI)} = \frac{\text{Weight of the child}}{\text{Weight of a normal child at the same height}} \times 100$$

Using the standard range for the two classifications, children are grouped into different grades of nutritional status as given below:

Forms of malnutrition	*Stunting (HAI)*	*Wasting* (WHI)
Normal	> 95	>90
Mild	87.5- 95	80-90
Moderate	80-87.5	70-80
Severe	<80	<70

Adult's Nutritional Status

Adult nutritional status anthropometrics have not been standardized in terms of reference data or choice of indicators for risk and response assessment as they have been done for children. Since adults are not growing in stature, their height will not be able to reflect synchronic nutritional shocks. But recent events effect fluctuations in weight in adults. So Body Mass Index (BMI) is recommended.[30] BMI is based on a weight-to-height ratio that is considered a good indication of body fat and protein stores, an indirect estimate of changes in energy balance.[31]

Body Mass Index: This intends to assess different levels of thinness (Chronic Energy Deficiency) and degrees of overweight in adults. This measure is age independent and is best used for individuals between ages of 20 and 65 years.

$$\text{BMI} = \frac{\text{Weight (in Kilogram)}}{\text{Height}^2 \text{ (in metres)}}$$

BMI is calculated for adults (18+ years) and are grouped into different nutritional grades as recommended by Collins *et al.* (2000).[32]

BMI Categories of Chronic Under Nutrition

BMI	*Nutrition Grade*
$\geq$ 18.5	Normal
17.0 - 18.4	Grade I (Mild)
16.0 - 16.9	Grade II (Moderate)
$\leq$ 15.9	Grade III (Severe)

In this analysis primary thrust is given to height-for-age, weight–for–height and weight/height^2 (m).

Although these can be supplemented by detailed measurements of other body parts and proportions like Arm circumference, Chest circumference, fat fold at triceps and head circumference, the addition of such measures does not improve the efficiency of height and weight. This researcher, while assessing children's nutrition status, collected data on Arm circumference for children below 15 years. Since the index showed below standard level for all undernourished children, this variable is not considered and also to prevent multiplication of analysis this variable is excluded.

The procedure of measuring height and weight is evolved after going through elaborate literature in the methods of measurement. The guidelines given by NNMB 1984 and ICMR are the basis for the procedure adopted. Using the respective anthropometric measures for children and adults, differentials of malnutrition in terms of stunting and wasting are assessed to know the nutritional status of the sample population. To find the extent of association between household and maternal factors with nutritional status of children and adults, Chi-square analysis of association of attributes is used. The indicators are found useful for isolating the under nourished from the normal-household.

Household Factors and Nutritional Status

Household level factors include occupational category, household income, per day per capita expenditure on food, family size and access to health and sanitary environment. These are now examined with respect to the study-villages.

The nutritional status of children 0-5 years, 6-18 years and adults (18+ years) in relation to *occupational category* is shown in Tables 9, 10 and 11 respectively for both the districts. It could be observed that in Sivaganga district, nutritional status has significant dependence on land holding, for majority of the well-nourished children and adults belong to the MF category, while in the case of under nourished children and adults majority belong to landless agricultural families. It is interesting to find that among the children of 0-5 years no case of severe form of malnutrition is found. But in 6-18 years and 18+ years, awfully severe form of malnutrition is noted in females of LAL category. Among NFW category households majority of children of 0-5 years is affected by mild under-nutrition and for other age groups, 6-18 years and 18+ years, nutritional status is found to be almost normal.

In Cuddalore district, on the contrary, children of 0-5 years and 6-18 years and adults especially males belonging to NFW category are observed to be the best nourished in terms of nutritional status. Adult's nutritional status is found to be normal for MF category too. Severely affected children (0-5 years) are found moderately in NFW category but this proportion is very high for LAL households, where it is found

Table 9
Incidence of Stunting and Wasting Malnutrition for 0-5 Years Children by Household Category

	MF				*NFW*				*LAL*			
Forms of	*MALE*		*FEMALE*		*MALE*		*FEMALE*		*MALE*		*FEMALE*	
Malnutrition	*S*	*W*	*S*	*W*	*S*	*W*	*S*	*W*	*S*	*W*	*S*	*W*
Sivaganga District												
Normal	2 (66)	2 (66)	2 (50)	3 (75)	1 (25)	1 (25)	-	-	-	1 (50)	-	-
Mild	-	-	2	1	2	1	3	1	1	-	-	1
Moderate	1	1	-	-	1	2	-	2	1	1	1	-
Severe	-	-	-	-	-	-	-	-	-	-	-	-
Total	3	3	4	4	4	4	3	3	2	2	1	1
Cuddalore District												
Normal	-	-	-	1 (25)	2 (40)	3 (60)	-	1 (25)	-	-	-	-
Mild	3	2	4	1	-	-	-	1	2	2	1	-
Moderate	1	1	-	2	2	1	3	1	2	2	1	1
Severe	-	1	-	-	1	1	1	1	2	2	-	1
Total	4	4	4	4	5	5	4	4	6	6	2	2

Source: Computed.
Figures in parentheses denote percentage to column total.

Table 10
Incidence of Stunting and Wasting Malnutrition for 6-18 Years Children by Household Category

Forms of	MF				NFW				LAL			
	MALE		FEMALE		MALE		FEMALE		MALE		FEMALE	
Malnutrition	*S*	*W*	*S*	*W*	*S*	*W*	*S*	*W*	*S*	*W*	*S*	*W*
Sivaganga District												
Normal	-	3	8	8	3	5	9	9	-	4	4	3
		(37)	(62)	(62)	(23)	(38)	(56)	(56)		(31)	(22)	(16)
Mild	6	5	4	5	6	5	4	6	8	6	7	10
Moderate	2	-	1		4	3	3	1	4	2	5	4
Severe	-	-	-	-	-	-	-	-	1	1	2	1
Total	8	8	13	13	13	13	16	16	13	13	18	18
Cuddalore District												
Normal	4	8	5	7	8	10	5	7	2	2	2	1
	(31)	(62)	(38)	(54)	(36)	(45)	(38)	(54)	(12)	(12)	(12)	(6)
Mild	7	4	7	3	11	9	5	4	9	11	10	10
Moderate	2	1	1	3	2	3	3	2	5	3	3	3
Severe	-	-	-	-	1	-	-	-	1	1	2	3
Total	13	13	13	13	22	22	13	13	17	17	17	17

Source: Computed.
Figures in parentheses denote percentage to column total.

more in females. In terms of nutritional status in this district, LAL category is the most disadvantaged group. The detailed findings for both districts reveal that occupational hierarchy is closely related with under-nutrition.

Table 11
Incidence of Chronic Undernutrition for Adult Population (18 + Years) by Household Category

Forms of Malnutrition	*MF*		*NFW*		*LAL*	
	Male	*Female*	*Male*	*Female*	*Male*	*Female*
Sivaganga District						
Normal	21	12	18	16	10	2
	(72)	(40)	(58)	(47)	(38)	(6)
Mild	7	12	11	6	7	9
Moderate	1	4	2	7	5	11
Severe	-	2	-	5	4	9
Total	29	30	31	34	26	31
Cuddalore District						
Normal	19	17	24	19	4	3
	(54)	(55)	(75)	(68)	(15)	(14)
Mild	16	5	6	3	17	8
Moderate	-	6	2	5	5	5
Severe	-	3	-	1	1	6
Total	35	31	32	28	27	22

Source: Computed.
Figures in parentheses denote percentage to column total.

Tables 12 and 13 show respectively for Sivaganga and Cuddalore districts the relationship of the *income of the household* to the nutritional status of the individual members. The association between these two variables is found to be highly significant at one per cent level in Sivaganga district. It is interesting to observe that most of the high income group individuals are well nourished and no severe case of stunting and wasting is observed in the 0-18 Years age group in middle and high income group. But chronic undernutrition is found in some cases of adult population.

In Cuddalore district, majority of the children and adults belonging to low income group are seen to be affected by incidence of stunting and wasting. 'P' value shows one per cent significant level for both the age groups of 0-18 years and 18+ years in the incidence case of 'wasting' malnutrition. It is found to be five per cent significant level for 'stunting' malnutrition in the age group of 0-18 years. Increase in the income level strongly influencing proportional increase in the nutritional status of individuals is also established by other researchers (World Bank 1981; Shariff 1995).[33-34]

Table 12
Level of Income and Nutritional Status: Sivaganga District

Forms of Malnutrition	*Low*	*%*	*Middle*	*%*	*High*	*%*	*Total*	χ^2
Stunting (0-18 Years)								
Normal	2	5	10	28	17	68	29	41.42 (0.000)
Mild	15	41	21	58	7	28	43	
Moderate	17	46	5	14	1	4	23	
Severe	3	8	0	0	0	0	3	
Total	37	100	36	100	25	100	98	
Wasting (0-18 Years)								
Normal	5	14	17	47	17	68	39	22.39 (0.001)
Mild	21	57	13	36	7	28	41	
Moderate	9	24	6	17	1	4	16	
Severe	2	5	0	0	0	0	2	
Total	37	100	36	100	25	100	98	
Chronic Undernutrition (18+ Years)								
Normal	8	14	32	43	39	78	79	55.20 (0.000)
Mild	18	32	27	36	7	14	52	
Moderate	17	30	11	15	2	4	30	
Severe	14	24	4	6	2	4	20	
Total	57	100	74	100	50	100	181	

Source: Computed.
Note: Figures in parentheses denote ' P' level significance.

A strong positive association is found between *food expenditure* and nutritional achievement. As observed earlier, economic position as measured by per day per capita expenditure on food is the important factor influencing

Table 13
Level of Income and Nutritional Status: Cuddalore District

Forms of Malnutrition	*Low*	*%*	*Middle*	*%*	*High*	*%*	*Total*	χ^2
Stunting (0-18 Years)								
Normal	4	10	15	30	9	29	28	14.79 (0.021)
Mild	16	41	27	54	16	52	59	
Moderate	14	36	6	12	5	16	25	
Severe	5	13	2	4	1	3	8	
Total	39	100	50	100	31	100	120	
Wasting (0-18 Years)								
Normal	2	5	23	46	15	49	40	27.25 (0.000)
Mild	17	44	20	40	10	32	47	
Moderate	13	33	5	10	5	16	23	
Severe	7	18	2	4	1	3	10	
Total	39	100	50	100	31	100	120	
Chronic Undernutrition (18+ Years)								
Normal	10	24	37	49	39	67	85	19.63 (0.003)
Mild	17	42	24	32	14	24	55	
Moderate	9	22	10	13	4	7	23	
Severe	5	12	5	6	1	2	11	
Total	41	100	76	100	58	100	175	

Source: Computed.
Note: Figures in parentheses denote 'P' level significance.

nutritional status at the household level. In Tables 14 and 15, a direct association is seen between higher levels of expenditure and improved levels in height-for-age and weight-for-height measurements in both the districts. 'P' value is highly significant at one per cent level. Improved nutritional status with increase in per capita expenditure on food has hitherto been established in empirical nutritional analyses.[35-36]

Tables 16 and 17 exhibit the incidence of stunting and wasting by *family size* in both the districts respectively. In Sivaganga district, the family size is found to influence the nutritional status of children especially in the incidence of 'wasting' malnutrition. A higher percentage of children and

Table 14
Per day Per Capita Expenditure on Food and Nutritional Status: Sivaganga District

Forms of Malnutrition	*Low*	*%*	*Middle*	*%*	*High*	*%*	*Total*	χ^2
Stunting (0-18 Years)								
Normal	6	10	16	67	7	58	29	34.53 (0.000)
Mild	33	53	5	21	5	42	43	
Moderate	20	32	3	12	0	0	23	
Severe	3	5	0	0	0	0	3	
Total	62	100	24	100	12	100	98	
Wasting (0-18 Years)								
Normal	16	26	13	54	10	83	39	17.96 (0.001)
Mild	30	48	9	38	2	17	41	
Moderate	14	23	2	8	0	0	16	
Severe	2	3	0	0	0	0	2	
Total	62	100	24	100	12	100	98	
Chronic Undernutrition (18+ Years)								
Normal	28	26	34	74	17	63	79	36.55 (0.000)
Mild	38	35	8	18	6	22	52	
Moderate	25	23	2	4	3	11	30	
Severe	17	16	2	4	1	4	20	
Total	108	100	46	100	27	100	181	

Source: Computed
Note: Figures in parentheses denote 'P' level significance.

adults in the small families are found to suffer. This is mainly due to the fact that when the size of the family increases, the level of nutritional condition of individual decreases. It might be due to the reason that the individual's share of food in the family becomes scarce with increase in the number of family members. So children of large size families are at a disadvantage. In Cuddalore district (Table 17) family size has no significant effect on the nutritional status of the individuals. A closer look at the data, however, shows that the number of persons affected by the occurrence of 'stunting' and 'wasting' malnutrition increases from small to medium size family.

Table 15
Per day Per Capita Expenditure on Food and Nutritional Status: Cuddalore District

Forms of Malnutrition	Low	%	Middle	%	High	%	Total	χ^2
Stunting (0-18 Years)								
Normal	4	9	20	33	4	29	28	18.74 (0.005)
Mild	21	47	29	47	9	64	59	
Moderate	13	29	11	18	1	7	25	
Severe	7	15	1	2	0	0	8	
Total	45	100	61	100	14	100	120	
Wasting (0-18 Years)								
Normal	8	18	27	44	5	36	40	18.11 (0.006)
Mild	16	35	26	43	5	36	47	
Moderate	13	29	7	11	3	21	23	
Severe	8	18	1	2	1	7	10	
Total	45	100	61	100	14	100	120	
Chronic Undernutrition (18+ Years)								
Normal	16	33	54	56	16	53	86	15 23 (0.018)
Mild	14	29	31	32	10	33	55	
Moderate	12	25	9	9	2	7	23	
Severe	6	13	3	3	2	7	11	
Total	48	100	97	100	30	100	175	

Source: Computed.
Note: Figures in parentheses denote ' P' level significance.

Severe under-nourishment and other forms of malnutrition are observed more in medium size families. The low incidence observed in this districts may be associated with increased income. This is perhaps the reason for large family size not observed to significantly affect the nutritional status in select occupational and income groups.

Table 18 and 19 show the association between the household's level of *access to health and sanitation* and nutritional status in the respective districts. The analysed data reveals that the health and sanitation environment of the household influences nutritional status of the population positively. In

Table 16
Family Size and Nutritional Status: Sivaganga District

Forms of Malnutrition	Small	%	Medium	%	Total	χ^2
Stunting (0-18 Years)						
Normal	11	33	18	29	29	5.420 (0.066)
Mild	18	55	25	38	43	
Moderate	4	12	19	29	23	
Severe	0	0	3	4	3	
Total	33	100	65	100	98	
Wasting (0-18 Years)						
Normal	18	55	21	32	39	9.837 (0.020)
Mild	10	30	31	48	41	
Moderate	3	9	13	20	16	
Severe	2	6	0	0	2	
Total	33	100	65	100	98	
Chronic Undernutrition (18+Years)						
Normal	35	52	44	39	79	3.910 (0.271)
Mild	16	24	36	31	52	
Moderate	11	16	19	17	30	
Severe	5	8	15	13	20	
Total	67	100	114	100	181	

Source: Computed.
Note: Figures in parentheses denote 'P' level significance.

Sivaganga district a strong association is found with height-for-age, and the level of significance is shown to be five per cent for children in 0-18 years and one per cent level is observed for currently nourished population in the age groups of 0-18 years and 18+ years. But in Cuddalore district, though a significant association of five per cent level is found in the incidence of 'stunting' and 'wasting' malnutrition of children in the age group of 0-18 years, it does not show any significant impact on the nutritional status of the adult group. Along with food intake, access to health and sanitary facilities is proven to reduce effectively the malnutrition of population.[37]

Table 17
Family Size and Nutritional Status: Cuddalore District

Forms of Malnutrition	*Small*	%	*Medium*	%	*Total*	χ^2
Stunting (0-18 Years)						
Normal	9	31	19	21	28	2.48 (0.288)
Mild	15	52	44	48	59	
Moderate	5	17	20	22	25	
Severe	0	0	8	9	8	
Total	29	100	91	100	120	
Wasting (0-18 Years)						
Normal	12	41	28	31	40	2.462 (0.482)
Mild	12	41	35	38	47	
Moderate	4	14	19	21	23	
Severe	1	4	9	10	10	
Total	29	100	91	100	120	
Chronic Undernutrition (18+ Years)						
Normal	32	56	54	46	86	2.446 (0.485)
Mild	16	28	39	33	55	
Moderate	5	9	18	15	23	
Severe	4	7	7	6	11	
Total	57	100	118	100	175	

Source: Computed.
Note: Figures in parentheses denote 'P' level significance.

Maternal Factors and Nutritional Status

Maternal factors consist of household headship, maternal education, nutritional knowledge, control over income, level of participation in decision making and percentage of time spent in food related activities. These factors are juxtaposed with the data on nutritional status of individuals to assess the extent of their influence. Inferences which are drawn will be used for policy suggestions. In this context, the hypothesis, *Maternal factors exert significant influence on the individual nutritional security,* is framed and subjected to statistical verification.

Table 18
Level of Access to Health and Sanitation and Nutritional Status: Sivaganga District

Forms of Malnutrition	*Low*	*%*	*High*	*%*	*Total*	χ^2
Stunting (0-18 Years)						
Normal	8	18	21	40	29	9.560 (0.022)
Mild	20	43	23	44	43	
Moderate	16	35	7	14	23	
Severe	2	4	1	2	3	
Total	46	100	52	100	98	
Wasting (0-18 Years)						
Normal	10	22	29	56	39	11.80 (0.003)
Mild	25	54	16	31	41	
Moderate	9	20	7	13	16	
Severe	2	4	0	0	2	
Total	46	100	52	100	98	
Chronic Undernutrition (18+Years)						
Normal	32	31	47	59	79	14.81 (0.002)
Mild	37	36	15	19	52	
Moderate	19	19	11	14	30	
Severe	14	14	6	8	20	
Total	102	100	79	100	181	

Source: Computed.
Note: Figures in parentheses denote 'P' level significance.

he nutritional status of children in the age groups 0-5 years, 6-18 years and adults (18+) is furnished in Tables 20, 21 and 7.22 respectively for both the districts by *household headship*. In Table 20, the data for 0-5 years children in Sivaganga district, reveal no incidence of severe or moderate malnutrition in FHH and it is interesting to observe that the higher proportion of nutritionally normal children are found only in these families. The data for Cuddalore district show that the incidence of severe malnutrition is prevalent in male headed households and a good proportion of children here is found to be affected by both 'stunting' and 'wasting' malnutrition.

Table 19
Level of Access to Health and Sanitation and Nutritional Status: Cuddalore District

Forms of Malnutrition	*Low*	*%*	*High*	*%*	*Total*	χ^2
Stunting (0-18 Years)						
Normal	12	17	16	34	28	9.488 (0.023)
Mild	36	49	23	49	59	
Moderate	17	23	8	17	25	
Severe	8	11	0	0	8	
Total	73	100	47	100	120	
Wasting (0-18 Years)						
Normal	21	29	19	40	40	8.820 (0.032)
Mild	25	34	22	47	47	
Moderate	18	25	5	11	23	
Severe	9	12	1	2	10	
Total	73	100	47	100	120	
Chronic Undernutrition (18+ Years)						
Normal	48	45	38	55	86	3.111 (0.374)
Mild	35	33	20	29	55	
Moderate	14	13	9	13	23	
Severe	9	9	2	3	11	
Total	106	100	69	100	175	

Source: Computed.
Note: Figures in parentheses denote 'P' level significance.

In the case of 0-18 years, presented in Table 21, it is quite interesting to observe that a good proportion of children under female headship in both the districts is seen to have attained normal nutritional status as measured in terms of height for their age and weight for height. Also no incidence of severe malnutrition is noticed in female headed families in Sivaganga district. But, on the contrary, in Cuddalore district, severe cases are of malnutrition are found in female headed households and the reason is that these families belong to low income and poverty stricken families of NFW and LAL categories.

Table 20
Incidence of Stunting and Wasting Malnutrition for 0-5 Years Children by Headship-wise

Forms of	FHH				JHH				MHH			
	MALE		FEMALE		MALE		FEMALE		MALE		FEMALE	
Malnutrition	*S*	*W*	*S*	*W*	*S*	*W*	*S*	*W*	*S*	*W*	*S*	*W*
Sivaganga District												
Normal	3	4	1	2	-	-	-	-	-	-	1	1
	(75)	(100)	(50)	(100)							(100)	(100)
Mild	1	-	1		2	1	4	3	-	-	-	-
Moderate	-	-	-	-	2	3	1	2	1	1	-	-
Severe	-	-	-	-	-	-	-	-	-	-	-	-
Total	4	4	2	2	4	4	5	5	1	1	1	1
Cuddalore District												
Normal	-	-	-	1	1	1	-	-	1	2	-	1
				(50)	(17)	(17)			(11)	(22)		(17)
Mild	-	-	1	-	3	2	1	-	2	2	3	2
Moderate	-	-	1	-	2	2	1	2	3	2	2	2
Severe	-	-	-	1	-	1	-	-	3	3	1	1
Total	-	-	2	2	6	6	2	2	9	9	6	6

Source: Computed.
Figures in parentheses denote percentage to column total.

Table 21.

Incidence of Stunting and Wasting Malnutrition for 6-18 Years Children by Headship-wise

	FHH				*JHH*				*MHH*			
Forms of	*MALE*		*FEMALE*		*MALE*		*FEMALE*		*MALE*		*FEMALE*	
Malnutrition	*S*	*W*	*S*	*W*	*S*	*W*	*S*	*W*	*S*	*W*	*S*	*W*
Sivaganga District												
Normal	1	5	11	9	1	5	9	9	1	2	1	2
	(12)	(62)	(61)	(50)	(6)	(31)	(45)	(45)	(10)	(20)	(11)	(22)
Mild	7	3	6	8	12	9	6	9	1	4	3	4
Moderate	-	-	1	1	3	1	4	1	7	4	4	3
Severe	-	-	-	-	-	1	1	1	1	-	1	-
Total	8	8	18	18	16	16	20	20	10	10	9	9
Cuddalore District												
Normal	8	8	4	5	5	9	5 (29)	9 (53)	1 (5)	3 (13)	3 (18)	1 (6)
	(57)	(57)	(40)	(50)	(31)	(56)						
Mild	5	5	2	2	10	5	12	6	12	14	8	9
Moderate	-	-	2	-	1	2	-	2	8	5	5	6
Severe	1	1	2	3	-	-	-	-	1	-	-	-
Total	14	14	10	10	16	16	17	17	22	22	16	16

Source: Computed.

Figures in parentheses denote percentage to column total.

With regard to adult nutritional status, as tabulated in Table 22, a higher proportion of adults in FHH is found to be in normal nutrition status in both the districts. Other grades of chronic energy deficiency are least visible in individuals belonging to families headed by females of this adult age group. The overall nutritional status is found to be normal in more males than females. Even severe chronic energy deficiency is found more in females. It is worth comparing the findings in the previous section on adequacy perspective which showed that nutrient adequacy in general is more for males than females. Equity perspective analysis on intra household allocation of food also revealed that female headship improves the nutrient intake of family members especially female children. Thus, female headship, an important variable at the household level, is proved to be a good proxy for children's health.[38] This confirms the finding of other researchers.[39-40]

Table 22
Incidence of Chronic Undernutrition for Adult Population (18+Years) By Headship-wise

Forms of	*FHH*		*JHH*		*MHH*	
Malnutrition	*Male*	*Female*	*Male*	*Female*	*Male*	*Female*
Sivaganga District						
Normal	17	17	23	8	9	5
	(59)	(45)	(60)	(22)	(47)	(25)
Mild	8	9	11	9	6	9
Moderate	4	9	2	10	2	3
Severe	-	3	2	10	2	3
Total	29	38	38	37	19	20
Cuddalore District						
Normal	11	10	19	14	17	15
	(65)	(58)	(36)	(54)	(38)	(39)
Mild	5	3	11	7	23	6
Moderate	-	2	2	4	5	10
Severe	1	2	-	1	-	7
Total	17	17	32	26	45	38

Source: Computed.
Figures in prentheses denote percentage to column total.

Another factor, *women's education,* is hypothesized to exert a major influence on health and nutritional status.[41] The data presented in Tables 23 and 24 district-wise for Sivaganga and Cuddalore respectively, show the positive and larger influence of maternal education in improving the nutritional status of children and adults. In both the districts. A higher per centage of mild and moderately malnourished children are seen to be born to mothers who are illiterates. A greater proportion of well-nourished children is known to belong to mothers with middle school and above. Maternal education is found to influence the nutritional status of adults also. A highly significant inverse relationship is observed between malnutrition and maternal education with higher level of education resulting in lower prevalence of malnutrition.

Table 23

Maternal Education and Nutritional Status: Sivaganga District

Forms of Malnutrition	*Illiterate*	*%*	*Primary*	*%*	*Middle*	*%*	*Total*	χ^2
Stunting (0-18 Years)								
Normal	3	16	15	27	11	46	29	13.14 (0.011)
Mild	8	42	22	40	13	54	43	
Moderate	8	42	15	27	0	0	23	
Severe	0	0	3	6	0	0	3	
Total	19	100	55	100	24	100	98	
Wasting (0-18 Years)								
Normal	6	31	18	33	15	63	39	8.970 (0.062)
Mild	7	38	27	49	7	29	41	
Moderate	6	31	8	14	2	8	16	
Severe	0	0	2	4	0	0	2	
Total	19	100	55	100	24	100	98	
Chronic Undernutrition (18+ Years)								
Normal	18	27	40	47	21	75	79	26.95 (0.000)
Mild	25	37	23	27	4	14	52	
Moderate	18	27	9	10	3	11	30	
Severe	6	9	14	16	0	0	20	
Total	67	100	86	100	28	100	181	

Source: Computed.

Note: Figures in parentheses denote 'p' level significance.

In Cuddalore district (Table 24), mother's education is seen to be amazingly improving the nutritional status of both children and adults, where 'p' level of significance is shown to be at one per cent. Studies have also documented the significant relationship between anthropometric, measures of child health and maternal education.[42-43]

Table 24
Maternal Education and Nutritional Status: Cuddalore District

Forms of Malnutrition	*Illiterate*	*%*	*Primary*	*%*	*Middle*	*%*	*Total*	χ^2
Stunting (0-18 Years)								
Normal	3	7	11	23	14	50	28	23.88 (0.001)
Mild	21	49	25	51	13	46	59	
Moderate	14	32	10	20	1	4	25	
Severe	5	12	3	6	0	0	8	
Total	43	100	49	100	28	100	120	
Wasting (0-18 Years)								
Normal	4	9	19	39	17	61	40	29.53 (0.000)
Mild	18	42	19	39	10	36	47	
Moderate	16	37	6	12	1	3	23	
Severe	5	12	5	10	0	0	10	
Total	43	100	49	100	28	100	120	
Chronic Undernutrition (18+ Years)								
Normal	20	29	36	54	30	77	86	26.13 (0.002)
Mild	28	41	19	28	8	20	55	
Moderate	14	20	9	13	0	0	23	
Severe	7	10	3	4	1	3	11	
Total	69	100	67	100	39	100	175	

Source: Computed.
Note: Figures in parentheses denote 'p' level significance.

Women's level of participation in *decision-making* and its relationship with nutritional status of family-members are shown in Tables 25 and 26 for the respective districts. The results reveal that the nutritional status of children and adults show significant dependence on the level of women's participation in the decision-making process. In Sivaganga district (Table 25), the prevalence rate of under nutrition is observed to be very high among the children belonging to families where women's participation level is very low. It is 85 per cent mild and moderate form in the case of stunting malnutrition and 62 per cent in the case of wasting malnutrition. It could be inferred from the data that when the level of women's decision making increases, the prevalence rate of under nutrition decreases and the proportion of nutritiously normal children increases. No one in families where women's participation level is shown to be high is found to be severely affected. This factor is observed to highly influence the nutritional status of children ($p<0.01$).

Table 25
Women's Participation Level in Decision-making and Nutritional Status: Sivaganga District

Forms of Malnutrition	*Low*	%	*Medium*	%	*High*	%	*Total*	χ^2
Stunting (0-18 Years)								
Normal	2	15	14	22	13	59	29	14.23 (0.006)
Mild	6	46	29	46	8	36	43	
Moderate	5	39	17	27	1	5	23	
Severe	0	0	3	5	0	0	3	
Total	13	100	63	100	22	100	98	
Wasting (0-18 Years)								
Normal	3	23	22	35	14	64	39	19.16 (0.001)
Mild	3	23	30	48	8	36	41	
Moderate	5	39	11	17	0	0	16	
Severe	2	15	0	0	0	0	2	
Total	13	100	63	100	22	100	98	
Chronic Undernutrition (18+ Years)								
Normal	7	23	50	44	22	59	79	15.46 (0.017)
Mild	10	32	36	32	6	16	52	
Moderate	8	26	14	12	8	22	30	
Severe	6	19	13	12	1	3	20	
Total	31	100	113	100	37	100	181	

Source: Computed.
Note: Figures in parentheses denote 'p' level significance.

Nutritional status of adults is also found to increase in proportion to the level of increase in women's participation in decision making. When an increase is recorded in the level of participation from low to medium level, the percentage of adults with normal nutrition status is also found to increase from 23 per cent to 44 per cent. And a still higher proportion of 59 per cent is found to be normal in children belonging to families where women's participation level in decision making is high. A close association is found between women's participation in decision-making and nutrition status and the statistical value observed is p 0.017 ($p<0.05$).

Table 26
Women's Participation Level in Decision and Nutritional Status: Cuddalore District

Forms of Malnutrition	*Low*	*%*	*Medium*	*%*	*High*	*%*	*Total*	χ^2
Stunting (0-18 Years)								
Normal	7	13	15	30	6	37	28	14.64 (0.005)
Mild	25	46	29	58	5	32	59	
Moderate	17	32	6	12	2	12	25	
Severe	5	9	0	0	3	19	8	
Total	54	100	50	100	16	100	120	
Wasting (0-18 Years)								
Normal	10	18	20	40	10	63	40	21.65 (0.000)
Mild	22	41	24	48	1	6	47	
Moderate	17	31	6	12	0	0	23	
Severe	5	10	0	0	5	31	10	
Total	54	100	50	100	16	100	120	
Chronic Undernutrition (18+ Years)								
Normal	37	39	41	67	8	44	86	18.86 (0.004)
Mild	34	35	15	25	6	33	55	
Moderate	19	20	3	5	1	6	23	
Severe	6	6	2	3	3	17	11	
Total	96	100	61	100	18	100	175	

Source: Computed.
Note: Figures in parentheses denote 'p' level significance.

Almost similar results are obtained for Cuddalore district (Table 26). The proportion of children affected by both 'stunting' and 'wasting' malnutrition is found to be very high and these children belong to families where the women's participation level in decision making is very low. It is also unusually observed that severe cases of malnutrition are found in children and adults where women's participation level is high. This may be attributed to low income, illiteracy and lack of nutritional knowledge of the women in spite of their high-level participation. Statistical results show greater significant at one per cent level for children and adults.

Adult nutritional status in the district also has significant association with women's participation level with the 'P' value at 0.004. Prevalence rate of under-nutrition for both mild and moderate nutritional status is 55 per cent among malnourished who belong to families with low women's participation and only three per cent among in families where women's participation level is high.

The close association of these variables is statistically tested and the findings support the view that maternal factor greatly influences the nutritional status of household members. Corresponding findings are reported from other developing countries.[44-45]

Tables 27 and 28 reveal the relationship between women's *control over income* earned by them and by other members of the family and the nutritional status of the household-members. In Sivaganga district (Table 27) the results are encouraging as no case of moderate and severe malnutrition is found among the children who are diagnosed as malnourished by height for their age and weight for their height. Majority of nutritiously normal children at 67 per cent and 87 per cent respectively for both age-groups belong to families where women have full control over the income. Even for adults, it is recorded at 68 per cent. And also the minimum number of malnourished is found in this bracket. Empirical test reveals a strong association control of income and nutritional status exactly at one per cent significant level.

In Cuddalore district (Table 28) also, a higher percentage of well nourished children are seen to belong to families where the income is controlled by women and the 'P' value shows

Table 27
Women's Control Over Income and Nutritional Status: Sivaganga District

Forms of Malnutrition	*Nil*	*%*	*Partial*	*%*	*Full*	*%*	*Total*	χ^2
Stunting (0-18 Years)								
Normal	2	9	17	30	10	67	29	41.28 (0.000)
Mild	6	22	32	56	5	33	43	
Moderate	15	58	8	14	0	0	23	
Severe	3	11	0	0	0	0	3	
Total	26	100	57	100	15	100	98	
Wasting (0-18 Years)								
Normal	3	12	23	40	13	87	39	37.38 (0.000)
Mild	10	38	29	51	2	13	41	
Moderate	11	42	5	9	0	0	16	
Severe	2	8	0	0	0	0	2	
Total	26	100	57	100	15	100	98	
Chronic Undernutrition (18+Years)								
Normal	6	13	48	48	25	68	79	41.29 (0.000)
Mild	14	32	31	31	7	18	52	
Moderate	10	23	17	17	3	8	30	
Severe	14	32	4	4	2	6	20	
Total	44	100	100	100	37	100	181	

Source: Computed
Note: Figures in parentheses denote 'p' level significance

five per cent and one per cent significance. From the results obtained for adults, it is observed that a higher percentage of nutritiously normal people, as measured by weight/ height^2(m), belong to families where women have full control of income. But, the severely under nourished in this group account for 15 per cent. Statistical value shows that control over income has no significant impact on the nutritional status of adults. It is the similar case with LAL households, where though the women have full control over income, their low income hindered their attempts to improve the nutritional status of their family members. During the field survey, it was

Table 28
Women's Control Over Income and Nutritional Status: Cuddalore District

Forms of Malnutrition	*Nil*	*%*	*Partial*	*%*	*Full*	*%*	*Total*	χ^2
Stunting (0-18 Years)								
Normal	2	12	18	21	8	44	28	13.39 (0.029)
Mild	8	50	47	55	4	22	59	
Moderate	6	38	16	18	3	17	25	
Severe	0	0	5	6	3	17	8	
Total	16	100	86	100	18	100	120	
Wasting (0-18 Years)								
Normal	2	12	29	34	9	50	40	21.67 (0.002)
Mild	7	44	36	42	4	22	47	
Moderate	6	38	17	20	0	0	23	
Severe	1	6	4	4	5	28	10	
Total	16	100	86	100	18	100	120	
Chronic Undernutrition (18+ Years)								
Normal	13	38	62	51	11	55	86	7.036 (0.317)
Mild	15	44	36	30	4	20	55	
Moderate	5	15	16	13	2	10	23	
Severe	1	3	7	6	3	15	11	
Total	34	100	121	100	20	100	175	

Source: Computed.
Note: Figures in parentheses denote 'p' level significance.

observed that women who are involved in trading activities control the income earned of their own labour, which is mainly spent for the well-being of children.

Findings of the surveyed data show that women's control over household income has been, found to influence children's and adult's nutrition positively. This result authenticates and, in term, is authenticated by the findings of Tripp.[46]

Tables 29 and 30 correlate mother's nutritional knowledge with nutritional status and show a positive relation between the nutritional status of the sample population and mother's nutritional knowledge. A strong association is found to

Table 29
Level of Mother's Nutritional Knowledge and Nutritional Status: Sivaganga District

Forms of Malnutrition	*Low*	*%*	*Medium*	*%*	*High*	*%*	*Total*	χ^2
Stunting (0-18 Years)								
Normal	6	22	11	28	12	38	29	14.45 (0.006)
Mild	9	33	15	38	19	59	43	
Moderate	10	37	12	31	1	3	23	
Severe	2	8	1	3	0	0	3	
Total	27	100	39	100	32	100	98	
Wasting (0-18 Years)								
Normal	9	33	9	23	21	66	39	14.60 (0.005)
Mild	12	45	20	51	9	28	41	
Moderate	4	15	10	26	2	6	16	
Severe	2	7	0	0	0	0	2	
Total	27	100	39	100	32	100	98	
Chronic Undernutrition (18+ Years)								
Normal	17	37	37	41	25	57	79	7.175 (0.305)
Mild	12	26	30	33	10	23	52	
Moderate	10	22	13	14	7	16	30	
Severe	7	15	11	12	2	4	20	
Total	46	100	91	100	44	100	181	

Source: Computed.
Note: Figures in parentheses denote 'p' level significance.

influence the nutritional status of children particularly. It is very encouraging to see that when the level of mother's nutritional knowledge is high no one is found to be severely malnourished amongst children of 0-18 years. It is also reckoned from the data that when the level of knowledge is increased, the proportion of children among of the 'normal' nutritional status category is also increased. Children's nutritional status is thus proved to be very closely associated with the level of nutritional knowledge. This suggests that nutrition knowledge may operate as a vigilant overseen in maintaining the health and nutrition of the children. This is, indeed, a practical policy oriented finding.

Table 30
Level of Mother's Nutritional Knowledge and Nutritional Status: Cuddalore District

Forms of Malnutrition	Low	%	Medium	%	High	%	Total	χ^2
Stunting (0-18 Years)								
Normal	7	13	9	21	12	48	28	19.14 (0.004)
Mild	23	44	24	56	12	48	59	
Moderate	17	33	7	16	1	4	25	
Severe	5	10	3	7	0	0	8	
Total	52	100	43	100	25	100	120	
Wasting (0-18 Years)								
Normal	4	8	19	44	17	68	40	33.34 (0.000)
Mild	27	52	14	32	6	24	47	
Moderate	13	25	8	19	2	8	23	
Severe	8	15	2	5	0	0	10	
Total	52	100	43	100	25	100	120	
Chronic Undernutrition (18+ Years)								
Normal	30	35	32	52	24	83	86	22.31 (0.001)
Mild	31	37	20	33	4	14	55	
Moderate	16	19	7	12	0	0	23	
Severe	8	9	2	3	1	3	11	
Total	85	100	61	100	29	100	175	

Source: Computed.
Note: Figures in parentheses denote 'p' level significance.

Surprisingly in the case of adult population in Sivaganga district, women nutritional knowledge does not show any significant impact. This could be due to the lack of information regarding food values and age-specific nutrient needs of the elderly or, perhaps, the adults disliked to be policed. Over all, the finding shows that in rural villages, to a greater extent women's traditional indigenous nutritional knowledge and knowledge gained through school education and information from other sources influence the nutritional status of family members. This result endorses the findings of few other researchers in this area.[47-48]

Tables 31 and 32 relate the association between the percentage of *women's time spent in food-related activities* and nutritional status of the family members in both the study districts. In both district, a negative relationship recorded. In Sivaganga and Cuddalore districts a higher proportion of normal children, as measured by height for age and weight for height, is found to belong to families where women's time spent in food related activities is more. Similar results are obtained in the case of nutritional status of adults. But the prevalence rate of under-nutrition in adults is more or less the same irrespective of the level of time spent by women in food-related work. This maternal factor is thus seen to have a negative influence on the long-term and short-term nutritional achievement of children and adults. This is shown by non-significant effect of the 'P' value.

Table 31
Percentage of Women's Time Allocated for Food Related Activities and Nutritional Status: Sivaganga District

Forms of Malnutrition	*Low*	*%*	*High*	*%*	*Total*	χ^2
Stunting (0-18 Years)						
Normal	9	19	20	38	29	4.184 (0.123)
Mild	23	50	20	38	43	
Moderate	11	24	12	24	23	
Severe	3	7	0	0	3	
Total	46	100	52	100	98	
Wasting (0-18 Years)						
Normal	18	39	21	40	39	0.011 (0.946)
Mild	20	44	21	40	41	
Moderate	8	17	8	16	16	
Severe	0	0	2	4	2	
Total	46	100	52	100	98	
Chronic Undernutrition (18+ Years)						
Normal	33	44	46	43	79	2.572 (0.462)
Mild	17	24	35	33	52	
Moderate	14	19	16	15	30	
Severe	10	13	10	9	20	
Total	74	100	107	100	181	

Source: Computed.
Note: Figures in parentheses denote 'p' level significance.

Table 32
Percentage of Women's Time Allocated for Food Related Activities and Nutritional Status: Cuddalore District

Forms of Malnutrition	*Low*	*%*	*High*	*%*	*Total*	χ^2
Stunting (0-18 Years)						
Normal	12	18	16	29	28	2.345 (0.504)
Mild	35	54	24	44	59	
Moderate	13	20	12	22	25	
Severe	5	8	3	5	8	
Total	65	100	55	100	120	
Wasting (0-18 Years)						
Normal	18	28	22	40	40	2.805 (0.422)
Mild	26	40	21	38	47	
Moderate	14	21	9	16	23	
Severe	7	11	3	6	10	
Total	65	100	55	100	120	
Chronic Undernutrition (18+ Years)						
Normal	34	47	52	51	86	0 94 (0.815)
Mild	23	31	32	31	55	
Moderate	10	14	13	13	23	
Severe	6	8	5	5	11	
Total	73	100	102	100	175	

Source: Computed.
Note: Figures in parentheses denote 'p' level significance.

This negative influence can be partly attributed to the fact that the nutritional status depends more on the nutrient content of the cooked food consumed rather than on the time and energy spent by women with regard to food supporting activities and cooking. The non-significant effect may perhaps be due to other factors such as lack of knowledge about food requirements, less time on caring of children and lower intake of food by adult women owing to heavy work burden. Women's high work load is also seen to negatively influence cooking habits and preparation of less nutritious food and loss of nutrients while cooking. Other Observation also suggest that women always readjust the number of meals or the kind of food provided to family based on work load.[49]

The verification of the fourth hypothesis shows that maternal factors have significant influence on the individual nutritional status.

After putting to evaluation the relationship of various maternal factors like mother's literacy, participation in decision-making, control over family income, nutritional knowledge, and percentage of time spent with nutritional status of individual members of the household, the fourth hypothesis, *maternal factors have significant influence on individual nutritional status* emerges vibrant and valuable.

KEY FINDINGS

- *Adequacy perspective of individual Food Security:* The protein-calorie adequacy status of both females and males is higher in Sivaganga district. Almost about half of the sample population suffer from calorie deficiency in both the districts. A similar percentile of respondents suffers from calorie gap in comparison with protein-gap.
- *Equity perspective of Individual Food Security:* Age-bias is significant only, in some JHH and MHH. The significant level is less pronounced in FHH. In Sivaganga district there is no sex-bias in general against females in terms of relative calorie and protein consumption within the household. But in Cuddalore district, gender prejudice is observed to exist within the household with favouritism towards males. Female headship has a positive effect on the relative nutritional allocation of its members towards equitable distribution.
- *Efficiency Perspective of Individual Food Security:* Nutritional status of children is greatly influenced by mother's nutritional knowledge. Nutritional status of the sample population is influenced greatly an positively by household income and level of expenditure on food. Maternal factors such as women's high-level participation in decision making, control over income and education strongly and positively contribute to individual nutritional status.

NOTES AND REFERENCES

1. Nutrition studies carried out by the Indian Council of Medical Researcher (ICMR), National Institute of Nutrition (NIN), International agencies like the World Health Organisation (WHO) and Food and Agriculture Organisation (FAO) and nutritionists have proposed a variety of approach for assessment of nutritional status of the community. Of them the direct parameters include (i) dietary intake, (ii) clinical assessment, (iii) anthropometric and (iv) biochemical analysis are considered. Of these the clinical assessment and biochemical analysis cannot be used to find mild and moderate forms of malnutrition.

   For further detail see, Visweswara Rao, K. (1980), "Efficiency of Anthropometric Indices for the Diagnosis of Malnutrition", *Currier,* Vol. 30, No. 2, 113-121.

2. Burgess, R.S.L. (1997), *A Novel Calorie Method for the Estimation of Equivalent Scales,* Oxford University Press, Mimeo.

3. Some household may allocate a greater proportion of higher costing, higher quality food to boys vs. girls. This only indicates the preferential treatment or parental valuation of boys and girls. However, the differential valuation does not translate into gender allocation of nutrients of boys vs. girls. And this preferences are irrelevant to individual welfare.

4. World Health Organisation (WHO) (1985), "Energy and Protein Requirements", Report of a Joint FAO/WHO/UNI/Expert Consultation, Technical Report Series No. 724, Geneva.

5. Starauss, John and Duncan Thomas (1998), "Health, Nutrition, and Economics Development", *Journal of Economics Literature,* Vol. 36, 766-817.

6. The method includes weighing the cooked food before eating it. The equipment used is an electronic weighing balance, which accurately measures the cooked weight of various dietary items before they are consumed. Based on the cooked weight and recipe used for formulating the dish, the weight of the raw ingredients is arrived at. And on the basis of the amount of raw ingredients used, calculations are made for different nutrients such as calorie and proteins.

   For details see, Gopaldas, T. and S. Seshadri (1987). *Nutrition: Monitoring and Assessment.* Oxford University Press, New Delhi.

7. ICMR (2002), "Nutrient Requirements and Recommended Dietary Allowances for Indian", A Report of the Expert Group of the Indian Council of Medical Research, NIN, Hyderabad: 9, 29.

8. Sha, C.H., S.D. Savant and B. Sangvi (1983), *Nutrition Gap An Economic Analysis*. Himalaya Publishing Work, Bombay.

9. National Nutritional Monitoring Bureau (1999), *Report of Second Repeated Survey-Rural 1996-97*, NIN (ICMR), Hyderabad.

10. Gopalan, C. (1984), "Classification of Under Nutrition Their Limitations and Fallacies." *Nutrition Foundation of India Bulletin*, Vol. 5, 2.

11. Carloni, Alice Stewart (1981), "Sex Disparities in the Distribution of Food within Rural Households", *Food and Nutrition*, 7: 3-12.

12. Leslie, J. (1991), "Women's Nutrition: The Key to Improve Family Health in Developing Countries?", *Health and Policy Planning*, Vol. 6, No. 1, 1 B9.

13. Sen, A. K. (1981), *Poverty and Famines: An Essay on Entitlement and Deprivation*, Calender Press, Oxford.

14. Abdulla, Mohammad and Erica F. Wherrel (1985), "Seasonal Variation and the Intra-household Distribution of Food in a Bangladesh Village", *American Journal of Clinical Nutrition*, Vol. 41, 305-13.

15. Chen, L.C., B. Huq and S. D'Souza (1981), "Sex Bias in the Family Allocation of Food and Health Care in Rural Bangladesh", *Population and Development Review*, Vol. 7, No. 1, 55-70.

16. Bruce, Judith (1989), "Home Divided", *World Development*, Vol. 17, No. 7, 972-92.

17. Gittel, John J. (1991), "Opening the Box: Intra-household Food Allocation in Rural Nepal", *Social Science and Medicine*, Vol. 33, No. 10, 1141-1154.

18. Becker, G. S. (1991), *Treatise on the Family*. 2nd ed. Mass, Harvard University Press, Cambridge.

19. Sanauer, B., M. Garcia and E. Jacinto (1988), "Determinants of the Intra-household Allocation of Food in the Rural Philippines", *American Journal of Agricultural Economics*, Vol. 70, No. 1, 170-179.

20. A sample household from Sivaganga district is chosen as an example for computation.

Relative Calorie Allocation

Work Type	*Age*	*Sex*	*Wt (in kg)*	*Calorie Actual (in kcal)*	*RDAs*	*ICAR*	*RCA*
Moderate	34	M	59.6	2620	2825	92.7	1.04
Moderate	23	F	56.0	2250	2356	95.5	1.07
Sedentary	5	F	17.0	1350	1643	82.1	0.92
Sedentary	2	M	10.8	990	1301	76.1	0.86

$$\text{HCAR} = \frac{7210}{8125} \times 100 = 88.7$$

Relative Protein Allocation (RPA)

Age	*Protein (in gm) Actual*	*RDA's*	*IPAR*	*RPA*
34	55	60	91.6	0.97
23	47	50	94.0	0.99
5	26	27.3	95.2	1.01
2	19.5	19	102.6	1.09

$$\text{HPAR} = \frac{147.5}{156.3} \times 100 = 94.3$$

21. Kennedy, E. (1988). *Effects of Sugarcane Production in South Western Kenya on Income and Nutrition.* International Food Policy Research Institute, Washington, D.C.

22. During the last one decade the National Nutrition Monitoring Bureau (NNMB) has been conducting diet and nutrition surveys on various age-sex groups in the rural areas in India. A look at the data suggests that women are not discriminated against as far as food intake goes.

    See also NNMB, (1999), *Report of Second Repeated Survey-Rural 1996-1997*, National Institute of Nutrition (ICMR), Hyderabad.

23. Haughton, Dominique and Joanathan Haughton (1997), "Explaining Child Nutrition in Vietnam", *Economic Development and Cultural Change*, Vol. 45, 541-56.

24. Kilander, Holger Fredrick (1951), *Nutrition For Health.* McGraw-Hill Book Company, New York, 3-5.

25. Visweswara Rao, K. (1977), "Analysis of Relative Importance of Factors Affective Body Weight Changes in Pre-school Children

by Nutritional Status", Proceedings of the International Statistical Institute Seminar, New Delhi.

26. Tara, Gopaldas and Sundandra Seshadri (1987), *Nutrition Monitoring and Assessment*, Oxford University Press, Delhi, 103-104.

27. Reynaldo, Martorell and J.H.O. Teresa (1984), "Malnutrition, Morbidity and Mortality", in Henry Mosely and Lincoln C. Chem, (eds.), "Child Survival Strategies for Research", *Population and Development Review*, Vol. 10, 49-51.

28. Chen, L.C., A.K.M.A. Chaudhury and S.L. Huffman (1980), "Anthropometric Assessment of Energy-protein Malnutrition and Subsequent Risk of Mortality Among Pre-school Age Children", *American Journal Clinical Nutrition*, Vol. 33, 1836-1845.

29. Waterlow, J.C., R. Bozina and W. Kallen (1977), "The Presentation and Use of Height and Weight Data for Comparing the Nutritional Status of Groups of Children under the Age of 10 years", *Bull WHO*, Vol. 55, 489-498.

    See also Jean Gerard Pelletier (1993), *Children in the Tropics, Severe Malnutrition: A Global Approach 1993*, 208-209.

30. Bowman, B., B. H. Irwin and M.D. Rosenberg (1982), "Assessment of Nutritional Status of the Elderly", *American Journal of Clinical Nutrition*, Vol. 35, 1142-1151.

31. Mitchell, C. and D. Lipschitz (1982), "Detection of Protein-calorie Malnutrition in the Elderly", *American Journal of Clinical Nutrition*, Vol. 35, 398-406.

32. Collins, S., A. Duffield and M. Myatt (2000), "Assessment of Nutritional Status in Emergency-affected Population: Adults", July, ACC/SCN, Geneva.

    BMI: A man who weighs 50.5 Kg. and a height of 1.538 cm would have a BMI of (50.5/1.538 x 1.538)=21.3

    See also, A. Ferro-Luzzi, S. Sette, M. Franklin, and W.P. James (1992), "A Simplified Approach of Assessing Adult Chronic Energy Deficiency", *European Journal of Clinical Nutrition*, Vol. 46, March: 173-186.

33. World Bank (1981), *World Bank Report*. Washington, D.C., 59-60.

34. Shariff, Abusleh and Namkee Ahn (1995), "Mother's Education Effect on Child Health: An Economic Analysis of Child Anthropometry in Uganda", *The Indian Economic Review*, Vol. 30, No. 2, 203-22.

35. Sukhatme (1987), "Economics of Nutrition", *Indian Journal of Agricultural Economics,* Vol. 32, No. 3, 1-11.

36. Alderman, H. (1990), "Nutritional Status in Ghana and its Determinants", *Social Dimensions of Adjustment in Sub-Saharan Africa Working Paper,* No. 3, World Bank, Washington, D.C.

37. World Health Organization (WHO) (1985), "Women, Health and Development", A Report by the Director-General WHO Offset Publication, No. 9, Geneva.

38. Gupta Rao,G. (1985), "Role Conflict and Coping Strategies. A Study on Indian Women", A Ph.D., Dissertation, Bangladesh University.

39. Blumberg, Rae (1991), "Income Under Female versus Male Control," in Rae Blumberg (ed.), *Gender, Family and Economy: The Trifle Overlap,* Sage Press, Newbury Park: 97-106.

40. Kennedy, E. and P. Peters (1992), "Household Food Security and Child Nutrition: The Interaction of Income and Gender of Household Head", *World Development,* Vol. 20, No. 8, 1077-1085.

41. Barrera, A. (1990), "The Role of Maternal Schooling and Its Interventions with Public Health Programs in Child Health Production", *Journal of Development Economics,* Vol. 32, 69-91.

42. Behrman, J.R. and B.L. Wolfe (1987), "How Does Mother's Schooling Affect Family Health, Nutrition, Medical Care, Wage, and Household Sanitation? ", *Journal of Econometrics,* Vol. 36, 185-204.

43. Alderman, H. and M. Garcia (1995), "Food Security and Health Security. Explaining the Levels of Nutrition in Pakistan", *Policy Research Working Papers,* No. 865.

44. Sen, Gita, Adrien Germaine and Lincoln Chen (1994), *Population Policies Reconsidered-Health, Empowerment and Rights.* Harvard University Press.

45. Smith, L.C., U. Ramaakrishnan, A. Ndiaye, L. Haddad, and R. Martorell (2003), "The Importance of Women's Status for Child Nutrition in Developing Countries", Research Report No. 20, IFPRI, Washington, D. C.

46. Tripp, R.B. (1982), "Farmers and Traders. Some Economic Determinants of Nutritional Status in Northern Ghana", *Journal of Tropical Pediatrics,* Vol. 27, No. 1, 15-22.

47. Piwoz, Ellen Gail and Fernando Viteri (1985), "Studying Health and Nutrition Behaviour by Examining Household Decision Making, Intra-household Resource Distribution and the Role of Women in these Processes." *Food and Nutrition Bulletin*, Vol. 7, No. 4, 1-30.

48. Devadas, Rajammal P., V. Chandrasekhar, S. Premakumari, and G. Geetha (1991), "Female Literacy and Female Improvement. Part 1. Correlation between Female Literacy, Birth Rate and IMR", The *Indian Journal of Nutrition and Dietetics*, Vol. 28, 70-77.

49. Prehm, M.S. (1991), "Developing Integrative Methods for Describing Food Production and Consumption Linkages", *Ecology of Food and Nutrition*, Vol. 25, 193-207.

8

Integrated Discussion and Policy Suggestions

This chapter attempts to integrate together the scooped out results obtained from the analysis of household entitlements, women's role and individual food security in the foregoing chapters of this study. This cartelisation, it is hoped, will help drawing up a basket of need-based policy suggestions and spotting out useful research needs of various dimensions of food security.

INTEGRATED DISCUSSION

The precision and analytical evidence with which this empirical evaluation of rural household food and nutritional security was done has provided a clear insight into the Household Food Path Model.

Household Food Security

A micro-level analysis of household food security from women's perspective inter-linked with socio-economic environment is considered essential to promote the nutritional status of the rural population. Household's background information such as household category, family size, sex, age composition and other external factors like asset, income, food consumption frequency, food storage, food habits, and maternal factors are necessary in the determination of household food security. Another component which is considered is women's access to resources such as land, income, credit and control over them, and their access to nutritional knowledge. Women's role as mediator in household food security is also assessed. In the present economic conditions, household food security depends more on the household's access to food than simply on availability. The main determinants of food security are the households' entitlements which influence the capacity of the household to obtain adequate quantities of food for its members. In relating the results to the causes of food insecurity, this study is indebted Sen's entitlement approach.

A household's adequate asset base is important for ensuring its food security as land provides direct access to food. Income generating assets such as land, large livestock and trees are one of the prime determinants of household food security. This income generating asset is found to be highly concentrated among the MF households which are also observed to have lower incidence of food insecurity. Land is the main form of wealth for MF households which accounts for 60 per cent in Sivaganga district and 70 per cent in Cuddalore district. The asset status of LAL households is very low and thus they lack the resource base for income generation. Liquid assets in the form of jewels and small livestock are found to be highly concentrated among the NFW households (see Chapter 5, Table 1). Scarce assets show the vulnerability of the poor to food insecurity.

Households possessing land consume home produced food to a larger extent. Further, it is found that poor farm households owning less than 0.75 acres produce less and are equipped to feed their members for a few months only and for future consumption they depend on the open market and PDS. Even the landholders of more than 0.75 acres are sometimes seen to market their home produced grains to meet out household's food and non-food expenditures. So food is seen to be ensured only in those households which retain their stock for the entire year's consumption. For MF households, resources for primary food consumption come from home production which is at around 70 per cent of the total for all the four study villages. Market dependency is higher for NFW households and LAL households who depend to a greater extent on PDS and open market hampers (see Table 5.4 p.119). Respondents are also observed to gather food from fields and forests and the gathered foods are processed and kept for future household consumption or sold to meet emergency monetary requirements.

Landless households derive their income from wage employment in farm and non-farm sectors and from petty trading and livestock rearing. Analysis of sources of income has revealed that for LAL households a large fraction of income originates from wage employment which is nearly 90 per cent of the total (see Chapter 5, Table 5). This income generating assets and liquid assets and wage income are the most important sources by which the rural households acquire food.

The food supply of rural households is ensured by a combination of two factors, namely, home production and household expenditure. The household food expenditure, to a great extent, determines the level of food consumption. Analysis of food expenditure shows a striking variation in the level of expenditure among the households which reflects the gross inequalities in income. Average monthly food expenditure is the highest for MF households, followed by NFW households, and it is the lowest for LAL households, in both the districts. In all sample households, the highest expenditure is on cereals which accounts for 36 per cent of the total consumption expenditure.

The share of expenditure on expensive food items like meat and milk products are higher for MF and NFW households than LAL households. Lowest share of expenditure is made on micro-nutrient rich foods like green leaves and fruits in all sample households which account for only two per cent (see Chapter 5, Table 6, Chapter 5, Table 7 and Chapter 5, Table 8). Some households with adequate income are also experiencing food inadequacy and the underlying cause is lack of knowledge about nutritional value of foods. Analysis on the frequency of food consumption has shown that frequency of pulse consumption is greater than meat and fruit for the rural poor households (see Chapter 5, Table 12 and Chapter 5, Table 13).

While considering the average storage of food items, the mean value of storage of cereals is found to be maximum for MF households at 404.0 kg and 317.0 kg for V_1 and V_2 of Sivaganga district and 440.0 kg and 292.0 kg for V_1 and V_2 of Cuddalore district respectively. This shows that home production exerts a positive influence on the storage of staple food (see Chapter 5, Table 14). MF households in V_1 of the both the districts retain the food grain stock in large quantities and they have the advantage of market accessibility to sell the grains whenever the need arises. Food habit matrix examines the number of cooking sessions, number of meals and food type during normal and lean season. It is unhappily observed that five households in Sivaganga district and eight in Cuddalore district have a mere one-square meal a day and majority of them belong to LAL households. Generally during lean season the respondents are seen to consume starchy staple food and during normal time they consume protein content foods (see Chapter 5, Table 15).

A theoretical focus on food security enlightens on factors related to supply and demand side and women's role which are crucial in achieving household food security. The supply and demand for food at the household level is determined by exchange entitlements and their interrelationship is evaluated by the framing of the first hypothesis which states that *household entitlements and food security move together.* Household food security is seen as an outcome of three different time-dimensions as past food security, current food security and future food security. Food frequency (which explains household's usage pattern) is taken as an indicator of past food security. Current state of household food security is measured by the adequacy of household's present consumption. Future food security is measured through current food storage which analysis is limited to storable foods. Multiple linear regression models are fitted and analysed separately for Female Headed Households (FHH), Joint Headed Households (JHH) and Male Headed Households (MHH) to assess the overall influence of the intervening variables namely PSIGLA, PCI, ARES, FS, and EDR on all the three time-dimensions of household food security for both the study districts. The same model is again applied to assess the overall influence of the various intervening variables on all the three components of household food security for both the districts (see Chapter 5, Table 16, Chapter 5, Table 17 and Chapter 5, Table 18).

The results of the above assessments given in (Chapter 5, Table 19) show that the exchange entitlements are highly contributing to household food security. All the intervening variables included in the model are observed to be contributing significantly for past, current and future food security of the sample households. The cumulative findings show that the exchange entitlements such as PSIGLA, PCI, ARES, HP/WIK, EDR, and FS exert influence and are highly contributing for Fpulse (71.7 per cent), QSC (90.2 per cent) and QSP (80.9 per cent), PUPC (60.6 per cent) and PUCC (52.6 per cent) in Sivaganga district, whereas in Cuddalore district these entitlements are contributing for Fpulse (73.7 per cent), QSC (80.7 per cent), QSP (70.9 per cent), PUCC (52.2 per cent), and Fmeat (57.7 per cent). It is observed that the regression co-efficient has the expected sign for family size showing negative influence with frequency of consumption of food and current consumption of cereals and pulses. Households with higher dependency ratios are seen to be more vulnerable from food security standpoint, indicating the importance of considerations of family type and composition for the purpose of food security targeting. Of all the entitlements, per capita income shows the highest explanatory power indicating a significant positive relation in achieving household food security. Women's access to resources also has shown a positive effect.

Women's Role in the Food Chain

Logical extension of this discussion on food security is the assessment of the potential of the women for improving household food and nutrition security at the household level through food chain activities. The obtained results indicate that women keep occupied for a long time on food chain activities. Comparatively, women in Sivaganga district are observed to allocate more time in household chores and remunerative activities. On an average women in MF households in this district spend 930 mins. in V_1 and 850 mins. in V_2 as against women in Cuddalore district who spend 860 mins. in V_1 and 760 mins. in V_2. Even women in NFW and LAL households in Sivaganga district are seen to allocate more time for this activity than women in Cuddalore district (see Chapter 6,Table 1, Chapter 6, Table 3 and Chapter 6, Table 5). It has been established from the survey data that women in Sivaganga district spend more time on water collection. Data on percentage share of food related activities indicate that more than 90 per cent of the work is carried out by women alone in both the districts (see Chapter 6, Table 2, Chapter 6, Table 4 and Chapter 6, Table 6). It is observed that on an average the total time women allocate to work on a yearly basis is around 10-11 hours per day in Sivaganga district and 8-10 hours per day in Cuddalore district. In peak season, they work for as long as 14-16 hours per day in Sivganga district and 10-12 hours per day in Cuddalore district.

The Household Economic Model considered the effect of women's role and bargaining power. Women's access to resources emerges as an important issue in this regard. Most of the women with less access to resources are concentrated among the poor strata of the LAL category households. Women in Sivaganga district show high level of participation in decision-making. The influence of women empowerment, measured through women's participation in the food chain and decision making processes, in improving the dietary status and achievement of household food security is the core of the second hypothesis, which reads, *women empowerment contributes positively to household food security.* The mean differences in DAR are tested between women empowerment groups and between ten food groups, namely cereals, pulses, green leafy vegetables, roots and tubers, other vegetables, fruits, fish, and poultry products, milk and milk products, fats and edible oils sugar and jaggery, using the Fisher's Two-way Analysis of Variance (ANOVA). The result show that as women empowerment ascends from low level, dietary adequacy status is also seen to ascend significantly (see Chapter 6, Table 16) and hence the hypothesis that women empowerment contributes to food is validated to be reliable.

Between food groups, the mean difference in DAR of cereals is found to be statistically significant in both low empowered households and moderately empowered households (see Chapter 6, Table 17 and Chapter 6, Table 18). Identification of food secured households based on the mean requirements of the nutrient intake such as calorie and protein consumption reveal that majority of LAL households fall under food insecure category. In Sivaganga district, of the 60 households, 24 are food secured households (13 in V_1 and 11 in V_2) aggregating 46 per cent. Category-wise distribution of households shows that 45 per cent of the MF households, 50 per cent of the NFW category and 75 per cent of the LAL households are food insecured. But in Cuddalore district, only 22 households (12 in V_1 and 10 in V_2) are found to be food secured aggregating only 37 per cent. Calorie intake shows that 90 per cent of LAL households suffer from calorie insufficiency.

The nutritionally insecure LAL households in terms of protein consumption is distributed in Sivaganga district at 55 per cent and at 60 per cent in Cuddalore district. A comparison of mean per capita consumption in relation to household headship leads to a strong conclusion that female headed households are much better than male headed households in terms of calorie/protein consumption (see Chapter 6, Table 20 and Chapter 6, Table 21). Investigations on the relationship of family size with nutrient intake reveals that the family size is closely but negatively correlated with nutrient intake (see Chapter 6, Table 25).

To overcome food insecure situations women in majority of the households are found to adopt Ex-anti and Ex-post coping mechanism (see Chapter 6, Table 26). Livestock rearing is observed to be a prominent Ex-anti coping strategy in the study villages followed by saving grains and maintaining household gardens. The number of households using these strategies is found to be more in Sivaganga district than in Cuddalore district. In Cuddalore district, borrowing and selling of livestock is considered an important Ex-post coping strategy by majority of the households. Women's education is also found to influence food consumption at the household level (see Chapter 6, Table 27).

Individual Nutritional Security

In a holistic household food security analysis, the nutritional status of every individual in the household is important. Three factors determining an individual's food and nutritional security are adequacy, equity and efficiency. Adequacy of nutrition of individuals in terms of nutrient intake (Calorie and Protein) is assessed to examine the relative positions of individuals according to age and sex. A comparative analysis of protein-calorie adequacy status (P^+C^+) presented in (see) Figure 1 show that the percentage of protein-calorie adequacy status of both male and females in Sivaganga district is higher than their counterparts in Cuddalore district. The protein-calorie inadequacy is found to be lower by 10 per cent for females in Sivaganga district. Overall nutrient adequacy status shows that a higher percentage of male population suffers from protein deficiency and female population suffers from calorie deficiency. The variations in the food intake by age and sex confirm the prevalence of inequity (see Chapter 7, Table 1 and Chapter 7, Table 2). This necessitated the need to make an analysis of intra-household food allocation.

Female headship as an important component in the nutrient intake of households has already been established. So the relationship of headship with intra-household allocation of food is empirically tested through the third formulated hypothesis that *female headship reduces age and gender bias in individual nutritional security.* Mean differences in relative nutrient (calorie/protein) allocation between males and females are computed to identify the extent of the sex bias and age bias of the intra familial food allocation. The empirical results show that female headship has a promotional effect on the relative nutrient allocation of its members equitably between age and gender groups. The analysis shows that there is no sex-bias against females in terms of relative calorie and

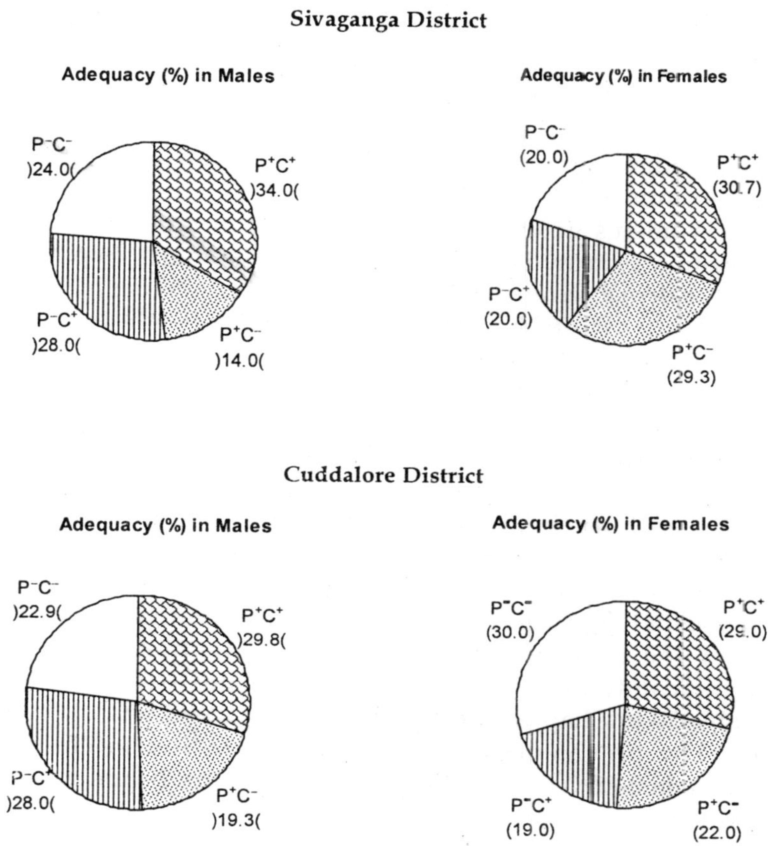

FIGURE 1
PROTEIN-CALORIE ADEQUACY STATUS (%) AMONG THE SAMPLE POPULATION

protein consumption within the female headed households for female's calorie/protein adequacy ratio is shown to be either equal to one or more than one. The hypothesis is validated and this is attributed to the single most important fact that women's participation in food allocation process is enhanced by their decision making level (see Chapter 7, Table 3 to Chapter 7, Table 8).

To ascertain the efficiency perspective of individual nutritional security, the household level determinants of food security such as per capita income, expenditure on food, family size, occupation, and access to health and sanitary conditions and maternal factors such as female headship, women's literacy, their control over household income, level of participation in decision-making, nutritional knowledge, and their time allocation in food related activities are examined.

Women's position as the mediators of family food and nutrition security is examined through the fourth hypothesis that *maternal factors have significant influence on the individual nutritional security*. Height-for-age index and weight-for-height index are the two anthropometric indices used for measuring the 'stunting' and 'wasting' malnutrition (diagnosing the long term and short term nutritional maladies respectively) in children. Body Mass Index is the index used for measuring the body composition of adults. The extent of association between household and maternal factors with nutritional status is measured by using Chi-square analysis of association of attributes. The result indicates that maternal factors such as women's high level of participation in decision-making, control over income, their headship, and education contribute significantly to individual nutritional status (see Chapter 7, Table 20 to Chapter 7, Table 30).

The prevalence of stunting malnutrition in children between 0-18 years represented in (see) Figure 2 show that the proportion of normal-nourished children is higher in Sivaganga district at 29.59 per cent than in Cuddalore district which is at 23.33 per cent. The extent of severe stunting is also the lowest in Sivaganga district at 3.06 per cent when compared to 6.67 per cent in Cuddalore district. Even in the case of wasting malnutrition a higher proportion (39.8 per cent) of under-normal category is found in Sivaganga district than in Cuddalore district (33.33 per cent). About 2.04 per cent of children are severely undernourished in Sivaganga district as against 8.33 per cent in Cuddalore district. But in adult population, surprisingly, the proportion of severe malnutrition is higher at 11.05 per cent in Sivaganga district than in Cuddalore district which is only 6.29 per cent.

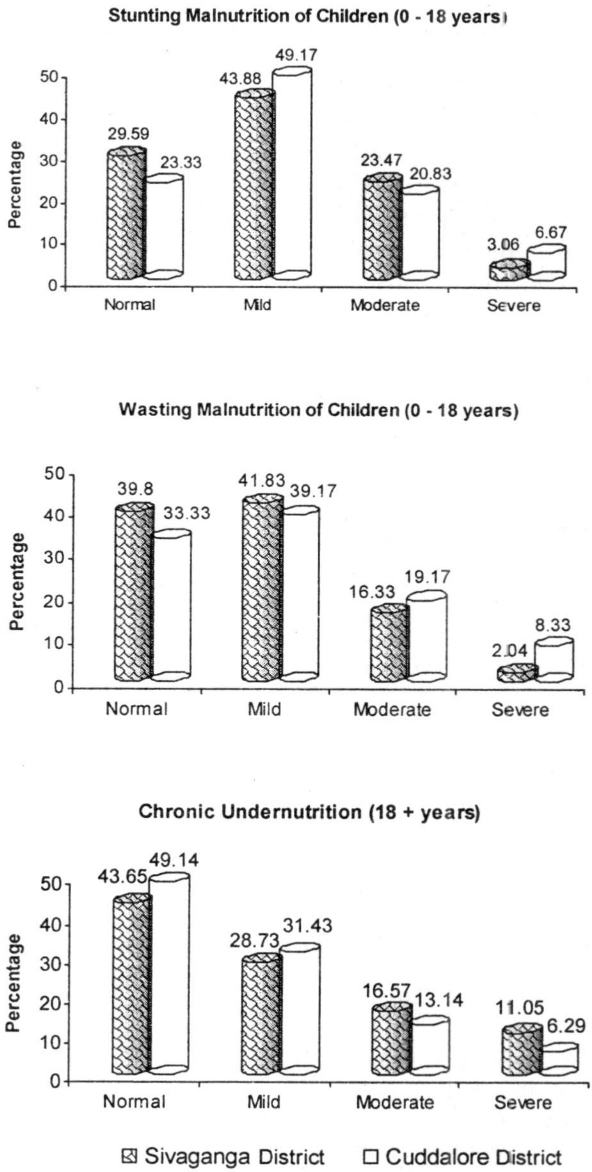

FIGURE 2
NUTRITIONAL STATUS OF THE SAMPLE POPULATION

Statistical verification of the data obtained in both the districts shows that the proportion of malnourished children and adults are low in families where women's control over income, nutritional knowledge and women's decision-making level are high. The analysis of rural household food security with women outlook would provide positive logistics to the food security intervention programmes.

Based on the investigations of determinants of household food security, nutrient intake levels and the nutritional status of individuals, this empirical research has led to the structuring of following household Food Path Model:

HOUSEHOLD FOOD PATH MODEL FOR FOOD SECURITY

Background Variables	*Intervening Variables*	*Proximate Variables*	*Criterion Variables*
I. Household Entitlements 1. Income Generating Assets 2. Women's Access to Resources	- Household Income - Women's participation in Decision-making →	- Per Capita Expenditure on Food - Women Empowerment →	Household Food Security (DAR) → ↓
II. Household Factors 1. Occupational Category 2. Family Type and Size	- Days of Employment - Earner Dependent Ratio - Sex ratio	- Per Capita Income - Nutrient Intake Levels	Individual Food Security (PCA/RNA) ↓
III. Maternal Factors 1. Task and Time Allocation 2. Maternal Education	- Female Headship Matrix - Nutritional Knowledge	- Food Habit Status - Intra-household Food Allocation	Nutritional (HAI/WHI/BMI)

Note: DAR–Dietary Adequacy Ratio
PCA–Protein Calorie Adequacy
RNA–Relative Nutrient Adequacy
HAI–Height-for-Age Index
WHI–Weight-for-Height Index
BMI–Body Mass Index

POLICY SUGGESTIONS

Diagnosis of the problems in food security has explicitly footaged the adverse effects of lack of household entitlements and promotional effects of women empowerment with regard to household food security and individual nutritional security. In this context, certain practicable short-run and long-run policy measures are suggested to build up coping strategies for household food and nutritional security using proximate variables. Proximate variables used include per capita income, expenditure on food, intra-household food allocation, food habit, nutrient intake level, and women empowerment. In making the policy suggestions, due importance is given to the comments and remarks of the women respondents who were interviewed for the survey. Each short and long-run suggestion is suffixed with the reason which necessitated the suggestion.

Short-run Policy Suggestions

The following are the measures suggested for improving food security and overcoming under-nutrition.

1. Legal changes in existing ownership and inheritance rules are one of the important coping strategies which would ensure women's continued access to land regardless of their marital status. In the study area, women do not inherit land, even if it is legally their right. Conventions of practice are seen to clash with legal rights. Lack of awareness on the part of women is another pothole. In this regard non-government organisations particularly women rights organisations should come forward to educate the women and to create attitudinal changes that are needed to change such traditional practices.
2. The Government should provide better storage facilities to farmers, and there by prevent them from selling grains just because of the risk of loss during storage. It is seen in the study villages of Cuddalore district that lack of storage facilities made the marginal

poor farmers to sell their grains immediately after harvest thus affecting their future food security.

3. Agricultural extension services are needed to disseminate knowledge on the income generating potentials to the rural people. They need to be advised on the low labour requirement crops, and crops that need minimum land preparation, weeding techniques and sources of irrigation. They should be educated to identify crops that are fit for direct consumption and easily encashable.
4. Women must be motivated to create and maintain household kitchen gardens to improve family nutrition and they should be made aware of their potential to generate additional income. Extension educators should give proper training and support to home gardens.
5. Co-operative marketing activities among women have to be encouraged because they are more feasible and successful than individual marketing. Such arrangements have the advantage of reducing the time and labour each individual has to spend on marketing their products. The trouble-spot for women involved in trading activities and productivity in the food chain was observed to be lack of opportunities for marketing their produce, whether it is processed or unprocessed food.
6. Child-care support for women is an important policy issue. So informal or more formal arrangements for child-care should be evolved. Most women from the lower socio-economic categories in the study villages are employed in the informal sector, which has no child-care services. During the agricultural season, they are away at work for more than six hours and are unable to provide complementary food to the child and the child is prone to become nutritionally deprived.
7. Rural Employment Guarantee Scheme (EGS) which would support local work programmes should be

established. This will be the single most important measure of social security for the rural poor. In the present study, it is found that women's access to and control over productive resources is very low particularly when days of employment are greatly limited from farm activities. Hence encouraging the participation of women in paid non-farm employment becomes imminent.

8. Micro-credit facilities should be examined as an effective and sustainable strategy for supporting women's livelihood. Women must be motivated to become a member of the self-help group in their respective villages. This is suggested because in the study area women's access to credit is found to be greatly limited to only formal sources like banks. Micro-credit intervention at the village level through self-help or women's groups is bound to help women to gain access to financial resources, which would facilitate them to gain better status within the family. Credit provision would result in increasing their income, which would have direct bearing on the nutritional status of the family.

9. The value of traditional foods, including coarse grains, needs to be revived and reevaluated. The importance of micronutrient rich foods like fruits and vegetables in improving the nutrition of the people should be emphasised through health workers attached to primary health centers or Non-Government Organisations (NGOs).

10. Inequality in the intra-familial food allocation should be eliminated through appropriate social safety nets involving NGOs. For low income groups, foods which can substitute more expensive alternatives should be suggested.

11. Public Distribution System (PDS) needs to be restructured ensuring more efficient food distribution. For the time-being Targeted Public Distribution

System (TPDS) should continue. However, in the context of numerous problems of TPDS, there is a need for the Government to re-examine this policy. The Government should try to adopt a universal system of distribution rather than TPDS so as to ensure that no section of the population is deprived of food. Exploring alternative options to the public distribution system like issue of food stamps to promote economic access of food to the poor and the vulnerable population especially in food deficit and dry land areas is considered necessary. Efficient targeting of the PDS should also try to eliminate macro and micro nutrient deficiencies. Food policy should be linked with population policy. In order to solve the problem of under nutrition there is a need to look for supra-food solutions. Non-nutritional factors such as access to safe drinking water and adequate sanitation should also be considered.

Long-run Policy Suggestions

1. Asset creation and non-farm livelihood opportunities for women should be prioritised. Asset creation is necessary because women belonging to economically under-privileged class are often over worked and under paid and they remain poor, because they have no productive assets. Since agriculture work is seasonal, non-farm livelihood opportunities provide a strong base for current and future food security which in turn may lead to sustainable food security at the household level.
2. Steps should be taken to eliminate wage disparities. The present study reveals that women in Sivaganga district receive very low wages for farm activities than women in Cuddalore district.
3. Interventions for increasing food production in the rural area should be implemented and these should aim at preserving and expanding irrigation systems, making unused land productive, preventing conversion

of productive lands for other purposes and extending soft loans to farmers.

4. Community afforestation programmes could be an important policy measure to increase the availability of fire wood for women. Empowering Panchayat Raj Institutions for encouraging afforestation is considered important. Another policy option is increasing the possibilities for developing a communal irrigation system combined with proper water management like rain water harvesting, which will significantly increase women's productivity while simultaneously reducing their burden of work.

5. Improving early nutrition and ensuring that the next generation has the best nutritional start is essential. Since low birth weight is a major constraint to stunting, the prevention of low birth weight should be considered an intermediate target. The primary focus of attention should be adolescent girls, who are the mothers-to-be and pregnant and lactating women. Nutritional needs of pregnant and lactating women should be recognized. Dietary prescriptions during these physiological states should be in the form of food taboos, which tend to render the diet less nutritious rather than improving. Breast-feeding needs to be encouraged. Dissemination of health and nutritional knowledge is essential and this should aim at ensuring appropriate feeding practices for children and these should be publicised through appropriate communication channels like television, radio, handbills, and billboards.

6. Nutritional campaigns should be organised in the villages to impart knowledge about the dietary diversification to meet the nutritional needs of the family. To avoid the incidence of age-bias, promoting appropriate intra-family distribution of food based on individual requirements of both the sexes is necessary. Campaigns should emphasize about the food that can be acquired and prepared with minimal resources and also on their cultural acceptability.

7. Enhanced female education is one of the successful approaches to improve the food and nutrition secured situation. Efforts to expand access to primary and secondary education are important. This has many further benefits such as raising literacy levels, delaying the age of marriage and child bearing, improved work opportunities and better dietary practices and use of health and nutrition services.
8. Nutrition Education has to be integrated with the science subjects in the school curriculum. Children should be made aware of the nutritive value of food. This is needed to develop desirable behavioural attitudes in children towards nutritional issues and to inculcate in them the good nutritional practices. Parents also should be made aware that malnutrition diminishes the quality of their life and that nutritious foods can play a creative role in providing a more prosperous future.
9. A holistic approach is needed in planning and implementing nutrition and health related programmes. The implementation of various Government programmes and their impact on the nutritional status of the population should be systematically monitored and evaluated. Empowering people with information about developmental programmes which are meant for them, is one of the strategies for ensuring effective implementation of programmes at the grass root level.

SCOPE FOR FUTURE RESEARCH

1. Information concerning women's nutritional status based on scientific research is limited, particularly with regard to causes or consequences of malnutrition linked to pregnancy or lactation. This is essential to prevent low birth weight babies. Research on this issue specifically on culture-specific and culture related nutritional behaviours with in households are needed.
2. Documented studies associating women's trading activities with food consumption and nutritional status of her own

and her children are insufficient. Studies of this type are essential, particularly for women of fishing communities on whom there is practically no studied information.

3. Studies have to be conducted to cartograph the reasons for regional variability in patterns of stunting, wasting and low weight-for-age so that their implications could be recorded for future programme planning and allocation of resources.

9

Conclusions

This microanalytical study on the role of women in rural household food security has mapped out important findings of theoretical value, which are not within the grasp of previous research studies. The findings would provide the logistics and the vital empirical support required for any future rainbow study on women and household food security. Major results and the unique features of the study are briefly and crisply summarised here.

Majority of the respondents is Hindus in all the study villages. Major community concentrated in Sivaganga district is the backward class (BC) and in Cuddalore district it is the most backward class (MBC). Most of the households adopt nuclear family system. Sex ratio is higher for Sivaganga district and it is lower for Cuddalore district, which reflects the national trend. Most of the households belong to medium size families. The number of males and females are found to be more in the middle age groups. Dependency ratio is lower whereas female literacy is greater for Sivaganga district. More female earners are found in Sivaganga district than in Cuddalore district. Female-headed households are comparatively more in number in Sivaganga district. Main source of borrowing in both the study districts is from private moneylenders. Borrowing for consumption purposes is higher for poor households in both the districts.

Income generating assets and liquid assets, and wage income are the important means by which rural households acquire food for consumption. Rice is the important crop which is grown once in a year. Very few households, less than 15 per cent of the total, indulge in crop diversification to reduce the risk against entitlement failure due to depleted water and productive resources.

Home production is the main source of food for majority of MF households. NFW households depend on the open market to a larger extent. LAL households purchase more from PDS as well as from open market. Majority of rural households are not satisfied with the working of PDS in their areas. People also gather secondary food from the fields and forest. The intensity and involvement in this food source is greater in Sivaganga district.

The maximum level of income and assets are in MF category households. NFW and LAL categories form the second and third levels in the hierarchy. Landlessness is identified by most of the LAL respondents as one of the cardinal reasons for food insecurity.

Food expenditure is positively related to income. Expenditure on cereals occupied the highest expenditure and the lowest is on fruits. Frequency of pulse consumption is greater than the frequency of consumption of meat and fruits for the sample rural households. 11.7 per cent of families in Sivaganga district and 15.7 per cent of families in Cuddalore districts do not consume milk whereas 20.2 per cent and 22.5 per cent of families in Sivaganga and Cuddalore districts respectively do not consume fruits. Home production exercises a favourable influence on storage of staple food. Proportion of households consuming starchy food type round the year is found to be higher in LAL households and poor MF and NFW categories. Variations are found in the number of cooking sessions, number of meals and food type among the household categories.

Operationalization of household food security for various exchange entitlements reveal that per capita income (PCI) influences household past, current and future food security positively. Family size affects the frequency of food consumption. Women's access to resources has a positive effect but not strong significance on food security.

On an average women in Sivaganga district allocate more time in household chores and remunerative activities. Percentage share of women's work is the greatest for food related activities in both the districts. Women's access to various resources is limited in both districts. Comparing the level of access to resources by score value, women in FHH are better.

Awareness about vaccination and immunization is found in women of both study areas. Educated women are found to have some functional knowledge on nutrition. Women in Sivaganga district take higher level of participation in decision making. Women's age, education and their level of access to resources influence positively the level of decision making in various household matters.

The Dietary Adequacy Ratio (DAR) improves as the level of women empowerment increases. Over all mean calorie consumption, headship wise is higher for FHH. Calorie consumption, occupational category wise, is higher for MF and NFW categories than LAL category.

When income increases, the food expenditure level also rises but the proportion of income spent on food declines. Saving grains is found to be an important ex-anti coping strategy for majority of MF households. Livestock rearing is identified as the most important ex-anti coping strategy whereas borrowing is the most important ex-post coping strategy in majority of the households in both the districts. Maternal education contributes to food security.

From the 'adequacy' perspective of individual food security, it is inferred that about a half of the sample population suffers from calorie deficiency in both the districts. The Protein-Calorie adequacy (P^+C^+) status of both females and males is higher in Sivaganga district. People in both the study areas suffer from calorie gap to a greater extent than protein gap.

The 'equity' perspective of individual food security indicates that in Sivaganga district there is no sex-bias against females in terms of relative calorie and protein consumption within the household. But in Cuddalore district, the existence of sex-bias is observed within the household favouring males. The sex-bias is significant only in MF and NFW households coming under JHH and MHH, confirming that female headship has a positive effect on the equitable nutritional allocation to its members. Age-bias against children is found but the effect is significant only in few households, which come under JHH and MHH. Its incidence is less pronounced in the FHH.

From the 'efficiency' perspective of individual food security it is found out that nutritional status of the sample population is influenced greatly by household income and level of expenditure on food. Maternal factors such as women's high-level of participation in decision making, control over income and education strongly contribute to individual nutritional status. Nutritional status of children is greatly influenced by mother's nutritional knowledge.

The obtained results suggest that to improve food security in low income rural households, national nutritional programmes should be developed. These programmes should target subsistence farmers and landless rural households and provide them opportunities for increased farm and non-farm employment. The distorting forces in the market should be kept under check. Two instruments need to be geared up, namely: (i) monetary mechanism, whose bearing on prices is obvious, and (ii) the public distribution system (PDS) whose role has to be strengthened, in terms of wider base and extended service.

The sustainable way of ensuring adequate food supplies to poor households is through keeping the food products affordable and by creating nutritional awareness. Empowering women with access to local productive resources should be the enshrined and holistic objective of a new plan to end malnutrition. At the household level policies should have this understanding as their backbone so as to enhance the chances of their success. Steps should be taken to improve the infrastructure of the poor to earn their livelihood with dignity.

This implies that the quality of human resource represented by these households will need to be improved through better health care and education.

Swami Vivekananda said, "So long as millions starve in hunger, I would hold every Indian a traitor." India has achieved self-sufficiency in food production such that it imports all food-grains except pulses, yet food insecurity remains unabated. In Human Development Index (HDI) India is rated only in the 124th position out of 171 countries. Because of its commitment to globalisation and liberalisation India is in the process of creating a silicon society, where the bazaars of the metros are abuzz with the ringing of a zillion cellphones, but far off in the rural pockets of the country, sun-baked peasants, mud colour their colour, are seen to toil to keep themselves fed. India is, indeed, a country of paradoxes:

With shadows cast on the light,
A morning tainted by the night,
This is not the morning we strove for.

The preferentials for a progressive democracy are "food for every palate, work in every hand, dream in every eye and peace in every mind". It is ardently wished that this holistic approach to food security brings them pleasure and prosperity.

Appendices

APPENDIX-1

Nutritive Value of Common Indian Food Preparations*

I.	Cereals	Weight **gm.	Calorieskcal	Proteingm.
1	Plain Rice	200	222	4.4
2	Curd Rice	253	221	6.0
3	Idli	136	130	4.6
4	Plain Dosai	100	216	4.1
5	Pongal	148	200	5.5
6	Chappatis	57	193	5.0
7	Puris	32	136	2.6
8	Ragi Puttu	146	422	4.4
II.	*Pulses*			
1	Bengal Gram Dhal	125	124	5.6
2	Black Gram Dhal	145	161	9.0
3	Green Gram Dhal	155	316	19.2
4	Lentil Gram Dhal	130	79	4.2
5	Red Gram Dhal	135	109	6.0
6	Kootu	155	147	4.7
7	Sambar	160	81	4.0
8	Dhal Rasam	196	29	1.5
9	Green Gram Sundal	142	259	13.1
III.	*Vegetables*			
1	Avial	140	123	2.2
2	Potato Curry	135	132	3.2
3	Vegetable Kurma	140	132	2.1
4	Dry Potato Curry	70	94	1.7
5	Brinjal and Potato	130	134	1.7
6	Ladies Finger	140	226	5.5

Contd...

		*Weight **gm.*	*Calorieskcal.*	*Proteingm.*
7	Pumpkin Curry	165	110	2.6
8	Cabbage	100	131	2.3
9	Fenugreek Leaves	100	121	2.2
IV.	*Meat, Fish and Poultry*			
1	Omelette	39	77	5.8
2	Fried Fish	85	218	18.2
3	Fish Curry	110	141	17.6
4	Meat Curry	142	339	21.8
5	Prawn Curry	145	219	18.4
V.	*Snacks*			
1	Awal	150	298	3.7
2	Bajji	58	280	3.8
3	Vada	43	138	6.1
4	Masala Vada	60	167	6.4
5	Potato Bonda	83	199	5.9
6	Samosa	65	207	2.5
7	Upma	80	130	2.9
VI.	*Chutneys*			
1	Coconut Chutney	55	125	2.0
2	Coriander Chutney	20	47	0.6
3	Groundnut Chutney	20	66	3.0
4	Mint Chutney	18	7	0.3
5	Tamarind Chutney	20	65	0.2
6	Tomato Chutney	50	32	0.9
VII.	*Milk Products*			
1	Coffee	200	104	3.8
2	Tea	200	72	1.4
3	Milk (Cow's)	200	130	7.0
4	Milk (Buffalo)	200	216	8.4
VIII.	*Fruits*			
1	Banana	70	116	1.2
2	Lime	85	57	1.0
3	Apple	84.6	59	0.2
4	Grapes	92	32	0.7
5	Mango	81	74	0.6
6	Jack Fruit	76.2	88	1.9
7	Pine Apple	87.8	46	0.4

Source: Swaran Pasricha (1989). *Count What You Eat.* National Institute of Nutrition, Hyderabad.

Note: *Nutritive value of food items restricted to those foods commonly consumed by the rural households in the study area.
** Weight refers to converted volumetric measure for one serving.

APPENDIX-2

Calorie Requirement of Children (Kcal/24hr)

Age (Years)	*Boys*	*Girls*
1+	1096	1078
2+	1301	1190
3+	1463	1310
4+	1531	1458
5+	1778	1643
6+	1948	1750
7+	2030	1858
8+	2034	1792
9+	2160	1848
10+	2140	1907
11+	2193	1956
12+	2248	2032
13+	2340	2037
14+	2468	2066
15+	2354	2065
16+	2586	2070
17+	2662	2061
18+	2677	2061

Source: I.C.M.R (2002). *Nutrient Requirements and Recommended Dietary Allowances for Indians : A Report of the Expert Group of the Indian Council of Medical Research.* National Institute of Nutrition, Hyderabad : 25.

APPENDIX-3

Calorie Requirements of Adults (Kcal/24 Hr)

	Age 18-30 years					
	Male Activity			*Female Activity*		
Body Weight (kg)	*Sedentary*	*Moderate*	*Heavy*	*Sedentary*	*Moderate*	*Heavy*
35	-	-	-	1536	1824	2400
40	1960	2328	3063	1648	1957	2575
45	2080	2470	3250	1760	2090	2750
50	2192	2603	3425	1872	2223	2925
55	2312	2746	3612	1984	2356	3100
60	2424	2879	3788	2096	2489	3275
65	2544	3021	3975	2208	2622	3450
70	2656	3154	4150	2320	2755	3625
75	2806	3335	4388	-	-	-

		Age 30+ to 59+yrs		*Age 60+ yrs*	
		Activity		*Activity*	
Sex	*Body Weight (kg)*	*Sedentary*	*Moderate*	*Heavy*	*Sedentary*
Male	45	2120	2518	3313	1664
	50	2208	2622	3450	1768
	55	2296	2727	3588	1872
	60	2376	2822	3713	1976
	65	2464	2926	3850	2072
	70	2552	3031	3988	2176
	75	2640	3135	4125	2280
Female	45	1792	2128	2800	1544
	50	1856	2204	2900	1624
	55	1920	2208	3000	1704
	60	1984	2356	3100	1784
	65	2056	2442	3213	1864
	70	2120	2518	3313	1944
	75	2184	2594	3413	2024

Source: I.C.M.R (2002). *Nutrient Requirements and Recommended Dietary Allowances for Indians : A Report of the Expert Group of the Indian Council of Medical Research.* National Institute of Nutrition, Hyderabad : 22-23.

APPENDIX-4

ICMR-Recommended Protein Requirement for Children/Adults (gm/24 hr)

		Protein Requirements	
Group	*Age Groups*	*Male*	*Female*
Children	1-3	22	22
	4-6	30	30
	7-9	43	43
	10-12	54	57
Adolescents	13-15	70	65
	16-18	78	63
Adults	18 + years	60	50

Source: I.C.M.R (2002). *Nutrient Requirements and Recommended Dietary Allowances for Indians : A Report of the Expert Group of the Indian Council of Medical Research.* National Institute of Nutrition, Hyderabad: 83.

APPENDIX-5

ICMR-Recommended Anthropometric Standards

	Boys		*Girls*	
Age (Years)	*Height (cm)*	*Weight (kg)*	*Height (cm)*	*Weight (kg)*
1+	80.07	10.54	78.09	9.98
2+	90.01	12.51	87.93	11.67
3+	98.36	14.78	96.21	13.79
4+	104.70	16.12	104.19	15.85
5+	113.51	19.33	112.24	18.67
6+	118.90	22.14	117.73	21.56
7+	123.32	24.46	122.65	24.45
8+	127.86	26.42	127.22	25.97
9+	133.63	30.00	133.08	29.82
10+	138.45	32.29	138.90	33.58
11+	143.35	35.26	145.00	37.17
12+	148.91	38.78	150.98	42.97
13+	154.94	42.88	153.44	44.54
14+	161.70	48.26	155.04	46.70
15+	165.33	52.15	155.98	48.75
16+	168.40	55.54	156.00	49.75
17+	173.00	57.91	156.90	50.42
18+	172.05	58.38	157.04	50.89

Source: I.C.M.R (2002). *Nutrient Requirements and Recommended Dietary Allowances for Indians: A Report of the Expert Group of the Indian Council of Medical Research.* National Institute of Nutrition, Hyderabad: 9.

Bibliography

Abdullah, A. (1989), "The Effect of Seasonality on Intra-household Food Distribution and Nutrition in Bangladesh," in D.E. Sahn (ed.), *Seasonal Variability in the Third World Agriculture: The Consequences for Food Security*. Johns Hopkins University Press, Baltimore.

Adato, M. and S. Felman (2001), *Safety Nets: In Empowering Women to Achieve Food Security*. A.R. Quisumbing and R.S. Meinzen-Disk. (ed.) 2020 FOCUS 6. International Food Policy Research Institute. Wahington, D.C.

Agarwal, B. (1994), *A Field of One's Own: Gender and Land Rights in South Asia*. Cambridge University Press, Cambridge, UK.

Alamgir, M. (1978), *Bangladesh: A Case of Below Poverty Level Equilibrium Trap*. Bangladesh Institute of Development Studies, Dhaka.

Austin, J.E. and M.F. Zeitlin (1981), *Nutrition Intervention in Developing Countries: An Overview*. Oelgeschlager, Gunn and Hain, Cambridge.

Balachander, J. (1993), "Tamil Nadu's Successful Nutrition Effort," in J. Rohde, M. Chatterjee and D. Morely (eds.), *Reaching Health for All*. Oxford University Press, Oxford: 158-184.

Bapna, S.L. (1990), "Food Security through PDS: The Indian Experience," in D.S. Tyagi and Vijay Shankar Vyas (eds.), *Increasing Assess to Food*. The Asian Experience. Sage Publications, New Delhi, 99-144.

Behrman, J.R. (1992), "Intra-household Allocation of Nutrients and Gender Effects: A Survey of Structural and Reduced-form Estimates," in S.R. Osmani (ed.), *Nutrition and Poverty*, Clarendon Press, Oxford.

Behrman, J.R. and A.B. Deolaikar (1988), "Health and Nutrition," in H.Chenery and T.N. Srinivasan (eds.), *Hand Book of Development Economics*, Vol. 1. Elsevier Science Publishers B.V., New York.

Bhagwati, Jagdish and T.N. Srinivasan (1993), *India's Economy Reforms*, Ministry of Finance, Government of India, New Delhi.

Braun, Von J., T. Telku, and P. Webb (1998), *Famine in Africa: Causes, Responses, and Prevention*. Johns Hopkins University Press. Baltimore.

Davis, O. and M. Witter (1986), *Issues in Food Security in Jamaica*, Caribbean Food and Nutrition Institute, Kingston.

Dey, J. (1984), *Women in Food Production and Food Security in Africa*, Rome: FAO.

Dreze, Jean and Amartia Sen (1989), *Hunger and Public Action*, Clarendon Press, Oxford.

Ehrlich, Paul R. and Anne P. Ehrlich (1995), "Growing Beyond Our Limits", *Triumph of Discovery: A Chronicle of Great Adventures in Science* (from the Scientific American), Henry Holt, New York: 181-182.

Gadomski, A. and R. Black (1988), *Child Survival Programs: Issues for the 1990's, Impact of the Direct Interventions*. Department of International Health, School of Hygiene and Public Health, Johns Hopkins University, Baltimore.

Gangulee, N. (1939), *Health and Nutritional in India*, Faber, London, 77-78.

Gibsow, R. S. (1990), *Principles of National Assessment*, Oxford University Press, New York.

Gopalan, C. (ed.) (1993), *Recent Trends in Nutrition*. Oxford University Press, New Delhi, 220.

Haddad, L., J. Hodinott and H. Alderman (1997), *Intra-household Resources Allocation in Developing Countries: Models, Methods, and Policy*. Johns Hopkins University Press, Baltimore.

Haq, Mahbub ul. (1997), *Human Development in South Asia 1997*. Oxford University Press, Oxford, New York.

Indrapal and S.C. Kalwar (1989). "Socio-economic Factors Leading of Changes in the Pattern of Food Production and Nutrition Availability in Rajasthan," in M. Shafi and A. Aziz (eds.), *Food Systems of the World*, Rawat Publications, Jaipur : 199-224.

Mitra, A. and S. Mukherjee (1981), *Population, Food and Land Inequality India: A Geography of Hunger and Insecurity*. Allied Publications, New Delhi.

Mukherjee, Amitava (1993), *Structural Adjustment Programme, Putting the First Things Poverty and Environment Last*. Segment Books, New Delhi.

Myers, Norman (1994), "Population and Bio-diversity," in F. Graham-Smith (ed.), *Population: The Complex Reality*, The Royal Society, London: 117-156

Pant, B. R. (1994a), *Food and Nutrition: A Study of Himalaya Region*, Anmol Publications, New Delhi: 195.

Radhakrishna, R. and K.H. Rao (1994), *Food Security, Public Distribution and Price Policy*, CESS, Hyderabad.

Sen, A.K. (1981), *Poverty and Famines, and Essay on Exchange Entitlements*, Clarendon Press, Oxford.

Sen, A.K. (1985), *Commodities and Capabilities*, North-Holland, Amsterdam.

Spurr, G. B. (1984), "Physical Activity, Nutritional Status, and Physical Work Capacity in Relation to Agricultural Productivity," in E. Pollitt and P. Amante. (eds.), *Energy Intake and Activity*. New York.

Swaminathan, M. S. (1986), *Sustainable Nutrition Security for Africa: Lessons from India*, The Hunger Project, San Francisco.

Tyagi, D.S. (1990), *Managing India's Food Economy: Problems and Alternatives*, Sage, New Delhi.

Venugopal, K.R. (1992), *Delivery from Hunger the Public Distribution in India*. Sage Publications, New Delhi.

Webb, P. and J. Von Braun (1994), *Famine and Food Security in Ethiopia: Lessons for Africa*, John Wiley, Chichester, U.K.

Abdullah, M. and E.F. Wheeler (1985), "Seasonal Variations and Intra-household Distribution of Food in a Bangladesh Village", *American Journal of Clinical Nutrition*, Vol. 41, No. 6, 1305-1313.

Adrian, J. and R. Daniel (1976), "Impact of Socio-economic Factors on Consumption of Selected Food Nutrients in the United States", *American Journal of Agricultured Economics*, Vol. 58, 31-38.

Ahluwalia, D. (1993), "Public Distribution of Food in India: Coverage Targeting and Leakages", *Food Policy*, Vol. 8, No. 1.

Alagh, Y.K. (1995), "Poverty and Food Security: Toward a Policy System", *Economic and Political Weekly*, Vol. 30, No. 52, A142-50.

Alderman, H. (1989), "Poverty and Malnutrition: How Closely Linked?", *Cuadernos de Economia,* August, 6.

Ali, M. (1997), "Pulses for Nutritional Food Security", *Indian Farming,* Vol. 47, No. 7, 32.

Arora, C.L and P.N. Bhat (1997), "Investing in Live-stock Production for Food Security", *Indian Farming,* Vol. 47, No. 7, 25.

Arrow, K.J. (1988), "Poverty and Hunger", *Economic Philosophy,* Vol. 4.

Bajaj, S. (1989), "The Nutrition Security System at the Household Level: Policy Implications", *Food and Nutrition Bulletin,* Vol. 11, No. 4, 6-12.

Behrman, J.R. (1987), "Will Developing Countries Nutrition Improve with Income?: A Case Study for Rural South India", *Journal of Political Economics,* Vol. 95, 452-507.

Behrman, J. R. (1988), "Intra-household Allocation of Nutrients in Rural India: Are Boys favored? Do Parents Exhibit inequality Aversion?", *Oxford Economic Papers,* Vol. 40, No. 1, 32-54.

Behrman, J.R. and A.B. Deolalikar (1990), "The Intra-household Demand for Nutrients in Rural South India : Individual Estimates, Fixed Effects and Permanent Income", *Journal of Human Resources,* Vol. 25, No. 4, 665-696.

Bhagwati, J. (1987), "Poverty and Public Policy", *World Development,* Vol. 16, 11-14.

Cairncross, S. and J.L. Cliff (1987), "Water Use and Health in Mueda, Mozambique", *Transactions of the Royal Society of Tropical Medicine and Hygiene,* Vol. 81, No. 1, 51-54.

Chakraborty, A.K. (1990), "Food Grain Sufficiency Pattern in India", *Geographical Review of India,* Vol. 60, No. 2, 208-228.

Chen, L. C., E. Huq and S. D'Souza (1981), "Sex Bias in the Family Allocation of Food and Health Care in Rural Bangladesh", *Population and Development Review,* Vol. 7, No. 1, 55-70.

Dahiya, P.S. (1997), "Food Security-Key Issues and Investments Strategies", *Indian Farming,* Vol. 47, No. 7, 12,13.

De Waal, A. (1989), "Famine Mortality: A Case Study of Darfur, Sudan 1984-95", *Population Studies,* Vol. 43, 469-90.

Feenstra, G. (1996), "Community Food Security: Improving the Nutritional and Social Health of Communities." *Communicators,* Vol. 19, No. 2, 3-4.

Ferro-Luzzi, A., S. Sette, M. Franklin, and W. P. James (1992), "A Simplified Approach of Assessing Adult Chronic Energy Deficiency", *European Journal of Clinical Nutrition,* Vol. 46, March: 179-186.

Ferro-Luzzi, A., F. Branca and G. Pastore (1994), "Body Mass Index Defines the Risk of Seasonal Energy Stress in the Third World", *European Journal of Clinical Nutrition,* Vol. 48, S165-178.

Garcia, S.E., L.L. Kaiser and K.G. Dewey (1990), "The Relationship of Eating Frequency and Caloric Density to Energy Intake among Rural Mexican Pre-school Children", *Journal of Clinical Nutrition,* Vol. 44, 381-387.

Geetha, S. and M.H. Suryanarayana (1993), "Revamping PDS: Some Issues and Implications", *Economic and Political Weekly,* Vol. 28, 41.

Gittelsohn, J. (1991), "Opening the Box: Intra-household Food Allocation in Rural Nepal", *Social Science Medical,* Vol. 33, 1141-54.

Gupta, Das P. (1997), "Nutritional Status, the Capacity for Work, and Poverty Traps", *Journal of Econometrics,* Vol. 77, 5-37.

Haddad, L., E. Kennady and J. Sullivian (1994), "Choice of Indicators for Food Security and Nutrition Monitoring", *Food Policy,* Vol. 19, 323-53.

Kaul, G.L. (1989), "Fruit and Vegetable Production in India", *Production Nutrition Society India,* Vol. 45, 147.

Kramer, M.S. (1987), "Determinants of Low Birth Weight: Methodological Assessment and Meta-Analysis", *Bulletin of the World Health Organization,* Vol. 65, No. 5, 663-737.

Krishnaji, N. (1981), "On Measuring the Incidence of Under-nutrition. A Note of Sukhatme's Procedure", *Economic and Political Weekly,* May 30: 989-92.

Krishnakumar, A. (1996), "Eradicating Hungers-The Quest for a Food Secure World", *Frontline,* Vol. 13, No. 32: 102.

Leonard, W.R. (1991), "Household-level Strategies for Protecting Children from Seasonal Food Security", *Social Science and Medicine,* Vol. 33, No. 10, 1127-1133.

Lindtjorn, B. and T. Alemu (1997), "Intra-household Correlations of Nutritional Status in Rural Ethiopia", *International Journal of Epidemiology,* Vol. 26, No. 1: 160-165.

Longhurst, R. (1986). "Household Food Strategies in Response to Seasonality and Famine", *IDS Bulletin,* Vol. 17, No. 3:27-35.

Monteio, C.A., L. Mondini, A.M. Torres, and I. M. Dos Reis (1997), "Patterns of Intra-familiar Distribution of Under-nutrition: Methods and Applications for Devolving Societies", *European Journal of Clinical Nutrition,* Vol. 51: 800-803.

Mooij. E. Jos (1994), "Public Distribution System as a Safety Net: Who is Saved?", *Economic and Political Weekly,* Vol. 29, No. 3.

Mrunthyunjaya (1997), "Food Security Issues and Options", *Indian Farming,* Vol. 47, No. 7: 7

Mukherjee, Neela and Amitava Mukherjee (1994), "Rural Women and Food Insecurity: What a Food Calendar Reveals", *Economic and Political Weekly,* Vol. 29, No. 11: 12.

Naidu, A.N. and N.P. Rao (1994), "Body Mass Index: A Measure of the Nutritional Status in India Populations", *European Journal of Clinical Nutrition,* Vol. 48, 131-140.

Rao, M.V. (1997), "Indian Agriculture, Future Challenges", *University News,* Vol. 35, No. 10:12.

Sen, A.K. (1977), "Starvation and Exchange Entitlements: A General Approach and Its Applications to the Great Bengal Famine", *Cambridge Journal of Economics,* 1.

Sen, Amartya (1992), "Life and Death in China: A Reply", *World Development,* Vol. 20, No. 9: 1305-1312.

Shafi, M. (1960), "Food Efficiency and Nutrition in India", *The Geographer,* Vol. 14: 23-27.

Shafi, M. (1983), "Food Production and Consumption in Developed and Developing Countries", *The Geographer,* Vol. 30, No. 1, 15-23.

Shah, C.H. (1982), "The Demand for Higher-Status Food and Nutrition in Rural India: The Experience of Matar Taluka", *Food and Nutrition Bulletin,* Vol. 8: 7.

Shah, C.H. (1983), "Food Preference, Poverty and the Nutrition Gap", *Economic Development and Cultural Change,* Vol. 31, 121-48.

Spurr, G. B. (1983), "Nutritional Status and Physical Work Capacity", *Yearbook of Physical Anthropology,* Vol. 26: 1-35.

Sundaram, S.I. (1996), "Feeding a Hungry World", *Social Welfare,* Vol. 43, No. 9: 11.

Suryanarayana, M. H. (1995), "PDS Reform and Scope for Commodity Based Targeting", *Economic and Political Weekly*, Vol. 30, No. 13: 10.

Swaminathan, M.C., K.V. Rao and D.H. Rao (1969), "Food and Nutrition Situation in the Drought-Affected Areas of Bihar", *Journal of Nutrition and Dietetics*, Vol. 6: 7.

Varshney, Ashutosh (1993), "Self-limited Empowerment: Democracy, Economy Development and Rural India", *Journal of Development Studies*, Vol. 29, No. 4, 177-215.

Waterlow, J. C. (1994), "Relationship of Gain in Height to Gain in Weight", *European Journal of Clinical Nutrition*, Vol. 48, S72-74.

ACC/SCN (1998), "Challenging for the 21st Century: A Gender Perspective on Nutrition Through the Life Cycle." Paper from the ACC/SCN 25th session Symposium. Nutrition Policy Paper No.17. ACC/SCN Geneva.

Acharya, S. and V.G. Panwalkar (1988), "The Maharashtra Employment Guarantee Scheme: Impacts on Male and Female Labour." Regional Research Paper, The Population Council, Bangkok.

Alderman, H. and M. Garcia (1993), *Poverty, Household Food Security, and Nutrition in Rural Pakistan*, International Food Policy Research Institute, Washington, D.C.

Chambers, R. (1980), "Rural Poverty Unperceived Problems and Remedies", *World Bank Staff Working Paper* No. 400.

FAO (1991), *Dynamics of Rural Poverty*. FAO, Rome.

FAO (1996), *The State of Food Insecurity in the World*. FAO, Rome.

Food and Agriculture Organisation of the United Nations (1992), *Production Year Book 1991*, Vol. 45, United Nations, Rome.

Gopalan, C. (1989), *Nutrition, Health and National Development*, Nutrition Foundation of India (NFI). Special Publication Series: 136.

Gopalan, C. and S. Kaur (eds.), (1989), *Women and Nutrition in India*, N.F.I. Special Publication Series, 5: 378.

Gopalan, C. and H. Kaur (eds.), (1993), *Towards Better Nutrition*, N.F.I. Special Publication Series, 9: 445.

Holmboe-Ottesen, Wandel M. (1992), *Household Food Security: Application of a Normative Concept in Research for Planning Review*, UNICEF and Food and Agriculture Organisation, New York and Rome.

Horton, S. "Opportunities for Investments in Nutrition in Low-income Asia." Paper Contributed to the ADB-IFPRI Regional Technical Assistance Project 5824 on Nutrition Trends, Policies and Strategies in Asia and the Pacific.

International Fund for Agricultural Development (1992), "Rural Poverty Alleviation and Nutrition: IFAD's Evolving Experiences", A Technical Paper, Technical Advisory Division. IFAD, Rome.

Jodha, N.S. (1989), "Management of Common Property Resources in Selected Areas in India", A Paper Read at the Seminar on Approaches to Particularly Development and Management of Common Property Resources, held on 10th March, 1989, at the Institute of Economic Growth, New Delhi.

Joshi, P.D (1998), "Changing Pattern of Consumption Expenditure in India and Some Selected States", Sarvekshana Analytical Report No. 2, Ministry of Planning and Programme Implementation, New Delhi.

Lipton, M. (1983), "Poverty, Under-nutrition and Hunger", *World Bank Staff Working Paper* No. 597, World Bank, Washington, D.C.

Mc Guire, J. and B.Popkia (1988), "Increasing Women's Resources for Nutrition in Developing Countries", Paper Prepared for the U.N. Co-ordinating Committee's Subcommittee on Nutrition on Nutrition Symposium on Women and Nutrition.

Parikh, Kirit (1992), *Food Security: Issues and Options*. XXI International Conference of Agricultural Economics, Tokyo, August: 22-29.

Sen, A.K. (1988), "Undernutrition in Sub-Saharan Africa: Is there a Sex Bias?", *Working Paper* No. 47, WIDER, Helsinki.

Senauer, B. and M. Gracia (1988), "The Determinants of Food Consumption and Nutritional Status among Pre-school Children: Evidence from the Rural Philippines." Staff Paper Series, No. P. 88-33, Department of Agriculture and Applied Economics, University of Minnesota.

Sharman, A. (1970), "Social and Economic Aspects of Nutrition in Padhold Dukedi District", Uganda. Ph.D., Dissertation, University of London, U.K.

Subbarao, K. (1989), *Improving Nutrition in India*, World Bank Discussion Paper No. 49.

Subbarao, *et al.* (1997), *Safety Net Programmes and Poverty Reduction: Lessons from Cross Country Experience*. The World Bank, Washington, D.C.

Sundaram, K. and S.D. Tendulkar (1981), "Poverty Reduction in the Sixth Plan", *Working Paper* No. 233, School of Economics, Delhi.

Tendulkar, S.D., K. Sundaram and L.R Jain (1993), *Poverty in India*, 1970-71 to 1988-89. ARTEP, New Delhi.

United Nations (1982), *Model Life Tables for Developing Countries*, United Nations, New York.

United States Department of Agriculture (USDA) (1988), "Economic Research Service Food Assistance", *National Food Review*, Vol. 11, No. 2: 37.

WHO (1998), *The World Health Report 1998: Life in the 21st Century: A Vision of All*, WHO, Geneva.

WHO (1998), *Health for All in the 21st Century EB 101/8*. WHO, Geneva.

Index